Contemporary Political Studies Series

Series Editor: John Benyon, *University of Leicester*

Published

DAVID BROUGHTON
Public Opinion and Political Polling in Britain

CLYDE CHITTY
Education Policy in Britain

MICHAEL CONNOLLY
Politics and Policy Making in Northern Ireland

DAVID DENVER
Elections and Voters in Britain

JUSTIN FISHER
British Political Parties

ROBERT GARNER
Environmental Politics: Britain, Europe and the Global Environment; 2nd edn

ANDREW GEDDES
The European Union and British Politics

WYN GRANT
Economic Policy in Britain

WYN GRANT
Pressure Groups and British Politics

DEREK HEATER and GEOFFREY BERRIDGE
Introduction to International Politics

DILYS M. HILL
Urban Policy and Politics in Britain

ROBERT LEACH
Political Ideology in Britain

ROBERT LEACH and JANIE PERCY-SMITH
Local Governance in Britain

PETER MADGWICK
British Government: The Central Executive Territory

ANDREW MASSEY and ROBERT PYPER
Public Management and Modernisation in Britain

PHILIP NORTON
Parliament in British Politics

MALCOLM PUNNETT
Selecting the Party Leader

ROBERT PYPER
The British Civil Service

Forthcoming

RAYMOND KUHN
Politics and the Media in Britain

D0434681

Other books by Philip Norton

Politics UK (with others), 5th edn, Pearson Longman, 2004
Parliaments and Citizens in Western Europe, Frank Cass, 2002
The British Polity, 4th edn, Longman, 2001
Parliaments in Asia (ed. with N. Ahmed), Frank Cass, 1999
Parliaments and Pressure Groups in Western Europe, Frank Cass, 1999
Parliaments and Governments in Western Europe, Frank Cass, 1998
Legislatures and Legislators, Ashgate/Dartmouth Publishing, 1998
The Conservative Party, Prentice-Hall/Harvester Wheatsheaf, 1996
The New Parliaments of Central and Eastern Europe (ed. with
    D. M. Olson), Frank Cass, 1996
National Parliaments and the European Union, Frank Cass, 1996
Does Parliament Matter?, Harvester Wheatsheaf, 1993
Back from Westminster (with D. Wood), University Press of Kentucky,
    1993
Parliamentary Questions (ed. with M. Franklin), Clarendon Press, 1993
New Directions in British Politics?, Edward Elgar, 1991
Parliaments in Western Europe, Frank Cass, 1990
Legislatures, Oxford University Press, 1990
The Political Science of British Politics (ed. with J. Hayward),
    Wheatsheaf, 1986
Parliament in the 1980s, Basil Blackwell, 1985
Law and Order and British Politics, Gower, 1984
The Constitution in Flux, Basil Blackwell, 1982
Conservatives and Conservatism (with A. Aughey), Temple Smith, 1981
The Commons in Perspective, Martin Robertson/Basil Blackwell, 1981
Dissension in the House of Commons 1974–1979, Clarendon Press, 1980
Conservative Dissidents, Temple Smith, 1978
Dissension in the House of Commons 1945–74, Macmillan, 1975

Parliament in British Politics

Philip Norton

palgrave
macmillan

This book is designed as a direct replacement for the author's *Does Parliament Matter?*, published by Harvester Wheatsheaf in 1993.

This edition published 2005 by
PALGRAVE MACMILLAN
Houndmills, Basingstoke, Hampshire RG21 6XS and
175 Fifth Avenue, New York, N. Y. 10010
Companies and representatives throughout the world

PALGRAVE MACMILLAN is the global academic imprint of the Palgrave Macmillan division of St. Martin's Press, LLC and of Palgrave Macmillan Ltd. Macmillan® is a registered trademark in the United States, United Kingdom and other countries. Palgrave is a registered trademark in the European Union and other countries.

ISBN-10: 1–4039–0666–1 hardback
ISBN-13: 978–1–4039–0666–3 hardback
ISBN-10: 1–4039–0667–X paperback
ISBN-13: 978–1–4039–0667–0 paperback

This book is printed on paper suitable for recycling and made from fully managed and sustained forest sources.

A catalogue record for this book is available from the British Library.

Library of Congress Cataloging-in-Publication Data
Norton, Philip.
    Parliament in British politics / Philip Norton.
        p. cm. – (Contemporary political studies series)
    Includes bibliographical references and index.
    ISBN 1–4039–0666–1 (cloth) – ISBN 1–4039–0667–X (paper)
        1. Great Britain. Parliament. 2. Great Britain–Politics and government–21st century. I. Title. II. Contemporary political studies (Palgrave Macmillan (Firm))
JN550.N67 2005
328.41–dc22   2005047558

10   9   8   7   6   5   4   3   2
14   13   12   11   10   09   08   07   06

Printed and bound in China

Contents

List of Figures and Tables

Preface

The purpose of this book is embodied in the title. First, it seeks to provide a rich description of the institution of Parliament. Parliament is a core institution in the political system. It is a distinct and institutionalized body, with its own members, practices and procedures. Though many people claim to have an interest in politics, few admit to knowing a great deal about Parliament and how it works. This book provides an introduction to the workings of Parliament in the twenty-first century. Second, it explains how Parliament functions as a key body within British politics. Parliament does not exist in a vacuum. What it does derives from its relationships with different bodies. One of these relationships, clearly, is with government. Much of the literature on Parliament focuses on that relationship. This work is distinctive in going beyond that relationship. The first edition of this text, published as *Does Parliament Matter?*, in 1993, looked at the relationship of Parliament to government *and* to the citizen. In this edition, I have sought to develop and expand that study and to put it in a more explicit theoretical framework. Over the past decade, Parliament has been affected by a great many changes, some essentially external to it, some internal. The former have included major changes within the European Union – from the creation of the EU itself through to the treaty on a European Constitution – as well as devolution of powers to elected bodies in different parts of the United Kingdom and the passage of the Human Rights Act. The latter have included an extension of pre-legislative scrutiny, the introduction of debates in Westminster Hall, the extension of committees in the House of Lords, and the removal of most hereditary peers from membership of the Upper House. This work examines these changes within the context of a clear analytic framework.

The changes have meant that the constitutional landscape of the United Kingdom has substantially altered. At the beginning of the 1990s, there was only one Parliament in the United Kingdom. It is now possible to talk of parliaments – and assemblies – within the UK. This work is confined to the Westminster Parliament, though putting it within the context of changes that have taken place. Although change is a characteristic of Parliament, so too is continuity. Much of what

Parliament does, and the terminology it employs, would be familiar to a member from a century or so before. Money voted by Parliament is still known as supply. Even though a number of committees are chaired by women, the title of chairman is retained in both Houses. As we shall see, continuity has important consequences. The fact that Parliament has a long, largely unbroken history is central to explaining its current role in the political process and how that role is popularly viewed.

In researching the material for this edition, I have drawn on a mix of quantitative and qualitative sources. Since the publication of *Does Parliament Matter?* I have become a member of the Upper House and have variously drawn on my parliamentary experience to inform my writing. I have retained as much as possible of the earlier text, ensuring that as far as possible each chapter is self-contained, thus allowing the reader to look independently at particular aspect of Parliament's work and in order to enable chapters to be utilized as appropriate for class assignments. Where there is an overlap of subject matter, I have identified the chapter where the principal material appears and, if necessary to maintain internal coherence, briefly mentioned the essential point of the earlier material.

In writing the book, I have incurred a number of debts. I am particularly grateful to Steven Kennedy of Palgrave Macmillan for his regular and enthusiastic reminders that a new work was necessary; without his prodding, this work would still be in preparation. My research has been facilitated by the availability of data produced within Parliament itself: much of the material, as will be apparent from the source citations, derives from parliamentary publications. I am also grateful to parliamentary colleagues – both members and officials – who have furthered my knowledge of the institution and have been only too willing to share their recollections and insights with me. Responsibility for any errors, omissions and distorted interpretations remains entirely with me.

PHILIP NORTON

University of Hull

The author and publishers would like to thank the following who have kindly given permission for the use of copyright material: Oxford University Press for Tables 10.1 and 10.2; Dod's Parliamentary Communications for Table 9.2; Tables 5.3, 6.1, 6.2 and 6.3 are Crown copyright material reproduced with the permission of the controller of Her Majesty's Stationery Office under click licence CO1W0000276.

1

Parliament in Perspective

It is common for a country to have a legislature – a body created to approve measures that will form the law of the land. Legislatures exist under a variety of names, of which Congress is the most popular. Some use the term National Assembly. Others use terms specific to their language. In the United Kingdom, and in Commonwealth countries influenced by British experience, Parliament is preferred.

Two assumptions inform contemporary perceptions of legislatures (Norton, 1990a, pp. 3–5). One is long-standing; that is, that legislatures exist to make law. The second, deriving from the late nineteenth century, is that legislatures are in decline.

The first perception derives from the very name *legislature. Legis* is the genitive of *lex,* meaning law; *lator* means carrier or proposer. A *legislator* was therefore someone who carried law. Legislatures have thus, by definition, been treated as bodies for carrying, or making, law. 'The legislative' declared John Locke in his *Second Treatise on Government* in 1689, 'is no otherwise legislative of the society but by the right it has to make laws for all parts and for every member of society, prescribing rules for their actions, and giving power of execution where they are transgressed' (Locke 1960). Baron de Montesquieu, in *The Spirit of Laws* published in 1748, a work that was to have a powerful influence in America, similarly defined legislative power as that of enacting temporary or perpetual laws, and the amending or abrogating of those already made (Montesquieu 1949). Law was thus created by legislatures. It was the very task that gave them their name and justified their existence.

The second assumption has existed for more than a century. Various nineteenth-century scholars, such as the English journalist Walter Bagehot (1867) and the American academic A. Lawrence Lowell (1896), identified the likely consequences for legislatures of the growth of party. However, it was to be a twentieth-century work by the scholar-statesman Lord Bryce that popularized the perception of decline. In

1

Modern Democracies, published in 1921, Bryce titled Chapter 58 'The Decline of Legislatures'. In the following chapter, he identified five 'chronic ailments' that had undermined representative assemblies, with party as the principal ailment. Though Bryce qualified his assertion, the notion of decline became associated with his work. It is one that has found a resonance in the subsequent study of legislatures.

The decline of legislatures

That there should be a perception of decline is not surprising. In the nineteenth century, legislatures grew in number and political significance. This growth in significance was not uniform, however; some countries, such as Germany, witnessed no 'golden age' of parliament. However, such countries were exceptional. Parliamentarianism was a feature of the century (Sontheimer, 1984). Yet no sooner had this condition been reached than it began to deteriorate. Legislatures were unable to withstand the various pressures favouring executive dominance in the formulation and determination of public policy.

Industrialization generated an increasingly urban population with no political voice. Pressure for such a voice was to result in the widening of the franchise and the growth of political parties. In Britain, for example, the 1867 Reform Act – which increased the size of the electorate by almost 90 per cent – spurred the creation of mass-membership parties. Parties served to aggregate the demands of an electorate that lacked the willingness and the sophistication to consider the merits of individual candidates. Parties were beholden to electors for their success, and successful candidates owed their position to the party label. Continued party success came to depend on parties being able to implement promises made to the electorate. Implementation of such promises depended on party loyalty in the legislature. Scope for independent action by the elected members was squeezed out.

Party thus came to dominate the electoral and parliamentary processes. The party chose the candidates, raised the money to fight elections, and set the agenda. Party leaders occupied the central positions of government and decided what measures were to be laid before the legislature for approval. Party thus ensured that the site of policy-making – of crafting coherent measures of public policy – was the executive, not the legislature.

Industrialization had a further effect. Not only did it generate a mass franchise, it also resulted in a more specialized society. Interests became more differentiated – and more organized. In Britain, trade associations grew in number in the first half of the nineteenth century, and various professional and employers' organizations were established. These organizations began to compete to protect their own interests. What was notable in the first half of the century became more pronounced in the second half. Organized groups became more extensive in number and more national in structure. Trade unions, legalized in the 1870s, began to organize. The greater and more specialized the demands made of government by these groups, the greater the specificity of government policy (Richardson and Jordan, 1979, pp. 44–5). The more specialized government policy became, the more government relied on groups for advice, information and co-operation in implementing policy.

The support of the party could usually be taken for granted by government: that of interest groups could not. Increasingly, groups were drawn into the policy-making process. In Britain, a number of groups were effectively co-opted into that process and given statutory representation on advisory bodies. The National Health Insurance Act of 1924, for example, gave the medical profession representation on bodies set up to administer the system of social insurance. Co-option was extended in succeeding decades, and groups continued to grow in number. Government itself became more specialized and increasingly dependent on a growing bureaucracy. Contact with government departments became frequent and institutionalized (Norton, 2001a, ch. 7). By the 1970s, the links were extensive.

Hence, in the process of making law, legislatures came to be seen as increasingly marginalized. Party – or parties – dominate in the legislature. As Hibbing (2002, p. 35) has noted, 'most objective observers would concede that party norms usually trump legislative norms – in the U.K. and in most other countries'. The thrust of public policy is determined by party and confirmed by the electorate at periodic elections. The specific measures of public policy are formulated by government departments following consultation with affected interests, and those measures are subsequently presented to the legislature for approval. The legislature will usually lack the political will to challenge them; a partisan majority will exist to pass them. It may also lack the resources to challenge them: if presented with a measure that has the support of the different groups affected by it, it may have no alternative source of information or advice to challenge the agreed package. Consequently, the measures are passed.

The paradox of legislatures

The position of legislatures, on the basis of this analysis, thus appears to be straightforward. They are marginal bodies in policy-making. Yet legislatures present us with a seeming paradox.

On the one hand, legislatures are in decline, yet on the other, they are ubiquitous. They span the globe. Of the 191 member states of the United Nations in 2004, all bar eight had a national parliament. They exist in large, populous countries and in small island states. Many have existed for decades; some for centuries. Furthermore, they show no signs of diminishing in number. As military regimes have been toppled or have handed over power, so legislatures have been established. Following periods of military rule, countries such as Brazil and Greece have reverted to elected legislatures. As the Iron Curtain has rusted and disappeared, the legislatures of the old regimes of central and eastern Europe have given way to new legislatures. Legislatures are appearing in countries of the Middle East, such as Bahrain, which have little or no history of creating such bodies. The creation of legislatures is seen clearly as being important.

The significance of legislatures is recognized by political leaders; indeed, to them, legislatures are considered to be necessary. Their importance is also acknowledged frequently by citizens, and is reflected in attitudes and in action. A survey of six European countries in 1983 found that in every one of them an absolute majority of respondents regarded their legislature as very important or important 'in the life of our country nowadays' (*Euro-Barometre* survey, reported in Conradt, 1986, p. 152). Despite their presumed marginality, citizens often petition their national legislature or spend time meeting or writing to members of the legislature. In some countries, members of the parliament will often find citizens coming to their local offices to seek their assistance. Pressure groups will often develop links with parties in parliament or lobby parliamentarians. The media will variously cover what goes on within a parliament. One of the events regularly covered by the British media, for example, is Prime Minister's Question Time in the House of Commons.

If legislatures are so marginal, why are there so many of them – notable not only for their number but also their resilience – and why do citizens attach importance to them? The paradox is resolved by fact that there is more to legislatures than law-making. Those who bemoan the decline of legislatures are adopting a narrow focus. This can be demonstrated by looking at legislatures in terms of power and the functions they fulfil.

The power of legislatures

Power is a contested concept. It is normally defined as A getting B to do what B would not otherwise do. In fact, there are different views of power (Lukes, 1974). Three principal views can be characterized as the *pluralist,* the *elitist* and the *institutional* (Norton, 2004a). Each has a utility in helping to explain the relevance of a legislature within the political system.

The *pluralist* defines power it in terms of the resolution of disputes once an issue has come on to the political agenda. Whoever achieves the outcome they desire has exerted power. Power in pluralist terms takes two forms: coercion and persuasion. Someone may achieve a desired outcome by acting in such a way that others feel they have no option but to comply. In other words, there is no choice. If someone points a gun at an innocent bystander and orders them to hand over their money, the bystander is likely to feel compelled to hand it over. That is coercion. If a beggar approaches a passer-by and asks for money, the passer-by may or may not give them money: there is an element of choice. If they hand over the money, then they have been persuaded to do so. Sometimes the dividing line between coercion and persuasion is a thin one, but the distinction is important.

It is a relevant distinction for the purpose of analysing legislatures. Legislatures have a coercive capacity through their ability to say 'no' to government. They can kill a measure by voting it down. Political bodies that have the capacity to block a measure have been characterized as veto players (Tsebelis, 2002). Legislatures have a veto. However, they also have a persuasive capacity. If the government is contemplating a particular action or policy, members of the legislature may – by speeches, motions or meetings with ministers – make clear their opposition. The government may decide not to proceed because of pressure from parliamentarians: ministers may feel they need to maintain the goodwill of the parliamentarians (especially if they are members of the same party) or they may find the arguments they advance compelling. Whatever the reason, they have been persuaded to act in a way contrary to that they had intended. They have exercised choice. It is thus possible for outcomes to be affected without the legislature having formally said 'no' to government.

The *elitist* approach sees power in terms of agenda-setting, rather than in terms of what happens once an issue is on the agenda. It defines power in terms of controlling access to the political agenda. A particular group – an elite – can serve as a gatekeeper, determining what can and, most important of all, cannot be allowed on to the political agenda. Shared attitudes on the part of the elite may determine that certain matters are too important to be allowed to get on the agenda. This has been characterized as 'non-decision making' (Bachrach and Baratz, 1962). However, this view of power generates methodological problems: trying to identify what has been kept off the agenda is clearly fraught with difficulty. How issues are resolved once they are on the political agenda can frequently be observed: conflict is often public, or reports of conflict (of internal cabinet or party fights) find their way into the public arena. It is difficult to identify the issues that are kept off the agenda through the actions of a particular body, especially when that body may itself not be clearly discernible or act in an organized manner. This view is thus problematic, but may none the less have some utility for the study of legislatures. This is not so much because legislatures form part of the elite, but because the actions – actual or anticipated – of the legislature may have some impact on an elite. Carl Friedrich (1963) identified the 'law of anticipated reactions'. If a governing body – a president, prime minister or cabinet – anticipates a negative reaction from the legislature, it may decide not to bring an issue on to the political agenda. As Cox and Morgenstern (2002, p. 446) have observed, 'the venerable "rule of anticipated reactions" makes even primarily reactive institutions, such as Latin American legislatures, relevant'. In the UK, a bill may not be brought forward because of an expected hostile reaction from government backbenchers or the House of Lords. A policy or action may not be pursued in case it is the subject of critical review by a select committee or is raised on the floor of the House. A governing elite may control access to the agenda and operate in its own interest, but self-interest may dictate anticipating the reaction to an issue once it is allowed on to the agenda.

The *institutional* approach is concerned with the impact of institutions on shaping outcomes. The focus is not so much the conflict over a particular issue but rather the structures and processes through which the conflict takes place. The result of a football match may be determined by a penalty shoot-out. From a pluralist view, the team with the player who scores the winning penalty has exercised power over the other team. However, the institutional view stresses that the goal is scored within the context of a clearly defined game with specific rules governing the use of the penalty shoot-out. Had some other rule been in place, then the outcome might have been very different. The institutional view covers both the fact that the rules and processes can affect outcomes, and the acceptance of the rules by players and observers. Acceptance of the process underpins stability.

In the context of legislatures, structures and procedures can affect outcomes (Norton, 2001b). The need for measures to go through several stages, or to be passed by a particular time, affects what is brought forward by the executive. The rules may create bottlenecks, limiting how many measures can be brought forward at any one time. Acceptance of the process, at both the elite and the mass level, also renders the legislature powerful, as it is accepted that a measure is not legitimate if it has not received the assent of the legislature. The courts enforce the law as passed by the legislature. It is especially powerful in systems where there is no recognition of any alternative to the legislature as the body for legitimizing measures of public policy.

It is thus apparent that the perception of the decline of legislatures derives from a particular view of power. Indeed, it can be claimed to be a narrow view, even within a pluralist framework, derived primarily from an emphasis on coercion. Because legislatures do not regularly say 'no' to the executive, and substitute policy of their own, they are deemed to be in decline. However, once we go beyond the pluralist view, then we can see legislatures in a new perspective. The very fact that there are so many of them suggests that there is more to them than law 'making'. Looking at the different definitions of power is suggestive of a wider relevance. That relevance becomes more defined if we look at the functions, or tasks, that legislatures perform.

The functions of legislatures

The generic name of legislatures masks rather than illuminates what they in fact do. Their core defining role, as suggested by our opening sentence, is not to *make* law but rather to *give assent* to it. For some that has not only been their core but their only function. The parliament of the former German Democratic Republic (East Germany), for example, sometimes met on only three days a year to approve measures put before it, an example of what Michael Mezey (1979) has defined as a 'minimal legislature'. With the collapse of the Soviet-dominated regimes of central and eastern Europe, the number of such legislatures has declined significantly. Furthermore, such legislatures have been exceptional. Most legislatures engage in other activities and have wider consequences for their political systems. Their significance lies not so much in law-making but rather in a range of other functions they fulfil. Those functions will vary in extent and significance over time, and from legislature to legislature. Indeed, even in central and eastern Europe during the era of Soviet domination, there was some variation in activity and consequences. The Polish parliament (the Sejm), for example, exhibited a capacity for some independent action that set it apart from its German neighbour.

There is, then, more to legislatures – much more – than formulating (making) law. This is apparent from a cursory observation of the demands made in Britain of the House of Commons and its members. The House of Commons spends as much time dealing with other items of business as it does with legislation. Question time and debates on declaratory motions are not part of the law-making process. Some of the most significant occasions in the House that have had a major political impact have had nothing to do directly with legislation: for example, Tony Blair's speech in 2003 justifying war with Iraq, and later debates about the wisdom of going to war. The most extensive media coverage, to which we have already referred, is of the partisan clash between the prime minister and the leader of the opposition during the prime minister's weekly appearance at the dispatch box to answer questions. Constituents will write to Members of Parliament (MPs) seeking their intervention in cases where benefits have not been paid or where some government department has apparently mishandled a request or complaint. No change in the law is being sought, yet members of the legislature – in their capacity as members – are expected to act, and *do* act, in pursuit of particular demands. In surveys of what constituents expect of their MP, the constituency service role ranks significantly higher than the collective task of law-making or exercising an oversight of the executive (Norton, 2002a, pp. 29–30). Expectations of MPs as constituency workers have increased markedly since the 1960s (Norton, 2002a, pp. 20–9).

Britain may enjoy a legislature that is distinctive for its longevity, but observation of other legislatures suggests that it is not unusual in the range of its activities and the demands made of it. Most parliamentary assemblies have a facility for asking oral questions on the floor of the House (Bruyneel, 1978). A fixed period for asking such questions – question time – is a feature of many European parliaments. In some countries, such as Austria and Finland, the procedure for asking questions is enshrined in the constitution. Constituency work occupies the time of parliamentarians in many – though by no means all – countries (see Cain *et al.*, 1987, Norton, 2002a).

Formally, then, as well as in practice, expectations of legislatures extend beyond involvement in the formal process of law-making. Hence the apparent paradox falls. Legislatures cannot be assessed solely in

Table 1.1   Packenham's legislative functions

Legitimation
   Latent (through meeting regularly and uninterruptedly)
   Manifest (the formal stamp of approval)
   'Safety valve' or 'tension release' (outlet for tensions)

Recruitment, socialization and training
   Recruitment
   Socialization
   Training

Decisional or influence functions
   Law-making
   'Exit' function (resolving an impasse in the system)
   Interest articulation
   Conflict resolution
   Administrative oversight and patronage (including 'errand running' for
      constituents)

Source: Derived from Packenham (1970).

terms of their capacity to make law. Given this, a prerequisite is to identify the functions that they variously fulfil.

In a seminal study, Robert Packenham (1970) identified a total of
eleven functions of legislatures. He defined functions in terms of
consequences for the political system. In other words, they were not
necessarily planned or formally delineated tasks undertaken by the legislature. The functions are listed in Table 1.1. Packenham drew on a
study of the Brazilian congress in order to identify them. His study of
that legislature allowed him to determine a rank ordering – those at the
top of the list had the greatest consequences for the political system, and
those at the bottom the least. The decisional functions such as law-
making, on which pluralists concentrate, came towards the end of the
ranking. Those functions would clearly rank higher in any analysis of
the United States Congress but, as Packenham observed, 'what knowledge we have suggests that the Brazilian case is much closer to the
mode than the U.S. Congress'. For Packenham, it is the other functions
that merit particular scrutiny. 'In fact, even if it [the Brazilian congress]
had no decision-making power whatsoever, the other functions which it
performs would be significant.'

Packenham's delineation is neither original nor exhaustive. Walter Bagehot, in *The English Constitution* (1867), provided a list of functions of the House of Commons more than a century before Packenham's work appeared. They were five in number: the elective (choosing the government); expressive ('to express the mind of the … people on all matters which come before it'); teaching ('to teach the nation what it does not know' and so alter society); informing (to raise grievances and make people hear 'what otherwise we should not'); and, finally, the legislative function, 'of which of course it would be preposterous to deny the great importance'. Parliament's responsibility in the sphere of finance he subsumed under the last heading listed here. A year short of a century after Bagehot's work appeared, Samuel Beer identified another function – that of support mobilization; that is, helping to raise popular support for a particular measure of public policy. It was, he contended, a function that was significant in the USA but not in the United Kingdom (Beer, 1966). It is a function that, to some extent, marries Bagehot's informing and teaching functions.

Nor are the functions Pakenham identified free of criticism. His inclusion of latent legitimation is open to criticism on the grounds that it should not rank alongside the other functions listed, but rather be regarded as a consequence of the fulfilment of the other functions. If a parliament carries out the tasks expected of it by citizens, then it may generate a latent body of support for the political system. Meeting regularly and without interruption – part of the process of institutionalization – may develop some familiarity on the part of citizens, but such consistency may not itself generate a significant body of support. Such characteristics did little to prevent the collapse of regimes in central and eastern Europe in the late 1980s. Some regularity in meeting may be necessary, but not sufficient to build up latent support.

Packenham's work none the less marked a major advance. It is significant for its breadth, sophistication and empirical support. It still provides the most extensive delineation of functions available in the field of comparative legislative studies. In an adapted form, it will provide the basic structure for this study. It will be adapted in two ways. First, it will be reworked to provide slightly greater breadth and sophistication. The category of seeking a redress of grievance will be employed, thus separating out – and going beyond – the errand-running activity identified by Packenham; the law-making category will be broken up into the various stages of the legislative process; and the study will be complemented by a consideration of parliament's capacity to educate and to mobilize support for particular policies. Second, it will not be utilized in the rank order provided by Packenham. Instead, the functions will be grouped under two basic heads: government and the citizen.

Parliament, like other legislatures, serves as a buckle between the citizen and the government, and the buckle may not always be a strong one. However, what is important for our immediate purposes is that parliament has two sets of relationships, one with the government and one with the citizen. The relationships are not mutually exclusive but they are analytically separable. The focus of scholarly attention has been on the link with the executive and, in particular, on the capacity of parliament to affect government in the initiation and formulation – the making – of public policy. In short, the focus has been a pluralist one, concerned with observable decision-making.

The relationship with the citizen has rarely been explored to the same extent as parliament's relationship with the executive. The literature is growing but is still relatively sparse. Yet the link is a vital one, underpinning the health of a political system. How parliamentarians act on behalf of citizens can generate a latent body of support. That action may involve persuasion. That persuasion may be two-way, with parliamentarians influencing the action of ministers on the one hand and citizens on the other. That persuasion may be at the collective level – parliamentarians influencing the policy or actions of government or of organized groups (attentive publics) or the wider citizenry (general public) – or at the level of the individual, where an MP's actions influence the behaviour of a minister or a citizen.

Political authority, according to Richard Rose, rests on the twin pillars of effectiveness and consent. 'An organization that cannot effectively influence the society around it is not a government. A government that acts without the consent of the governed is not a government as we like to think of it in the western world' (Rose, 1979, p. 353). A government needs to be able to govern, and it needs to be powerful in pluralist terms. However, its legitimacy as a governing body derives, in a parliamentary system, from its relationship to the legislature. Any government normally requires the assent of the legislature to get its measures enacted. It may – in most cases, usually does – receive this assent, but the process by which it does so has to be accepted as legitimate by the population. The legislature thus needs to be powerful in institutional terms. Institutional structures and processes can serve as an important constraint on government. The latent body of support that Packenham identifies as an important element of legitimation may, as we have suggested, derive from the fulfilment of the other functions he identifies. By fulfilling a range of functions, legislatures may thus underpin popular support for the political system.

Explaining Parliament in Britain

The role of legislatures is thus more complex than that suggested by pluralist writers. This work seeks to give shape to that complexity. It does so by following the structure already identified: first, the relationship of Parliament and the executive; and, second, the relationship of Parliament and the citizen. The foregoing analysis helps shape the structure of the book. It also provides the basis of the analytic framework. Legislatures have proved to be adaptable bodies. Some have a history dating back several centuries: the English Parliament (which later combined with the Scottish one to form the British Parliament) and the Icelandic parliament (the Althingi) compete for the claim to be among the oldest. As we shall see, Parliament in Britain has had a chequered history, weathering a number of conflicts, but it has adapted and endured. It has been characterized by continuity and change, with the balance between the two frequently proving problematic. The basic premise of this study is that Parliament has adapted in recent times in a particular way. Recognition of Parliament's power to determine the outcome of public policy has moved, to a large degree, from the coercive to the persuasive. Its capacity to persuade has become more significant in giving voice to the needs and demands of citizens. Political stability rests on its capacity to make its voice heard, and in a way that meets the expectations and concerns of citizens.

Parliament and government

In Part I, we draw on Packenham's taxonomy in looking at the consequences of Parliament for recruitment and training, legislation (the law 'making' function), and scrutiny of government (oversight). We look first at Parliament as the recruiting agency for executive office. It is one of the functions that makes Parliament powerful – in institutional terms – in that it has a virtual monopoly as a recruiting agency for executive office. We then devote most of the section to legislation, analysing the pre-legislative stage (initiation and formulation) and the legislative process within Parliament. Again, the importance of the study is to be found in the institutional as well as the pluralist view of power. Measures requiring parliamentary approval are laid before Parliament and go through a specified process. Both Houses have highly developed rules and procedures. Every bill has to go through several stages in each House. It is at the stage of debate and approval that Parliament becomes most visible in the legislative process. The government is normally assured of getting the measures it wants, but the content of those measures may be influenced by the actions of MPs and peers. The need to go through the highly institutionalized legislative process limits government.

We conclude by looking at scrutiny of government. We also look at it beyond the level of the nation state. Parliament's relationship with executive bodies has been confined traditionally to the British government. This remains the central focus of its activities and hence also of Part I of this volume. However, that relationship is no longer so confined. Decision-making competences have been transferred from central government to the institutions of the European Union, and to elected bodies in different parts of the United Kingdom. The Human Rights Act 1998, incorporating the European Convention on Human Rights (ECHR) into British law, has also arguably transferred some power from Parliament to the courts. This seepage of power to other bodies has major implications for Parliament, and these will be considered in the concluding chapter of this section.

Parliament and citizen

In Part II, we look at the relationship of Parliament to citizen. We open by examining the importance of Parliament as a representative body. We then focus on MPs as the principal link between the individual and government, serving as 'grievance chasers' (in traditional terminology, seeking a redress of grievance) and as a safety valve for constituents wanting to give vent to particular problems and concerns. In Chapter 9 we look at Parliament's role as a means of expressing particular interests and demands channelled through parties and, at a more particular level, through pressure groups. We then go beyond organized interests to consider the extent to which Parliament fulfils a similar role for sectors of society that are not organized, a category that on occasion includes majority opinion. Having looked at the relationship of citizen to Parliament, we address the relationship of Parliament to citizen and consider how the institution informs and educates the public.

We conclude by looking at the extent to which Parliament is or is not meeting the challenge of adapting to the changing nature of British society. Enoch Powell, a distinguished parliamentarian, argued that

Parliament was the means through which the people spoke to government and government spoke to the people (Powell, 1982). That neatly encapsulates the various roles of Parliament. Parliament is not the government, though remains vital to the polity as the body through which government is chosen. Between elections, Parliament is needed by government to pass laws and thus achieve its policy goals. Parliament scrutinizes what government is doing and what it proposes. It serves as the body that ensures the government pays heed to the needs and expectations of citizens. The vital question is: to what extent does government hear, and act upon, what Parliament is saying?

2

The Development of Parliament

In legal terms, Parliament is not just the House of Commons and House of Lords: it is the Queen-in-Parliament. The assent of the monarch is necessary for a measure to be recognized by the courts as constituting an Act of Parliament. However, the queen, as sovereign, occupies a position distinct from the two Houses, forming what Bagehot referred to as a 'dignified' element of the constitution. Her actions as sovereign are determined almost exclusively by convention (Norton, 2004b). As such, her actions are predictable, involving little, if any, real scope for independent, and hence partisan, judgement. The role of the monarch will not form part of our enquiry. That will accord with popular perceptions of what constitutes Parliament: few electors would include the monarch if asked to define the term.

Many electors, though, would tend to define Parliament in terms of the House of Commons. It is not uncommon for writers on British politics to use 'Parliament' as a synonym for the House of Commons. In this study, though, the focus is on both Houses occupying the Palace of Westminster. The House of Lords may be a poor relation, but it is still part of the family.

However, though both Houses may be part of the same family, they are certainly not twins. Compared to other legislative bodies, both are extremely active chambers, each typically sitting for more than 150 days each year. Few other legislatures can match this figure (Select Committee on Sittings of the House, 1992). They are also large bodies. The Commons has 646 members and the House of Lords just over 700. No other bicameral legislature comes close in terms of the combined membership. However, compared to one another, the two chambers differ markedly. They have different origins, different practices and procedures, different roles and – formally since 1911 – different powers. The House of Commons is not dissimilar in character to many other elected first chambers; indeed, some legislative chambers in Commonwealth countries are modelled on the House. The House of Lords, as an

unelected chamber, is not unique, but the nature of membership (appointment for life in most cases) and its practices and procedures render it
distinctive. The unelected chamber is subordinate to the first. In the
event of conflict, the House of Commons can, if it insists, eventually get
its way. The United Kingdom thus has what is termed asymmetrical
bicameralism. Historically, it has not always been thus.

The House of Commons

The House of Commons is the younger, but now the more politically
significant, chamber. However, it is only in the years since 1832 that it
has established itself as the politically superior chamber.

Origins

The House has its origins in the thirteenth century. There was a practice
of the king holding a royal court on special occasions, to which leading
figures were called, supplemented in between by summoning the
principal prelates and tenants-in-chief (usually earls and barons) to offer
their counsel in the kings' court, the *Curia Regis*. In 1254, when the King
needed money, two knights from each shire were also summoned to
Court 'to consider what aid they will be willing to grant us in our great
need' (McKenzie, 1968, p. 15). Ten years later, at a time of considerable
conflict, Simon de Montfort – then the most powerful baron and effectively ruling the country – issued writs in the king's name for the return
of four knights from each shire to discuss the state of the realm. The
following year – 1265 – he issued writs for the return not only of two
knights from each shire but also of two leading figures (burgesses) from
each borough. This, as McKenzie noted, is often seen as the beginning
of the House of Commons: 'the Commons had arrived' (McKenzie,
1968, p. 15).

In 1275, Edward I held his 'first general Parliament', to which
knights, burgesses and citizens were summoned in addition to the
barons and leading churchmen (McKenzie, 1968, p. 17). He held some
thirty Parliaments during the first twenty-five years of his reign.
However, those summoned from the local communities, or *communes*
(Commons), played no part in the deliberations on high policy. Nor
were they always summoned. There is no evidence, for example,
of their having been summoned to more than four of Edward's
Parliaments. However, their attendance became more regular under

Edward II, and they were summoned regularly after the accession of Edward III in 1327. 'Having for a long time been accorded *some* significance, the presence of the Commons in Parliament had at last come to be regarded as essential' (Roskell, 1993, p. 7). The Commons grew in importance in the fourteenth and fifteenth centuries. There were various clashes between the king and Parliament, not least over taxation. There was pressure for Parliament to be summoned on an annual basis. The king tended to summon it only when he felt he needed it, usually to vote for more money. Relations between Henry IV and his Parliaments were 'constantly uneasy and fraught' (Roskell, 1993, p. 2). The king not only decided when Parliament would meet but also where it would sit. A number of cities were the sites for parliamentary sittings, though the most frequent venue was Westminster. Some sittings were very short, but a number lasted for weeks at a time. There were reigns when the number of Parliaments summoned was considerable.

There was also one other significant development in the fourteenth century. At various times, the knights and burgesses met separately from the churchmen and nobles, and so there developed the separation of the two chambers. It was also during this time that the Commons acquired functions that are still associated with it today.

Early functions

The knights and burgesses had initially been summoned to confirm the assent of local communities to the raising of additional taxation. There was no suggestion that they had the power to refuse that assent. Nor was such assent sought for all forms of taxation. However, in 1341, the king agreed that the people should not be 'charged nor grieved to make common aid or to sustain charge' without the assent of Parliament (White, 1908, p. 364). Granting money – known as supply – thus became an important parliamentary function.

Even before the measure of 1341, Parliament had begun to use its power of the purse to ensure that public petitions were accepted by the king. Citizens had the right to petition the monarch for a redress of grievances. Parliament presented such petitions and began to make the voting of supply conditional on a redress being granted. The first known instance of this was as early as 1309 (White, 1908, p. 369). From such petitions developed what came to be called statutes, which required the assent of the Commons, the Lords and the king, and were thus distinguishable from ordinances, which were the product solely of the king.

Statute law soon displaced ordinances as the most extensive form of written law, and in the fifteenth century the task of writing statutes was taken from the King's scribes and undertaken instead by the Commons.

Those returned to Parliament also began to take an interest in how money was being collected as well as how it was spent. As early as 1340, commissioners were appointed to audit the accounts of the collectors of subsidies. Where public officials were found wanting, Parliament used its power to remove them through impeachment, with the Commons voting impeachment, and the Lords trying the case. Though impeachment has since fallen into disuse, it provided the basis for the development of Parliament's scrutiny of administrative actions.

Sixteenth to eighteenth centuries

Parliament's position was strengthened under the Tudors, when monarchs needed supply and the support of Parliament in their various political and religious battles. Henry VIII had little difficulty gaining the support he wanted in his battles with Rome, but in so doing he accorded Parliament a significant status in helping to determine the high policy of the realm. During the Tudor era, a seat in the House of Commons became something to be sought after, rather than service in the House being treated simply as an expensive chore. It was also during this era that there were the first signs of embryonic specialization by the Commons. In 1571 there is the first official reference to a bill being sent to a committee of the House. Committees to undertake particular enquiries – select committees – were often employed in both Tudor and Stuart Parliaments.

The seventeenth century witnessed the clash between an assertive Parliament and a monarch believing in the divine right of kings. James I and, more especially his son, Charles I, variously denied the privileges of Parliament, and the clash between Charles and Parliament resulted in civil war. The defeat of the royalist forces brought in its wake not only the abolition of the monarchy but also of the House of Lords. The country was ruled by a council of state, elected by what came to be known – for fairly self-evident reasons – as the Rump Parliament, followed by military dictatorship. With the Restoration in 1660 came a revival of traditional institutions: there was a deliberate attempt to revert, unconditionally, to the position as it had been at the beginning of 1642.

Further tension between Crown and Parliament ensued, resulting in the clash between James II and a Parliament resistant both to his claims to the divine right of kings and to his Roman Catholic faith. In 1685, the

Commons refused to grant the king money to maintain a standing army. It also refused to repeal the Test Acts, which restricted public office to Anglicans. James decided to dispense with the services of Parliament and began to rule by prerogative powers, 'suspending' various laws, including the Test Acts. His actions incited leading politicians to invite the Protestant Dutchman, William of Orange, James' son-in-law, to bring a military force to England. He did so and James fled the country.

On the invitation of peers and former members of the Commons, William summoned a convention that proceeded to offer him and his wife, Mary, the throne, which it declared James to have abdicated. However, the offer was conditional. The convention promulgated a declaration of right, embodying thirteen articles affecting the rights of Parliament. The suspending of laws without the approval of Parliament was declared to be illegal; the dispensing power – to exempt individuals or groups from the provisions of particular acts – was forbidden; and the levying of taxation without the assent of Parliament was prohibited.

On 13 February 1689, William and Mary accepted both the throne and the declaration of right. The declaration was subsequently embodied in statute as the Bill of Rights and the convention turned, retrospectively, into a Parliament. According to G. M. Trevelyan (1938), James II had forced the country to choose between royal absolutism and parliamentary government. It chose parliamentary government.

The dependence of the monarch on Parliament was thus established. Increasingly, the monarch withdrew from the tasks of parliamentary management. Those tasks were assumed by the King's ministers, and the eighteenth century witnessed the emergence of a cabinet and a prime minister, and a powerful but not overly assertive House of Commons. Many MPs sat for rotten boroughs controlled by members of the aristocracy. The combination of aristocratic control and royal patronage was usually sufficient to ensure a majority for the king's ministry.

The nineteenth century

During this period, parliamentary politics was confined to a political elite. The aristocracy and the landed interests had a political voice, but few others had. Industrialization, as we noted in Chapter 1, created powerful pressures. There were demands for reform, and at the beginning of the 1830s, the Whigs – who had been the 'outs' in politics for a quarter of a century – found themselves in power and in a position to introduce a reform bill. The 1832 Reform Act enlarged the electorate by 49 per cent. In so doing, it helped to loosen the grip of the aristocracy on the Commons, but did not enlarge the electorate to such an extent that large-scale party organization was necessary to contact and mobilize electors. The consequence was a greater scope for independent action by MPs. The Act thus heralded what has been described as a 'golden age' of Parliament. MPs turned governments out and put new ones in (Bagehot's elective function), and variously overruled government policy: 'There was always a possibility that a speech might turn votes; the result of a division was not a foregone conclusion' (Campion, 1952, p. 15).

Too much should not be made of this golden age. The domain of public policy was very limited – most bills passed were private, rather than public – and defeats were not excessive in number. Furthermore, the period was a short-lived one. Pressure from a burgeoning urban middle class and from artisans contributed to a further major Reform Act in 1867. This was followed by measures to restrict corrupt practices and to introduce secret ballots. With the passage of the Representation of the People Act in 1884, the majority of working men were allowed to vote. The measures transformed the political landscape, as mass parties developed in response to the new situation. In the words of Richard Crossman (1963, p. 39), 'organized corruption was gradually replaced by party organization'.

The consequences for the House of Commons were profound. On the one hand, its superiority over the unelected Upper House was established, but on the other, it effectively lost two of the functions ascribed to it by Bagehot. The elective function passed to the electorate, and the legislative function passed, in effect, to the cabinet. Party came to dominate parliamentary activity. Government achieved control of the timetable. Whips – MPs appointed to keep fellow supporters informed of business and to ensure that they turned out and voted – became prominent figures in the life of members (Norton, 1979, pp. 10–14). By the start of the twentieth century, party cohesion was a well-established feature of parliamentary life: MPs voted loyally with their parties (Lowell, 1924, pp. 76–8). The outcome of votes was predictable: 'The task of the House of Commons became one of supporting the Cabinet chosen at the polls and passing its legislation ... By the 1900s, the Cabinet dominated British government' (Mackintosh, 1977, p. 174).

The twentieth century

The party leadership in government was able to utilize its parliamentary majority to ensure that those features of the nineteenth-century House that were to the benefit of government were retained, while those that were seen as a hindrance were diminished or removed. Hence the emphasis on an amateur House, with issues being debated on the floor, was maintained. A majority was easier to deploy on the floor. A few critical voices could be lost among the cries of loyal supporters. The use of investigative select committees facilitated critical scrutiny. What use there had been of select committees was reduced drastically.

However, the use of standing committees for taking the committee stage of legislation was extended. Standing committees were to the benefit of the government's legislative programme: more bills could be considered at the same time, avoiding a queue for detailed consideration on the floor of the House. From 1907, all bills were referred to a standing committee unless the House voted otherwise. Government was able to deploy its majority in a standing committee. Before the 1940s, a minister's parliamentary private secretary (an MP who was a minister's unpaid helper) used to act as an unofficial whip, but after 1945 it became standard policy to appoint whips to standing committees.

Government also became less willing to divulge information to the House. Increasingly, MPs were expected to defer to the superior knowledge of government. As government bills came to dominate the legislative agenda, and as those bills became more complex, the House failed to generate the resources to keep pace with those developments. Hence, in its relationship with government, the House exhibited the limitations mentioned in the introduction. It lacked both the political will and the institutional resources to challenge the measures formulated by government.

In terms of the relationship with citizens, the twentieth century witnessed some significant developments. One was the enlargement of the electorate.Under the provisions of the Representation of the People Act 1918, the franchise was extended to women aged 30 years and over. It was extended to encompass women aged 21 and over – thus bringing the female franchise in line with the male – in 1928. The voting age was lowered to 18 years by the Representation of the People Act of 1969.

However, for much of the century, an increased electorate did not entail a significant increase in the demands made of local MPs. MPs frequently were amateurs for whom parliamentary service was not a career occupation (see King, 1981; Riddell, 1993). For many Conservatives, it was a public duty and something often to be combined with other activities, such as practising at the Bar or serving as a company director or landowner. For some Labour MPs, it was essentially an end-of-career activity, a reward for long service in the cause of the party or a trade union. Where there were demands made of MPs by constituents, they were not always welcome. Even if many had wanted to be more active in dealing with their constituencies, there was the problem of limited resources. Payment for MPs was introduced only in 1912 (the princely sum of £400 a year) and saw few increases thereafter. Indeed, it was in fact reduced for three years in the 1930s because of the Depression.

For many MPs in post-war Parliaments, service was not always particularly rewarding, and for some without independent means it was difficult to survive. For those achieving ministerial office, and those amateurs who took some delight in watching – as one put it in the title of her autobiography – 'from the wings' (Cazalet-Keir, 1967), parliamentary life had some purpose. For others, Westminster offered little more than 'corridors of frustration' (Teeling, 1970). Members had little opportunity to influence public policy. Constituency activity absorbed some of an MP's time, but being recognized as a 'good constituency Member' was seen as an admission that one was not destined for government office. Serving as the link between citizens and government was not seen as the most rewarding, or productive, of activities. The link was essential, but not necessarily strong.

Recent changes

Since the 1950s there have been a number of changes that have relevance for our later analysis. There have been significant developments both inside and outside Parliament which have changed both the nature of the institution and the political environment in which it operates. We shall return shortly to those external to Parliament. The changes within the House can be grouped under five headings. The first three – background; resources; and behaviour – cover members and what they do. The other two – structures and visibility – relate to the institution. Each is important; in combination, they have changed the nature of the House of Commons.

Background

There has been a notable change in the background of MPs. This has been seen to some extent in terms of socioeconomic background, but even more so in terms of career aspirations.

Members of Parliament have become more middle class in background, a continuation of a trend. There was a substantial change in the background of Conservative MPs in the nineteenth century (Rush, 2001, pp. 97–100). The landed interest gave way to business and the professions. Those with private means have largely disappeared. In recent decades, the Conservative Party has, if anything, become more middle class than before (see Nott, 2002, p. 129). 'Traditionally, the Conservative may be regarded as the party of business, but it is even more the party of the middle class' (Rush, 2001, pp. 98–9). Conservative MPs are more likely to be university-educated than before, those drawn from non-Oxbridge universities becoming more prominent in the party's ranks. (The non-Oxbridge MPs have replaced MPs who had not had a university education rather than those who were Oxbridge educated.) The number educated at the leading public schools and Oxford or Cambridge universities has declined, most notably so in recent years. Though most Conservative MPs are public-school and university educated, only a small number are now drawn from the leading public schools; in 2001, only 14 out of 166 Conservatives elected had been to Eton (Criddle, 2002), once the breeding ground of future Tory MPs and prime ministers.

The proportion of manual workers in the ranks of the parliamentary Labour Party (the PLP) declined from 1945 to 1979 – from approximately one in four to one in ten – with only slight variations thereafter. Of the 412 Labour MPs elected in 2001, 12 per cent were drawn from manual backgrounds (Criddle, 2002, p. 204). The number of university-educated MPs on the Labour benches increased – from just over a third in 1945 to over half by 1970, and to two-thirds by 2001. The typical Labour MP in 2001 was educated at secondary school and university (or polytechnic); 62 had been educated at public school and university.

Members of both parties are now typically drawn from middle-class professions (Criddle, 2002, p. 204). Lawyers are to be found on both sides of the House, as are political organizers and journalists. Labour MPs are also drawn from the ranks of public-sector professionals, lecturers and teachers. The Conservative benches are supplemented by company executives and directors. Not only are there very few industrialists, landowners or miners, there are also relatively few scientists, engineers, architects, doctors or accountants.

The explanation for the dearth of MPs drawn from highly specialized professional backgrounds can be found in the fact that not only has there been something of a convergence in social background, but there has also been a convergence in terms of career goals. There has been a marked growth in the number of career politicians. These are politicians who, in Max Weber's words, 'live for politics'. For them, parliamentary life is long-term and more important than any other pursuit (Buck, 1963; King, 1981). Britain has always had career politicians, but what has been notable has been the growth in their number in recent decades, squeezing out the MP for whom parliamentary service came at the end of another career or, indeed, preceded going off to do something else with one's life (Riddell, 1993, 1995). Career politicians devote themselves to Parliament, or rather to their parliamentary careers. They serve as political researchers, advisers or consultants before being elected (Judge, 1999a, pp. 107–8). For them, re-election is a necessary but not sufficient condition for political advancement. They therefore apply themselves to raising their constituency profile. For promotion to the front bench, they need to impress their party leaders, so they busy themselves raising their profile in the House. This often entails asking questions, speaking in debates, and tabling motions (see Rush, 2001, Ch. 6). For the career politician, being an MP is a full-time, and often demanding, job.

Resources

Before the 1960s, MPs had few resources other than their salaries and travel allowances and, for most, a school-type locker in which to keep their papers. When not in the chamber, they found seats in the library or held meetings on seats in the corridors. Conditions improved from 1964 onwards, however. Their salary was increased in 1964, from £1,750 to £3,250 a year, and in 1969, a secretarial allowance of £500 a year was introduced. Members were also allowed to make free telephone calls within the UK. A subsistence allowance was introduced in 1972. The secretarial allowance evolved into an office cost allowance and has been increased variously since. Members' salaries have been increased. By 2004, the office cost allowance had been disaggregated into a range of allowances. In addition to their parliamentary salary (£57,485 in April 2004), MPs could claim more than £100,000 in allowances: an incidental expenses provision (£19,325 to cover costs of accommodation for office or constituency surgery and other services), a staffing allowance (between £66,458 and £77,534) and an additional costs allowance (£20,902 to cover overnight accommodation when away from home on parliamentary business). Certain MPs could also claim a London supplement of £1,618. MPs are also entitled to claim travel costs (including travel to EU institutions three times a year) and to have computer equipment for parliamentary use.

These changes have meant that MPs now have the capacity to hire secretarial and research staff, and to maintain offices in Westminster and their constituencies. Given the technology now available, many MPs concentrate their office resources in the constituency. In the 1950s and 1960s, concentrating resources in the constituency usually meant having the spouse do the administrative work while the MP replied in longhand to letters from constituents.

Physical resources have expanded. Extra office space has been created in the Palace of Westminster. The old Scotland Yard buildings – on the Victoria embankment a hundred yards (about 750 cm) from the Palace of Westminster – were taken over to provide more office space. They have been complemented by two major office buildings: No. 1 Parliament Street, a complex of modern offices built behind the original façade of several buildings, and Portcullis House, a large, purpose-made building dominating Bridge Street, opposite the Clock Tower of the Palace of Westminster. As a result of these developments, each MP now has an office.

Library and data-retrieval facilities have also been expanded. In 1972, the House of Commons Library had a staff of fifty-five; by the year 2000, it had a staff of 200. The Library offers not only a traditional library service, but also a research service, staffed by highly-qualified researchers who are able to provide extensive independent briefing packs for MPs at short notice. The Library has a Parliament and Constitution Centre, created in 1999, to provide a focus for its work in the field of Parliament and the constitution. The Library also publishes a wide range of debate packs and research notes for use by parliamentarians. MPs are great consumers of Library services. In 1973, the Library dealt with 3,291 enquiries; by 1999–2000, the number was 34,759, with a further 31,009 made at its branch library (in one of the outlying buildings), mainly by MPs' researchers (Rush, 2001, p. 130).

MPs are now able to work in dedicated offices, supported by secretarial and research staff, and use television sets to follow proceedings in the chamber, and their computers to access library research material and other data available on the parliamentary intranet.

Behavioural changes

The behaviour of MPs has changed in recent decades, especially in the chamber and the voting lobbies. Given the rise of the professional politician, there is far more competition in catching the Speaker's eye. There is far greater demand to take part in debates and question time (Rush, 2001, p. 154–7; Franklin and Norton, 1993). Most significant of all, though, has been the change in behaviour in the voting (division) lobbies. Members have proved to be relatively more independent in their voting behaviour. As we have seen, cohesion was a marked feature of parliamentary life by the end of the nineteenth century. This cohesion was maintained throughout the first seven decades of the twentieth century, reaching a peak in the 1950s. In two sessions (parliamentary years) in the 1950s, not a single Conservative MP voted against the party line. In the 1960s, one distinguished American commentator was able to declare that cohesion had increased so much 'until in recent decades it was so close to 100 per cent that there was no longer any point in measuring it' (Beer, 1969, pp. 350–1). Shortly afterwards, it did become relevant to measure it.

The early years of the 1970s saw a significant increase in cross-voting by Conservative MPs (Norton, 1975, 1978a). They voted against their own leaders more often than before, in greater numbers and with more effect. On six occasions, despite the government enjoying an overall majority of seats in the Commons, cross-voting resulted in the government being defeated. Cross-voting also became a feature of Labour MPs after a Labour government was returned to office in 1974, contributing to most of the forty-two defeats suffered by the government in the 1974–9 parliament (Norton, 1980, 2004c). The number of defeats on the floor of the House, combined with defeats in standing committee, ran into three figures (see Norton, 1980; Schwarz, 1980). The defeats took place on a number of important issues, including economic policy and the government's key constitutional policy of devolving powers to elected assemblies in Scotland and Wales (Norton, 2004c).

Some degree of independent voting has been maintained in succeeding Parliaments (Norton, 1985; Cowley and Norton, 1999; Rush 2001, pp. 170–76). In 1986, the government lost the second reading of the Shops Bill (Regan, 1987; Bown, 1990), when seventy-two Conservative MPs voted with the Opposition to defeat it, the first time in the twentieth century a government with a clear overall majority had lost a second reading vote. The Conservative government of John Major (1990–7) suffered four defeats as a result of cross-voting by Conservative MPs. Following a major defeat on the Maastricht Bill in 1993 – on the social chapter of the Maastricht Treaty – it had to seek a vote of confidence.

Though large majorities achieved by the Labour government in 1997 and 2001 served to absorb dissent by Labour backbenchers, the Blair Government – especially since 2001 – has witnessed significant back bench rebellions (Cowley, 2002a; Cowley and Stuart, 2004a, 2004b). In March 2003, 139 Labour MPs voted against the government on the issue of war with Iraq, the largest rebellion by government backbenchers in modern British history (Cowley and Stuart, 2004a). In the first two sessions of the 2001 Parliament, the government experienced a greater level of dissent by government backbenchers than had any previous post-war government (Cowley and Stuart, 2004b; p. 311). More than two-thirds of Labour backbenchers rebelled on one or more occasions. In 2004, the government narrowly avoided defeat on the issue of student fees, surviving a crucial vote on the Higher Education Bill by only five votes. Such was the frequency of rebellion by Labour MPs in the 2001 Parliament that some of the larger revolts went largely unreported (Cowley and Stuart, 2004b, p. 311). Independence in voting behaviour has been a more significant feature of the House of Commons than is popularly recognized.

The cause of this behavioural change has been the subject of considerable debate (Norton, 1978a; Schwarz, 1980; Franklin *et al.*, 1986; Norton, 1987; Rush, 2001, pp. 176–83). Clearly, issues are crucial. European integration has been the subject of considerable dissent, especially on the Conservative benches (Cowley and Norton, 1999). Issues, however, are necessary but not sufficient conditions to explain the change in behaviour. Some of the issues were not new but the willingness to vote against the government on such a scale, and to rob it of its majority, was. The behavioural change has been ascribed to the changing background of MPs – a generational explanation – as well as to the relaxation of the convention that a defeat necessarily involves the government's resignation. However, the changing background of MPs does not explain the sudden change in behaviour in the 1970s; there was little correlation between a new generation of MPs and dissenting behaviour. There was no change in the convention covering government defeats in the division lobbies. A government defeat *per se* was not sufficient to trigger a resignation or a general election; the defeat had to be on a vote of confidence for that to happen (Norton, 1978b). There was nothing new in this; it had been established in the nineteenth century. The remaining explanation is the 'poor leadership' thesis, advanced by this writer, ascribing the triggering effect for the dissension to Edward Heath's style of prime ministerial leadership in the 1970–4 Parliament (Norton 1978a). Heath ignored his backbenchers on important issues, generating such a degree of resentment and frustration that some of his supporters found themselves impelled to express their disagreement, publicly and forcefully, by voting against the government, and on occasion denying it a majority. Once triggered, such behaviour developed a momentum, ensuring that it outlived the prime minister responsible for unleashing it. As one dissenter stated, when you had voted against the government once, it was much easier to do it a second time.

These behavioural changes should not be exaggerated, as cohesion remains a very marked feature of parliamentary behaviour (Cowley, 2002a, p. 6). Even in the rebellious 2001 Parliament, the government was able to mobilize a unified Labour lobby in four out of every five votes (Cowley and Stuart, 2004b, p. 311). Party loyalty ensured that not it was defeated on a whipped vote. The change in behaviour is relative. Prior to 1970, a government with an overall majority was guaranteed a majority if it pressed ahead with a measure. Since then, it has usually been assured a majority but cannot quite take it for granted.

Structures

The late 1970s and 1980s saw some MPs flexing their new-found political muscle in order to extend their resources and to create a more specialized infrastructure. In 1986, MPs voted – against government advice – to increase their secretarial and research allowance by 50 per cent; and they repeated the exercise six years later. The House also approved various new procedures and new structures (Norton, 1986). Among the latter was the National Audit Office, to undertake efficiency audits of government departments, and – within the House itself – a series of departmentally-related select committees.

The committees were created in 1979 and marked a major departure from the chamber-orientated House that had been dominant since the advent of party government. Their introduction constituted the most important reform of the latter half of the twentieth century; possibly of the whole century. They exist to 'examine the expenditure, administration and policy' of the relevant department and associated public bodies. Fourteen were established in the 1979–83 Parliament, covering most government departments, and they have been increased in number since; for every department, there is now a departmental select committee. During the 2004–5 session there was a total of eighteen. The committees have become a permanent, and indeed a pervasive, feature of the parliamentary landscape. They are now central to the task of pre-legislative scrutiny (see Chapter 4) and administrative oversight (Chapter 6). They absorb the energies of almost a third of all MPs: 204 MPs serve on them. They are complemented by a number of other investigative committees, including Public Administration, European Scrutiny and the long-standing Public Accounts Committee. They are active bodies, choosing their own topics for inquiry, meeting usually weekly, engaging in extensive evidence-taking, and publishing a raft of reports, formally to the House but in practice directed at government (see Drewry, 1989; Dawes, 1993; Jogerst, 1993).

Their activity is reflected not only in the number of reports they publish – usually more than fifty a session – but also in the physical expansion of the parliamentary estate. Such has been the demand for them in the Palace of Westminster that a second floor of committee rooms has been built above the main committee corridor, and this has now been complemented by a floor of state-of-the-art committee rooms in Portcullis House.

Committee meetings are not the only parliamentary activity that draws MPs from the chamber. The House in 1999 introduced a parallel chamber, an idea borrowed from the Australian Parliament. Meetings are held each week in the grand committee room off Westminster Hall – the sittings are styled as meetings in Westminster Hall – to hold short debates on topics raised by private members as well as on select committee reports. The meetings are open to all MPs who wish to attend. Unlike the chamber, no votes are permitted and the room has fixed desks arranged in a semi-circle around a raised dais. Though meetings attract few MPs, they provide the opportunity for those with a particular interest to attend and speak.

Visibility

The other major change is in the visibility of proceedings. Until the 1970s, the press were admitted to the chamber and to public meetings of committees, but the broadcast media were excluded. One could read about debates but not listen to them, other than by sitting in the public gallery. In the mid-1970s, there was an experiment where debates were broadcast, and sound broadcasting of the debates in both Houses began on a permanent basis in 1978. People could now listen to what went on in Parliament, though the effect was not necessarily positive: the sound of MPs bellowing support or dissent proved to be unattractive. But pressure built up to admit television cameras, and the House of Lords admitted them in 1985. The House of Commons lagged behind, voting to admit them in 1988, and with the cameras beginning to transmit proceedings the following year. The cameras record proceedings on the floor of the House and, selectively, in committee, both select and standing. The television coverage initially proved both more extensive than had been anticipated, and also more popular, both with MPs and the viewing public. What had started out as an experiment was soon made permanent.

Televized broadcasting, as we shall see in Chapter 12, has also been supplemented by new technology. Proceedings may now be accessed via the internet, for example. In addition, transcripts of committee hearings are placed on the internet shortly after they become available. Committee reports are available on the internet. Some committees have also used the internet to undertake consultations on particular proposals.

These changes are essentially ones to have taken place within the House. The House has also been operating within a changing political environment and one in which greater demands have been made of it. The continuing demands made of government have ensured that the volume of legislation has continued to grow. The consequences of membership of the European Union (EU) have included EU business occupying parliamentary time, either on the floor of the House or in committee, and pressure groups have lobbied MPs on a more extensive basis than before (Norton, 1999b). Constituents have also become more demanding, writing more often to their MPs and having greater expectations – or appearing to local parties and to members to have greater expectations – of members spending more time than before in their constituencies (Norton and Wood, 1993; Rush, 2001, pp. 207–11). These changed conditions have significant consequences both for the activity of MPs and for the various functions of the House.

The House of Lords

The House of Lords can claim to have its origins in the earliest medieval courts, the Anglo-Saxon *Witenagemot* and its successor, the Norman *Curia Regis* of the twelfth and thirteenth centuries, summoned by the king to help discern and declare the law and to proffer advice before the levying of new taxes. As we have noted, the *Curia* comprised the leading barons and churchmen of the kingdom. If a baron attended regularly, it became common for his heir to be summoned following the baron's death. The court thus acquired a body of attenders there by virtue of being their fathers' sons rather than in their own right as tenants of the king.

In the thirteenth century, as we have seen, the king summoned knights and later burgesses to court. In the fourteenth century, the barons and churchmen started to deliberate separately from the knights and burgesses, thus creating the two bodies we now recognize as the House of Lords and the House of Commons.

Formally, the two Houses were co-equal, though the principle of the Commons being responsible for initiating taxation was soon conceded. Henry IV affirmed the position in 1407 and the Commons defended it after the Restoration when the Lords attempted to initiate bills to raise taxes. Indeed, the Commons extended its privilege, denying the right of the Lords to amend money bills (McKenzie, 1968, p. 70). In other matters, the House of Lords was equal to the Commons.

Indeed, in political terms, their lordships came to exert considerable influence over members of the Commons, not formally but through their control of parliamentary seats. Most, though not all, of the MPs returned for 'pocket' boroughs owed their positions to the patronage of peers. A table compiled about 1815 showed that 471 parliamentary seats were controlled by 144 peers and 123 commoners (Ostrogorski, 1902, p. 20). Some members of the Lords preferred to make their political presence felt through their surrogates in the Commons rather than through their own House. In the Lords, each had one voice. In the Lower House, they might control several.

Franchise and boundary reforms undermined this control. The House of Lords, though, remained a powerful body. It used its powers to initiate and, perhaps more importantly, to vote down bills. It continued to use this power despite the fact that its legitimacy as a co-equal body was undermined by the widening of the franchise. An unelected chamber had difficulty withstanding the claims of an elected chamber. As Lord Shaftesbury noted during the passage of the 1867 Reform Bill, the House might get away with voting down a particularly unjust or coercive bill, but to do so more than once would not be permitted. 'It would be said, "The people must govern, and not a set of hereditary peers never chosen by the people"' (quoted in Norton, 1981, p. 21). The House – Conservative-dominated, as it had been since William Pitt the Younger created a record number of Tory peers in the late eighteenth century (Baldwin, 1985, p. 96) – did vote down more than one contentious Liberal bill, and the outcry that Shaftesbury had anticipated was heard. The latter half of the nineteenth century saw calls for the reform, or even the abolition, of the Upper House. The policy of 'mend or end' became popular in Liberal circles. In 1893, the Lords threw out the Home Rule Bill. The following year, the Liberal Party conference voted in favour of abolishing the Lords' power to veto bills.

The nineteenth century thus ended in a situation where the House of Commons could claim political but not legal supremacy over the unelected House of Lords. The situation was likely to prove untenable in the event of the return of another Liberal government, and so it proved. The twentieth century saw major reform to the second chamber. In the first half of the century, under a Liberal and then a Labour government, the reform was of its powers. In the second half of the century, under a Conservative and then a Labour government, it was of composition. What started out at the beginning of the century as a co-equal chamber comprising predominantly members sitting by virtue of inheritance ended as a subordinate chamber composed predominantly of members chosen in their own right.

Reform: powers

The Liberal Government of 1906 introduced a number of measures that proved too radical for the tastes of the Conservative majority in the Upper House. The Lords threw out or emasculated several major bills, including an Education Bill, before finally rejecting the Budget in 1909 'until it had been submitted to the judgement of the country' (quoted in Norton, 1981, p. 22). The government called an election on the issue not of the Budget but of the House of Lords. The result, after two elections, was the passage of the Parliament Act of 1911. The king had agreed to create a sufficient number of new Liberal peers should that be necessary in order to ensure a majority for the bill. In the event, it was not necessary: the number of Conservative 'hedgers' outnumbered the 'ditchers' – those who wanted to make a last-ditch stance against reform.

The 1911 Act provided that a non-money bill could be delayed by the Lords for a maximum of two successive sessions, the bill being enacted if passed by the Commons in the next session. Money bills – those dealing exclusively with money and certified as such by the Speaker – were to become law one month after leaving the Commons, whether approved by the Lords or not. The subordinate position of the House was thus enshrined in statute. In succeeding decades, the House essentially acknowledged its position as a politically inferior chamber and rarely challenged the principle of measures sent to it by the Commons.

The subordinate position of the House found further confirmation during the period of Labour government from 1945 to 1951. Shortly after the return of the Labour government, the Conservative leader in the Lords, Lord Cranborne, later Lord Salisbury, expressed the view that the House should not reject the second reading of a bill promised by the government in its manifesto. What became known as the Salisbury convention has remained in force ever since, and indeed, been extended to cover any bill in the government's programme for the session. The formal powers of the House have also been further limited. Under the Parliament Act of 1949, the two-session veto on non-money bills was reduced to one session.

Reform: composition

Reform of composition in the latter half of the twentieth century took place in two stages. The first entailed the introduction of life peerages and the second the removal of most hereditary peers.

The inferior position of the House after 1911 appeared to limit peers' interest in taking part in its activities. In the 1940s, the House had a membership of over 800, but of those 'only about 100 attend regularly and of these perhaps sixty of them take an active part in its business' (Gordon, 1948, p. 139). The House rarely met for more than three days a week, and on those days would often not sit for more than three hours. Votes were rare and when they were taken peers voted on party lines (Bromhead, 1958). Limited powers and limited activity led to little outside interest in the House. Even MPs gave it little attention, some looking upon it as providing, through its gallery, no more than a convenient place for depositing unwanted guests. When it did attract attention it was from critics who wanted to reform it or – the preference of some Labour MPs – do away with it altogether.

Rather than allow the chamber to atrophy, the Conservative government of Harold Macmillan decided to invigorate it, and in 1958 achieved the passage of the Life Peerages Act, which introduced the provision for peerages to be held solely for the lifetime of the holder. This allowed for the elevation to the peerage of many, such as trade unionists and other Labour supporters, who objected to the hereditary principle. The addition of life peers – the number of new creations increasing over the years – added to the size of the House (by 1998, the number exceeded 1,200) as well as the activity; life peers were disproportionately active in the work of the chamber. Having introduced an Act to enable new peerages to be created, the same Conservative government was also responsible for an Act – the 1963 Peerages Act – that allowed hereditary members of the Upper House to renounce their peerages. The measure had been championed for some years by the second Viscount Stansgate – Tony Benn – who wanted to give up his peerage in order to return to the House of Commons. However, the act also worked to the advantage of two Conservative peers (Lords Home and Hailsham) who, given the facility to renounce, could then seek the Conservative leadership following Harold Macmillan's resignation in 1963. Lord Home was the successful candidate for the succession and renounced his peerage in order to contest a seat for the elected House.

The second major change came in 1999. The Labour government in 1968 had attempted to reform the composition of the House by phasing out the membership of hereditary peers, who continued to dominate the House. The bill to reform the House ran into opposition: some opponents on the left thought it did not go far enough (they preferred an elected chamber or no chamber at all), while some on the right thought it went too far, preferring to leave things as they were. The opponents combined to delay the bill and – while it was never defeated in a vote (the opponents simply wore the government down) – the government

Table 2.1   The changing membership of the House of Lords, 1999–2004

Grouping	1 January 1999	1 December 2004
Conservative	473	203
Labour	168	201
Liberal Democrat	67	68
Cross-bench	310	173
Law Lords*	12	12
Lords Spiritual**	26	26
Other***	0	10

Notes: Excludes peers on leave of absence.
* Judges appointed under the Appellate Jurisdiction Act 1876 to fulfil the judicial functions of the House.
** The two Archbishops and the Bishops of London, Durham and Winchester, and the twenty-one most senior Bishops in the Church of England.
*** Includes unaffiliated peers such as Lord Archer of Weston-super-Mare (the novelist Jeffrey Archer).
Source: Data derived from House of Lords website.

decided not to proceed. There was no further major reform attempt for another thirty years. Then, in January 1999, another Labour government – secure in a large majority in the House of Commons – introduced a bill, the House of Lords Bill, to remove hereditary peers from membership of the House. In order to ensure the passage of the bill through the House of Lords, the government agreed to an amendment to retain 92 hereditary peers in the House (90 to be chosen by peers and two to sit ex officio). The bill was passed successfully and was enacted at the end of the 1998–9 session.

The House of Lords Act removed more than 600 hereditary peers from membership. From November 1999, the House has comprised predominantly life peers. The change also affected the party composition of the House, transforming it from one with a preponderance of Tory members to one in which no single party dominated. Further creations of life peers in 2004 helped to bring the number of Labour peers close to parity with Tory peers. The scale of the change, in terms both of numbers and party strength, can be seen from the data in Table 2.1 contrasting the pre-reform position with that at the end of 2004. Of the members in December 2004, 561 were life peers. (A further twenty-nine members were law lords and former law lords created under the

Appellate Jurisdiction Act 1876.) The House is clearly different from that existing before 1999 and has been transformed compared with the Tory-dominated house of hereditary peers that existed prior to 1958.

The changing nature of the House

The changes in the powers and composition of the House are not the only changes to have occurred in the Upper House. There are other changes which have taken place, some related to, the others independent of, the change in the composition of the House.

Behaviour

The House of Lords has seen something of a revival in terms of attendance and activity. The introduction of life peers represented a major spur to greater activity, as they proved to be relatively more active than hereditary peers; as a result of the influx of life peers, attendance has increased. By the end of the 1980s, the average daily attendance exceeded 300. More than 700 peers attended one or more sittings each year, and of those, more than 500 contributed to debates (Shell, 1988). In other words, well over half of all peers made the effort to turn up one or more times during each session. The relative position improved after 1999, with the disappearance of most hereditary peers, and the hereditary peers selected to remain were among the most active. In the early 2000s, the average daily attendance in each session exceeded 350 (House of Lords, 2004, p. 41). Not only was this more in absolute terms than the figure in the 1980s, expressed as a proportion of the membership it marked a significant shift, from a quarter to more than half. There is a substantial body of regular attenders. In 2003–4, 39 per cent of members attended three-quarters of the sittings, and 50 per cent attended 65 per cent or more of the sittings (Review Body on Senior Salaries, 2004, p. 36). The House is usually packed for Question Time and for major debates on contentious issues. The increase in attendance has also made possible the creation of more committees.

The greater activity of the House is reflected not only in attendance but also in sittings. The House now sits on more days, and for longer hours, than it did in previous decades. It sometimes sits for slightly more days a session than the House of Commons. (In 2002, for example, it sat for 156 days and the Commons for 150.) As the House itself has noted, 'The House of Lords is one of the busiest legislative chambers in the world' (House of Lords, 2002–3, p. 11).

There has also been a change in voting behaviour, though the change is not that obvious on the surface. When Labour was in power in 1974–9, it suffered numerous defeats at the hands of the House of Lords (a total of 362; see Baldwin, 1995, p. 241). Although the Conservative government from 1979 to 1997 also suffered at the hands of the Lords – a total of 241 defeats – the frequency was far less than under a Labour administration. Since 1997, the House has imposed defeats on the Labour government – a total of 353 up to the end of the 2004–5 session – but, after November 1999, in a situation that differs notably from the previous period of government. Previously, Labour had suffered defeats at the hands of a predominantly Conservative House. It was now suffering defeats in a House in which no one party enjoyed a majority. (Of the 353 defeats, 283 were in the period after November 1999.) While some Labour peers compared the number of defeats with previous periods of Conservative government, it was not a valid comparison. The valid comparison will be with a future Conservative government, which – like the Labour government – will face a House in which it can be outvoted by a combination of the opposition parties or the main opposition party supported by cross-bench peers. The two main parties are thus in a similar position, in a way that they were not prior to 1999.

Structures

Most business in the Lords, including the committee stage of bills, continues to be conducted on the floor of the House. However, the House has created a number of select committees and more recently has experimented with the use of Grand Committees for the committee stage of some bills.

Until the 1970s the House was very much a chamber-orientated body. This changed with the creation of a European Communities Committee to consider documents emanating from the European Community. This has developed into an extremely active committee (now titled the European Union Committee). It can consider the merits of documents and it works through a number of sub-committees: the number was increased to seven in 2004. About eighty peers are engaged in the regular scrutiny of EU documents, and it has established a formidable reputation for its work (see Chapter 7). It has been complemented by other select committees, including the Science and Technology committee, the Delegated Powers and Regulatory Reform Committee, and – in 2001

– the Economic Affairs Committee and the Constitution Committee. The House also joined with Commons in 2001 to set up a Joint Committee on Human Rights. In 2004, it established a Merits Committee to consider Statutory Instruments. These committees have been supplemented by *ad hoc* committees appointed to consider particular issues; these have included in recent years the Chinook helicopter crash, scientific experiments on animals, and religious offences. The House also now utilizes Grand Committees for the committee stage of some non-contentious bills. The Grand Committees are held in committee rooms, and can sit while the House is sitting, thus saving some of the time of the House. Any member of the House can attend, though only those particularly interested in the measures tend to do so, and no votes can take place. Any contested amendment on which members wish to vote has to be considered again when the bill returns to the chamber for the report stage.

Resources

The House now has an active body of committees complementing what takes place in the chamber and absorbing the commitment of a wide range of members. This activity places a strain on the relatively limited resources of the House. Though ostensibly occupying half of the Palace of Westminster, it has far less space at its disposal than has the House of Commons. Both the House and its members have to maximize the use of the limited space.

Recent years have seen some improvements in the resources available to the House and its members, but these have been limited. Peers receive no salaries, only allowances, and these are paid on the basis of attendance, though some allowance can be claimed to cover parliamentary work during recesses. The allowances have been increased in recent years, but remain modest (see Review Body on Senior Salaries, 2004). Apart from travel, the daily allowances are capped: from November 2004, peers have been able to claim £150 for overnight accommodation in London, £75 for subsistence and £65 for secretarial support. For their income, peers tend to rely on the jobs they hold outside the House. While the House of Commons is increasingly a House of career politicians, the Lords sees itself as being a House of experience and expertise, utilizing the experience and skills of members drawn from a range of backgrounds. (Members are usually appointed to committee because of their expertise in the area covered by the committee.) Opposition parties – as in the Commons – also receive money now to support them in fulfilling their parliamentary duties, though there is no payment to individual members of the Opposition front bench, other than the leader and chief whip.

Office space has increased in recent years, with the House acquiring two new buildings – Millbank House and Abingdon House – across the road from the Lords. The pressure on space means that peers do not have individual offices, but instead have to share accommodation. Most who want a desk have one, though some peers, by choice or necessity, work instead in the Library or other working areas, such as the Royal Gallery or the Peers' Writing Room. The facilities may not appear generous, though the pressure on space is compensated to some extent by the attractiveness of the surroundings. The House also has its own Library, with research staff, and members are entitled to computers and printers and, like MPs, have access to the Parliamentary intranet.

Visibility

The other major change is, as in the Commons, that of the televising of proceedings. As we have already noted, the Lords admitted the cameras in 1985, four years ahead of their entry to the Commons. In the first four years, Lords debates received late-night coverage and, despite the timing, relatively good viewing figures, but the coverage was largely squeezed out once the cameras started recording proceedings in the Commons. Lords debates, and some committee meetings, are carried on the Parliament Channel. All committee meetings are now webcast in audio and, as with committees in the Commons, transcripts of evidence are placed on the internet, along with committee reports and other material.

The House of Lords has thus seen major changes since the start of the twentieth century, not only in terms of its powers and composition, but also in terms of its operation. It has been characterized as a full-time House of part-time members – an active chamber drawing on members whose expertise derives from work normally pursued outside the House. It has changed in its relationship to the first chamber from being a co-equal to being a complementary chamber. As an unelected chamber, it remains the subject of proposals for reform. An attempt to move towards a partly or wholly elected House failed in a number of votes in the House of Commons in February 2003 (Norton, 2004d) but critics of the House continue to press for reform.

The changing constitutional environment

Both Houses have thus experienced notable changes in recent years. These changes, as we have noted, have taken place in the context of significant developments in the wider polity. Parliament is no longer the only legislature engaged in debating measures that will be applicable in part or the whole of the United Kingdom. The European Parliament is now a major law-effecting body, and a substantial body of law in the UK derives from European legislation. Membership of the European Community/Union has added a judicial dimension to the British constitution (see Chapter 7). Parliament has approved legislation creating a Scottish Parliament, a National Assembly for Wales, and a Northern Ireland Assembly. In the case of Scotland and Northern Ireland, both executive and legislative powers have been devolved (though in the case of Northern Ireland, the devolved institutions have at the time of writing been suspended; see Chapter 7), and in Wales executive powers only. The functions normally ascribed to Parliament on which it previously had a virtual monopoly (almost but not quite, because for fifty years from 1922 to 1972 Northern Ireland had its own parliament at Stormont), are now being exercised by a range of bodies.

At the same time, there has been a perceived centralization of decision-making power within British government. The prime minister has become, according to some commentators, more presidential, meaning that he has become more detached from his own party and his own cabinet (Foley, 1993; Norton, 2003b), operating as if elected directly by the people and hence deriving his authority from them rather than from Parliament. The result has been a declining engagement with Parliament by the prime minister (Dunleavy and Jones, 1995). This presidential tendency has been compounded since 1997 under the Blair government by a limited knowledge of government itself and by a tendency for ministers to follow the prime minister in focusing on executive rather than parliamentary duties (Norton 2003b). The presidential tendency, combined with devolution, has contributed to a fragmentation of power, leaving a range of power sources located at some distance, constitutionally as well as geographically, from Parliament.

These developments challenge Parliament's hegemony as the body for giving approval to measures of public policy. There are now other elected bodies that confer assent and which can claim to speak for the people in deliberations on measures of public policy. Parliament has to compete with other bodies to make itself heard by the institutions of the European Union. With the concentration of executive authority in

Downing Street, Parliament faces a challenge also to make itself
heard by the British government. The challenge has been to adapt to a
changing constitutional environment.

Conclusion

Both Houses of Parliament have a history spanning several centuries,
and they have had significant consequences for the political system. At
times, they have been important allies – and on occasion adversaries –
of the monarch. In the seventeenth century, Parliament was a major
actor in shaping the nation's constitution.

Though the institution, like other Western legislatures, has not been
able to withstand the forces identified in the introduction, it remains a
central part of the body politic. It is not, and never has been for any continuous period in its history, a policy-making body. It continues, though,
to have important consequences for the political system. Neither House
is a static body. Recent years have seen remarkable changes both inside
and outside Parliament. Both Houses are more active, more specialized,
better resourced, and more visible than before. The specialization of
Parliament – with both Houses operating through committees – has
been especially important in transforming the institution. On the face of
it, Parliament should be in a better position than before to make itself
heard and to influence government. The need to do so is greater as
it faces challenges from changes in executive authority and a more
crowded political landscape. The remaining parts of this work examine
whether or not Parliament has met the challenge.

Part I
Parliament and Government

3

Recruiting Ministers

Government ministers are drawn from, and remain in, Parliament. The significance of this well-known fact is often overlooked, but it has fundamental implications for the ways in which government and Parliament function.

Ministers in Parliament

It is a convention of the constitution that ministers must normally be drawn from the ranks of MPs and peers. There is no legal requirement. It is something that has derived from political circumstance. Monarchs needed the support of Parliament (see Chapter 2) and it was therefore prudent to have their ministers in a position to marshal and contribute to that support. In modern British politics, MPs expect ministers to be answerable to them for their actions; that means coming to the dispatch box to answer questions and respond to debates. Exceptionally, a prime minister may appoint someone who is not in Parliament. However, once appointed, the minister is usually brought into Parliament. Traditionally, this has been achieved by elevating the minister to the peerage or engineering election to the Commons through a by-election; nowadays, prime ministers tend to stick to the former route, since victory in a by-election cannot be guaranteed.

An attempt was made through the Act of Settlement of 1701 to sever the link between ministers and Parliament by making 'placemen' – holders of office of profit under the Crown, a category that includes ministers – ineligible for membership of the Commons. This provision, though, was not to come into effect until the death of Queen Anne, in 1714, and was modified before then by an Act of 1706. This allowed ministers to retain their seats provided they sought re-election.

> Though this put them to trouble and expense and was not repealed until as
> late as 1926, only very occasionally did it result in the officeholder's defeat,
> since the convention was soon established that it was ungentlemanly to
> oppose a member seeking re-election. (Cannon and Griffiths, 1988, p. 441)

The succession to the throne of the Hanoverian George I, who spoke no
English, added enormously to the king's dependence on ministers to
manage Parliament. The most stable administrations proved to be those
led by ministers who enjoyed the confidence of both the monarch and
the House of Commons.

The practice of ministers being drawn from, and remaining in,
Parliament is thus long-standing. What has been noteworthy about
the twentieth century and later has been, first, a decisive shift to the
Commons as the pool from which ministers are drawn; and, second, the
increase in ministerial numbers. Ministers have become less aristocratic
and more numerous.

The shift to the Commons

As the franchise was extended and the Commons became the dominant
of the two chambers, so the greater was the emphasis on having ministers in the Lower House, answerable to elected representatives. In the
nineteenth century, it was not uncommon to have a preponderance of
peers in the cabinet and, indeed, for the prime minister to be a peer.
The twentieth century opened with the third Marquess of Salisbury still
occupying the premiership. Since then, there has been a decisive, but
not necessarily rapid, shift of emphasis to the Commons.

In 1923, George V had to choose between Viscount Curzon and MP
Stanley Baldwin for the premiership. He chose the latter, principally
because the Labour Party had become the official Opposition and had
no members in the Lords. However, the King's action has been taken as
establishing the convention that the prime minister must be drawn from
the Commons. This was, in effect, confirmed in 1940 when Lord
Halifax, favoured by some Labour members for the premiership, recognized that his membership of the Upper House precluded him from the
post.

We have already alluded to the events of 1963 (see Chapter 2), when
the Queen sent for the fourteenth Earl of Home to ask him to form a
government: he relinquished his title and, as Sir Alec Douglas-Home,
was returned to the Commons at a by-election (see Shepherd, 1991,

pp. 149–59). The occasion was exceptional and only made possible by the passage of the Peerages Act 1963. Lord Home was eligible to renounce his peerage within the time limit stipulated. He was also the beneficiary of the fact that the Conservative Party had no formal means of electing a leader, with the choice being left to the monarch in the event of no obvious leader emerging. Today, election of the leader is by party members – from 1965 to 1997 it was by Conservative MPs – and members of the House of Lords, no longer joining the House by reason of inheriting their titles, cannot renounce their peerages. (The 1963 Act applied only to hereditary peers and, furthermore, stipulated a time period; all the hereditary peers remaining in the Lords are now out of time.) The choice of leader, in other words, must fall on a member of the Lower House.

The emphasis on being answerable to an elected House has also resulted in fewer peers serving in the cabinet. Churchill included six peers in his first peacetime cabinet in 1951. Harold Macmillan included five in his cabinet in 1957. He was the last premier to have a duke (his own nephew-in-law, the Duke of Devonshire) in his government as a junior minister. In both cases, the numbers were in fact quite generous and included a qualitative dimension: a number of peers were given senior positions. Since then, no prime minister has drawn as heavily on the Upper House for members of the cabinet.

Two members of the cabinet were, up to 2005, necessarily drawn from the Lords – the Lord Chancellor and the Leader of the House of Lords – with the minimum number also usually, though not always, constituting the maximum. The cabinets of Margaret Thatcher occasionally contained a departmental minister who was in the Lords; the most senior was Lord Carrington as Foreign Secretary (1979–82). Tony Blair briefly had a departmental minister in the House – Lady Amos as International Development Secretary (2003) – but the instance was exceptional. Even the minimum figure ceased to be sacrosanct in 2005 when the reform of the office of Lord Chancellor meant that the holder of the office need not be drawn automatically from the Upper House.

Below cabinet level, peers are more numerous in ministerial ranks. It is useful for prime ministers to appoint a peer as one of the ministers in a department, as it means that there is then a minister free from constituency duties and therefore someone who can carry most of the routine ministerial tasks during an election campaign, when the other ministers are busy campaigning. None the less, as we shall see, peers still constitute a minority – usually about a fifth – of government ministers.

Growth in numbers

Over the twentieth century and into the twenty-first, the size of the cabinet has not changed significantly, usually comprising twenty or so senior ministers. In 1901, the cabinet had nineteen members; in 2004, it had twenty-one. There have been some variations, partly reflecting a variation in the number of government departments, and conditions of war have seen the formation of an inner, or war, cabinet, but the basic membership has shown no significant increase. Where there has been an increase has been in the number of ministers outside the cabinet.

 At the beginning of the twentieth century, the number of ministers of cabinet rank (senior ministers not in the cabinet, such as the Paymaster General) and junior ministers (such as the parliamentary secretary to the local government board) was not much larger than the number of ministers in the cabinet. Indeed, the number was only larger because of the inclusion of the whips. Since then, the growth in government responsibilities has resulted in a significant increase in the number of ministers. At the beginning of the twentieth century, there were thirty ministers outside the cabinet; by 1997 there were eighty (Theakston, 1987, pp. 42–3; Brazier, 1997, pp. 12–13). The growth has been especially pronounced in the years since 1945, and the change has been qualitative as well as quantitative. A new post of minister of state – just

Table 3.1   Number of government ministers in Parliament, August 2004

Rank	House of Commons	House of Lords	Total
Cabinet ministers (including PM)	19	2	21
Ministers of state[a]	25	3	28
Law officers	2	1	3
Under-secretaries of state[b]	29	8	37
Whips[c]	15	8	23
Total	**90**	**22**	**112**

Notes: (a) Includes the Chancellor of the Duchy of Lancaster, the Paymaster-General and the Financial Secretary to the Treasury.

(b) Includes the Economic Secretary to the Treasury.

(c) Excludes Chief Whip in the Commons, who is a Cabinet member.

Source: Data derived from published lists of ministerial positions.

below cabinet rank – was created in 1950, and most departments now have one or more of them, in addition to the more traditional parliamentary secretaries.

The number of ministers, in total and by rank, in the Labour government in 2004 is shown in Table 3.1. In three departments – Education, the Home Office, and Trade and Industry – there were in fact six ministers in addition to the cabinet minister: each department had three ministers of state and three under-secretaries. A further five departments each had five ministers under the cabinet minister in charge. In 1901, no department had more than one junior minister attached to it.

Consequences for ministers

The fact that ministers are drawn from, and remain within, Parliament – and are drawn predominantly from the House of Commons – has a number of consequences in terms of the recruitment and training of those who are to form the government of the United Kingdom.

Ministerial recruitment

Politicians seek membership of a legislature because they believe that such membership will be of value to them: 'Membership may have immediate political value, long-range career value, and financial value, as well as value calculated in less tangible ideological and psychological terms' (Mezey, 1979, p. 224).

Of these, the long-range political career is the most important for our purposes. It is also distinctive. For anyone seeking to undertake public service, there are alternatives to serving in Parliament. For anyone seeking financial gain, there are far more remunerative positions to pursue than that of being an MP or, for that matter, a minister. (Indeed, there are various instances of people turning down offers of ministerial jobs or being highly selective because they were being paid more for doing other jobs; see, for example, Nott, 2002, p. 124; Renton, 2004, p. 3.) For anyone seeking to have some influence on public policy, there are again alternatives to being an MP: for example, a senior civil servant, policy adviser (in, for example, the No. 10 Policy Directorate) or head of an influential pressure group. For anyone seeking to find a platform for a particular ideological viewpoint, there are again alternatives: journalism, or serving in a policy research body or think tank. However, for anyone wishing to become, and make a career of being, a government minister or, ultimately, to occupy the premiership – the top of what Disraeli called the greasy pole – there is only one route. Parliament, in effect, enjoys a virtual monopoly in terms of recruitment.

As we have noted, someone – usually not a politician – may be elevated to ministerial office without being in either House at the time of appointment. However, such instances are exceptional and – equally important in this context – unpredictable. In other words, anyone *seeking* a career as a minister cannot plan to do so through a route other than membership of the House of Commons.

The House of Commons thus serves as a magnet for those wanting to exercise political power as ministers. As one American observer noted, 'the British House of Commons may play an insignificant role in policy-making … [but] as the only channel to top executive office it has the special attractiveness of "the only game in town" for the politically ambitious' (Matthews, 1985, p. 22). In institutional terms, the House is a powerful body.

This thus distinguishes Parliament from political systems where the executive and legislature are elected independently of one another. In the USA, for example, there are multiple career lines. For anyone seeking the presidency or a cabinet post there is no single and predictable career course to follow, but rather a range of options: state politics (primarily the governorship), the federal legislature (House or Senate), public service, education or business. Congress therefore does not constitute the exclusive pool from which cabinet officers or presidential candidates are drawn. Of recent presidents, for example, Ronald Reagan, Bill Clinton and George W. Bush did not serve in Congress. None the less, members of the House or Senate may be chosen for cabinet posts. In the European Parliament, there is no such likelihood: '[T]he European Parliament's situation has remained unchanged since 1979; it offers no links to "external" governmental opportunities for upward mobility. The only way up is out' (Westlake, 1994, p. 6). Consequently, the European Parliament has not been able to retain a body of long-serving members able to form a clear and cohesive political elite (Westlake, 1994).

The first act of a politician in Britain wanting ministerial office is therefore to obtain a parliamentary candidature. In order to stand any chance of election, this means getting selected as a candidate for one of the main parties. That is the first, but not the only step to take, for election by itself is rarely sufficient. Exceptionally, a new MP – whose reputation for particular qualities has preceded him (never, as yet, her)

– may be offered a ministerial post straight away, but in practice, most members have to serve an apprenticeship in the House before being offered a government post. Once elected, they are socialized into the parliamentary process through various rituals and procedures, such as the maiden speech, using certain modes of address in the chamber, and conventions on where to sit. For the purpose of advancement, they need to learn how to use the practices and procedures to their benefit. Some have difficulty in doing so, some may not want to, but for those seeking office it is usually a necessity.

There are more MPs on the government side of the House than there are posts to be filled: the ratio is usually in excess of three to one. Consequently, there is competition for places on the treasury bench (the traditional name for the government front bench). This was especially the case following the 1997 general election, when the number of Labour MPs elected was 419 – over 60 per cent of the total membership – with approximately 90 ministerial posts to be filled. The chamber and the committee rooms serve as arenas in which ambitious members seek to get themselves noticed by those with the capacity to influence their promotion to office. This means the prime minister, senior ministers and – most important of all for getting a foot on the first rung of the ministerial ladder – the whips. There is always a whip present in the chamber, and the whips play a central role in advising the prime minister on the performance of members. In the words of one former whip, they are 'vital in determining whether Members climb the parliamentary ladder to senior positions, slip from high office, or remain for ever on the back benches waiting in hope' (Major, 1999, p. 78; see also Brandreth, 1999, p. 369; Renton, 2004, pp. 62–9, 79–83).

To establish a reputation in the House, members may focus on the chamber – making speeches, tabling oral questions and generally making themselves visible, as well as being obliging to the whips (Shephard, 2000, pp. 85–6) – or on making a mark as an effective committee member. Serving as a member, or chair, of a select committee – or as an officer of a back bench party group – can also help to establish a member's reputation. Exceptionally, a member may get noticed and promoted on the basis of a particular speech. Francis Maude was given office in 1985, two years after being elected to Parliament, reputedly because he made a speech that was noticed by Margaret Thatcher, who happened to be in the chamber at the time. More usually, reputations – and contacts – are made over a period of time.

A member may be promoted to ministerial office straight from the back benches, or go via the position of parliamentary private secretary

(PPS). A PPS is an unpaid assistant to a minister, helping with the minister's political arrangements, providing a link with back bench opinion, and ferrying messages between the civil servants' box in the chamber and the minister on the front bench. (PPSs by convention sit on the bench behind the treasury bench.) A PPS can acquire some knowledge of how a department is run and at the same time acquire a ministerial champion who can mention his or her particular qualities to the whips and the prime minister. Becoming a PPS is often seen as the first rung to achieving ministerial office, and MPs are variously chosen as PPSs because they are perceived to have ministerial potential (Norris, 1996, p. 147; see also Norton, 1994a). That potential is not always realized – perhaps they fail to shine, or their patron does not carry clout with the PM – and for some the height of their political career is serving as the parliamentary private secretary to a minister of a state, the length of the title being in an inverse relationship to its political importance.

A training ground

The fact that ministers are drawn from the ranks of parliamentarians ensures that Parliament serves as the recruiting agency for ministerial aspirants. However, equally significant is the fact that ministers remain within Parliament. A consequence of this is that Parliament is important not only for nurturing future ministers but also serving as a training, or testing, ground for ministers.

The fact that ministers will remain within Parliament may itself be a significant factor in influencing the choice of backbenchers for ministerial office. Skills that are appropriate to handling oneself in the House may take precedence over other qualities. A good speaker or someone who in committee has demonstrated a good grasp of detail may hold an advantage over a colleague who may be a good administrator but who cannot hold the House during debate or has a poor grasp of what is being discussed in a standing committee.

Once in office, a minister is expected to be able to perform competently at the dispatch box during debates and at Question Time. A good performance can contribute to a minister's standing and future career prospects, while a poor speech can mar advancement. 'Several ... ministers would find it hard to win a prize for parliamentary oratory ... As a result, they often had a far more difficult time than they deserved' (Norris, 1996, p. 82). On occasion, it can contribute to a minister's downfall. Nicholas Fairbairn, for example, ceased to be Solicitor

General for Scotland in 1982 after his disastrous handling of a debate on a controversial legal case.

Given the emphasis on performance in the chamber, ministers tend to take seriously their appearances at the dispatch box. Some prepare rigorously; and some get very tense. One junior minister recalled that her secretary of state was not only meticulous in preparation but 'was also nerve-racked before questions and debates, refusing to eat, and smoking enormous numbers of cigarettes. He infected the rest of us with pre-appearance nerves, especially me, as a brand-new minister not over-endowed with parliamentary confidence' (Shephard, 2000, p. 137). A poor speech at the dispatch box can undermine the morale of the parliamentary party and, in the process, the minister's reputation and that of the government. A good speech can lift it and enhance a reputation. Following particularly important debates, senior ministers sometimes hold post mortems to discuss how a speech at the dispatch box has been received (see, for example, Lang, 2002, p. 289; Nott, 2002, p. 267).

Performance outside the chamber is also important. A minister needs to be able to master the detail of legislation when it is going through committee, and to handle questions from critical MPs – usually, but not always, opposition MPs – when appearing before a select committee. It is important for ministers to maintain good relations with their own supporters. An ability to mix easily – to be clubbable – is not a pre-requisite for achieving and retaining office, but it is an advantage. A minister can generate goodwill by spending time chatting to MPs in the Commons tea room or when they are going through the division lobbies. A minister may invite worried backbenchers to come and discuss their concerns. If a policy or measure looks likely to upset members, the minister may write what is known as a 'Dear Colleague' letter (a letter sent to all MPs in the parliamentary party explaining the reasons for bringing the proposal forward). Goodwill can prove to be a protective shield. A poor standing with backbenchers can make a minister vulnerable in the event of a policy or administrative mistake.

Ministers may attract criticism because of a particular speech or, more likely, a particular pattern of poor performances at the dispatch box. A minister who lacks confidence at the dispatch box, who fails to gauge the mood of the House, or who is obviously not in command of the facts will attract mutterings from the back benches and these will be noted by the whips. In his first government reshuffle, for example, Tony Blair removed one cabinet minister who had a reputation for indecisiveness as well as for being a poor performer at the dispatch box.

On occasion, ministers may lose office not simply because there are private mutterings on the back benches but because there are public demands for them to go. Various ministers during the period of Conservative government from 1979 to 1997 resigned after losing the confidence of Conservative MPs. These included the Foreign Secretary, Lord Carrington, in 1982, Trade and Industry Secretary, Leon Brittan, in 1986; and National Heritage Secretary, David Mellor, in 1992. Some ministers in Tony Blair's government have left office after criticism not only from Opposition MPs but also from government backbenchers. One example was Geoffrey Robinson, the Paymaster General, in 1998 (Robinson, 2000, p. 233).

Remaining as members of a body which may not choose them but can influence their future has, then, a significant influence on ministers. Resignations as a result of upsetting backbenchers may be few in number but serve as a salutary reminder to other ministers. It is an exceptionally thick-skinned minister who is unconcerned about his or her parliamentary reputation, and it is a rare, and usually imprudent, minister who neglects government backbenchers.

Parliament is thus a vital training ground or, to put it perhaps more accurately, an environment in which ministers have to learn to survive. Most do so without undue difficulty, but knowing they have to survive in that fairly closeted environment influences both their perceptions and their behaviour.

Wider consequences

The fact that ministers are drawn from and stay within Parliament also has other consequences for Parliament and for government. One of the benefits that flow to government, in the form of control, represents a problem for Parliament. However, there are beneficial consequences for both. For Parliament, there are what may be seen as essentially beneficial consequences in terms of career attractiveness, stability in membership, proximity to ministers, and socialization. For government, there are important consequences – mainly, but not wholly, beneficial – in terms of control, ministerial selection and legitimation.

Parliament

Career attractiveness

As we have seen, for anyone seeking to influence public policy through holding national ministerial office, there is little or no alternative to seeking a seat in the House of Commons. Gaining a parliamentary majority is essential for a political party to carry out its programme. Being in Parliament is essential to forming part of the government.

The hold of the Commons over ambitious politicians is remarkable. The main parties have a large pool from which to select their parliamentary candidates; the number of applications to succeed a retiring MP often runs to three figures. Recent years, as we have noted (Chapter 2), have seen as rise in the number of career politicians. The result, as we shall see, has been a more active House.

The attraction of sitting in the House is reflected not only in quantitative but also in qualitative terms. Those holding influential positions in government or other bodies continue to give up their posts to become MPs. Despite the growing power of the European Parliament to determine EU legislation, British politicians are more likely to view membership of the European Parliament as a stepping stone to a seat in the House of Commons, rather than the other way round. Leading government advisers and journalists seek parliamentary candidatures. In 1994, the Chancellor of the Exchequer's economic adviser, Ed Balls – regarded as a powerful influence on the Chancellor's thinking – gave up his post to be selected as Labour candidate for a safe Labour seat. At the same time, an assistant editor of *The Times,* Michael Gove, was selected as a Conservative candidate to fight a safe Tory seat.

For some politicians, being an MP is an end in itself (see Searing, 1994). For others, it is a means to an end, usually deciding public policy as a minister or, failing that, influencing those who are ministers. So long as government is drawn from, and remains within, Parliament, then a seat in Parliament remains highly prized by ambitious politicians.

Stability in membership

A stable membership allows for some degree of continuity. Experience can be drawn on, and there is the potential for a corporate spirit to develop. There would thus appear to be some advantage to the House in having some measure of continuity in its membership.

Given that those intent on a political career have no alternative path to pursue, the Commons loses relatively few members as a result of competing job opportunities. Some younger members have left the House because they felt there was little prospect of promotion from the back benches, or because they found the environment less than congenial, but these are few in number. The injection of new blood into the House is achieved predominantly through a change in electoral fortunes and in the retirement of members at the end of their political careers.

Very few MPs under the age of 65 voluntarily give up their seats. The greater career orientation of members appears to have contributed to longer parliamentary careers, especially in the years since 1945 (Rush, 2001, p. 131).

Stability is obviously affected by a massive swing in political fortunes at a general election. The general elections of 1906, 1945 and 1997 resulted in a large body of new MPs, but other elections have not had such a dramatic effect. Whereas the 1997 election produced an extensive turnover of members – 39 per cent of the membership was new – the 2001 general election was remarkable for its low turnover. Very few seats changed hands and a relatively small number of MPs retired; the consequence was that only 15 per cent of the MPs in the 2001 Parliament were new. Hence, by 2005, the overwhelming majority of MPs had been members for at least eight years, and most for much longer than that. (Three had each been in the House for more than forty years.) Consequently, members wanting to make a career in the House have usually had an opportunity to do so. The result is a House of Commons with a stability in membership that is relatively high by international comparison. Most MPs will continue in post from one Parliament to the next.

Ministerial ambition is not the sole explanation for such stability. Many ex-ministers remain in the House, as do some backbenchers who know their chances of promotion to office are slight. The fact that ministers remain in Parliament may be a partial explanation for the presence of those not destined for future office. They remain close to those who are in office.

Proximity to ministers

The fact that ministers remain in Parliament is valuable to other members in that it ensures a closeness that can be utilized by each House collectively, and by members individually. Ministers have offices in the Palace of Westminster as well as in their departments. MPs can arrange to see them in the House. Some ministers will also spend time meeting members in the tea room, and smoking and dining rooms, not least for reasons of raising their profile among potential back bench supporters. In the 1997–2001 Parliament, Home Secretary Jack Straw was described as 'the senior minister most often in the tea rooms' (Cowley, 2002a, p. 160). Ministers will be present in the House to take part in debates and answer questions; the minister replying to a debate normally remains throughout to listen to the speeches. Some will attend to listen to other ministers in debate.

Given that they are members, ministers are also entitled to vote. They are thus present during divisions. As the process of voting takes several minutes – on average, about twelve minutes for each division – ministers spend some time rubbing shoulders with back bench supporters in the division lobbies. This presents an opportunity – and a much-used one – for backbenchers to talk to ministers and put over particular points. Conversely, ministers often utilize the opportunity to track down members they want to see. Such opportunities for face-to-face contact are recognized by members as invaluable for increasing the likelihood of a positive response to a request: a minister finds it more difficult to say no when facing the member making the request.

Socialization

The fact that ministers start life as MPs and remain as members ensures – or is likely to ensure – that they are familiar with parliamentary norms and expectations. Aspirant ministers have to know their way round the institution. A survey by the Study of Parliament Group of new MPs first returned in the 1992 general election found that approximately half of them regarded themselves as 'very familiar' or 'somewhat familiar' with parliamentary procedure. Once elected, they face the same demands and pressures as their other colleagues. And once elevated to ministerial office, those demands do not necessarily cease. Ministers in the House of Commons retain constituency responsibilities (see Chapter 9). They have to carry out tasks as MPs and not solely as ministers. They have to contact fellow ministers in their capacities as constituency MPs, and fellow ministers may approach them in a similar capacity.

There is thus socialization into the parliamentary process of those who are to form the political elite. Though ministers are answerable to Parliament, they are also members of the very institution to which they are answerable. They mix with backbenchers, rubbing shoulders with them – sometimes literally – when they vote. They are themselves likely to return to the back benches at some stage, be it by choice or by prime ministerial diktat. This reduces the likelihood of ministers ignoring and not understanding Parliament's needs and expectations. Indeed, not understanding those needs and expectations may facilitate a speedy return to the back benches. Some ministers may be poor at handling the House, but they generally grasp and are integrated into its practices and procedures. They are an integral part of the institution. This contrasts with those political systems where there is a separation of executive and legislature, increasing the potential for misunderstandings between the two.

Government

Control

Party dominates Parliament and political behaviour. We have seen in preceding chapters the conditions that made this possible. For its continuance in office, government is dependent on a parliamentary majority. Formally, this should ensure parliamentary control of the executive, but in practice, the flow of control is the other way. In the eighteenth century, control could be achieved through royal patronage and placemen in the Commons, but since the last third of the nineteenth century, it has been achieved through party.

The presence of ministers in Parliament is not the cause of party control (see Crowe, 1986) but serves to facilitate it. Being in Parliament means ministers have a platform to lead and to persuade their supporters. Ministers can serve as an important reference group for loyal and ambitious backbenchers. 'Some MPs model themselves after the front-bench group, especially those backbenchers who seek higher office themselves' (Crowe, 1986, p. 164). Ministers alone can introduce bills making a charge on the public revenue. In debate, frontbenchers are the focus of attention. And ministers collectively constitute a significant voting force.

Ministers are bound by the convention of collective responsibility, a convention requiring that ministers do not oppose a policy once it has been agreed. Some uncertainty existed in the nineteenth century as to whether the convention applied to junior ministers. In the twentieth century and since, there has been no such ambiguity (Norton, 1989b, pp. 34–5). It encompasses all ministers, and in recent years has been employed to constrain the activities of parliamentary private secretaries (Norton, 1989a, pp. 234–6; 1989b, pp. 35–6); PPSs voting against the government can usually expect to lose their posts. The result is a block vote at the disposal of government. Given the increase over the twentieth century in the number of ministers, and the increase in recent decades in the number of PPSs (from twenty-nine in 1979 to fifty-seven in 2004), it is now a sizeable block. In the parliament returned in 2001, it constituted 36 per cent of the Parliamentary Labour Party. In the event of an expected difficult vote, as over Iraq in 2003 and student fees in 2004, this block vote – normally referred to as the payroll vote, even though it includes unpaid PPSs – is much in evidence.

The government can also exercise control through patronage. Research shows that, in the 1997–2001 Parliament, there was a correlation between those with ambitions for ministerial office and voting loyally for the government (Cowley, 2002a, pp. 109–10). Those disclaiming ambition for office were more likely to rebel.

Ministerial selection

The fact that ministers must be drawn from the ranks of MPs and peers – predominantly the latter – has important consequences for British politics. It limits the pool from which the prime minister can select ministers. In the USA, the president has a very wide pool: cabinet members may be drawn from a wide range, extending not only beyond Congress but also beyond politics. The president may appoint academics, lawyers and leading bankers. A prime minister has no such luxury; ministers are chosen from the prime minister's own party and, within this party, from those who are usually within a certain profile in terms of age, experience and political acceptability. The only latitude there is to go beyond the pool is by appointing someone to the Lords, something Tony Blair has done occasionally.

Though the limited pool facing the prime minister may be seen as extremely constraining, it does mean that the prime minister will know well those he or she chooses to serve in the cabinet. S/he will have a good idea before taking office whom s/he wants in cabinet (and, perhaps equally important, wants to keep out). There will already have been an opportunity to work with them and observe them in action. So too will the whips.

Thus, as we have noted already, the fact that ministers have to survive within a parliamentary environment has some effect on ministerial selection. An ability to handle oneself in the House is an advantage for anyone keen to become a minister. A prime minister is also influenced by the support a potential or existing minister has on the back benches. Some ministers are deemed to be immune from dismissal because of their support on the back benches. Others may be vulnerable if they have little support and depend for their patronage solely on the prime minister or another senior minister.

For a potential or serving minister, then, parliamentary skills are highly prized. Arguably, they may be too highly prized. There is the danger that parliamentary skills may be elevated over skills that may be just as necessary to control and lead a government department. A minister capable of strategic thinking, with a good grasp of future policy requirements, and a capacity for hard work and administration, may make little progress – indeed, may lose office – if these are not matched by a capacity to handle oneself in debate and in one's relations with backbenchers. Indeed, as one former minister noted, the emphasis on parliamentary skills may have a negative effect on running a department:

> Performance at the dispatch box, or in debate, gave no indication of the ability of a minister to get things done in his department. Indeed, I came to believe that the ability to carry the House of Commons led individuals to think that they needed to put less effort into running their departments. (Golding, 2003, p. 19)

On this analysis, therefore, it is possible to argue that, far from lacking power, Parliament is too powerful. Ministerial membership in Parliament imposes constraints in ministerial selection, with a prime minister unable to exploit alternative avenues – because none exist – in ministerial recruitment. It also dictates attention to parliamentary performance to the potential detriment of effective departmental management and innovative thinking. Some highly intelligent ministers have been poor performers at the dispatch box.

Legitimation

The fact that ministers are drawn from the ranks of parliamentarians and remain within Parliament contributes to the legitimation of government. Membership of the legislature confers some status on ministers, over and above that accruing from being ministers. That ministers in the Commons have fought elections to be returned to Parliament as MPs gives them a particular status; and the knowledge that they are subject individually to re-election as members adds to their presumed sensitivity to electors' opinions. Membership in Parliament, with procedures geared to ministerial leadership, also provides an authoritative platform for ministers. Press conferences may give them greater media coverage, but making a statement in the House confers greater legitimacy.

Remaining within Parliament also adds a particular burden to the workload of ministers (see James, 1992, pp. 19–29). They have variously to be present, not just to take part in Question Time and debates, but also to vote and to support fellow ministers in important debates. As MPs, they have to pursue constituency casework. Douglas Hurd recalled that when he was foreign secretary: 'Foreign colleagues were amazed in an interval of some international conference to watch me signing replies to individual constituents on their personal problems, and to learn that I had earlier dictated these replies myself' (Hurd, 2003,

p. 312). The burden on individuals is heavy and they may therefore have mixed feelings about having to shoulder the twin burden of ministerial office and parliamentary membership. It can also create problems for government in that ministers cannot devote their energies exclusively to running their departments, though the existence of several ministers in a department now helps to spread the burden. However, from the perspective of government, the balance of advantage clearly favours the present integration of ministers in Parliament.

Conclusion

The Act of Settlement of 1701 almost resulted in a formal separation of ministers from Parliament. However, that was avoided and ministers continue to be selected from and remain within the ranks of MPs and peers.

From a pluralist view of power, that has rendered Parliament a weak body in policy-making. The governing party has its leaders in Parliament. Procedures are structured in order to facilitate ministerial leadership. Ministers open and close debates. Only ministers can move certain motions, especially those relating to money and to sittings of the House. The presence of ministers and PPSs ensures that the government has a substantial payroll vote at its disposal. Because ministers are drawn from the ranks of parliamentarians, the prime minister enjoys extensive patronage powers: those seeking advancement are likely to follow his or her wishes. If government supporters show signs of wavering, the whips – and ministers – are able to move quickly to respond and to persuade them to stick with the government. Mass parties and the existence of parliamentary government – government being drawn from and remaining within Parliament – has ensured the hegemony of government over Parliament.

However, viewed from an institutional perspective, the position makes Parliament powerful. Those wishing to change British society through control of public policy have to acquire office through the House of Commons. This applies collectively – that is, to parties – and individually – that is, to those seeking ministerial office. Parliament enjoys a monopoly as a recruiting agency for government. Within Parliament, ministerial aspirants are socialized into parliamentary life and have to demonstrate their skills as debaters. As we have noted, this not only renders Parliament powerful, but possibly too powerful; it limits the pool from which ministers can be drawn. Able people outside the House are excluded from consideration. Some able people in the House may also be excluded, or have short ministerial careers, because they are poor performers at the dispatch box. Some commentators, and indeed politicians have described parliamentary life as theatre. However, in this case, the players have the opportunity to influence who have the leading parts.

4

Policy-making: The Early Stages

The capacity of legislatures to affect the content of public policy is, as we noted in Chapter 1, a central concern of legislative scholars (see Olson and Mezey, 1991). From empirical observation, it is clear that the capacity to affect policy varies from one legislature to another.

In terms of their impact on public policy, three types of legislature can be identified: policy-making, policy-influencing, and those with little or no policy affect. The essential characteristics of each are identified in Table 4.1. Policy-making legislatures can involve themselves in the drawing up – the making – of policy. Policy-influencing legislatures have the formal capacity to amend, even to reject, measures of public policy placed before them, but they are essentially dependent on government to put forward those measures. Even if they reject a measure, they look to government to formulate and bring forward a replacement.

Table 4.1   Types of legislatures

Policy-making legislatures
Have the capacity to amend or reject policy brought forward by the executive, and the capacity to formulate and substitute policy of their own.

Policy-influencing legislatures
Have the capacity to amend or reject policy brought forward by the executive, but lack the capacity to formulate and substitute policy of their own.

Legislatures with little or no policy affect
Lack the capacity both to amend or reject policy brought forward by the executive and to formulate and substitute policy of their own. They confine themselves to assenting to whatever is placed before them.

Source: Norton (1990a, p. 178).

The legislature itself does not seek to generate – to make – policy. It lacks the political will, the institutional resources or even, in some cases, the constitutional power to do so. Legislatures with little or no policy effect exist primarily to give assent to measures laid before them.

For most of its history, Parliament has not been a policy-making body. The monarch came to depend on Parliament to assent to both supply and legislation (see Chapter 2). Demanding a redress of grievance before granting supply could be construed as initiating some change in the monarch's policies. But for most of the centuries of its existence, Parliament has looked to the executive – first the monarch, then the king's government – to bring forward measures for it to consider. Even in the wake of the Glorious Revolution of 1688, those responsible for the Bill of Rights wanted 'a real, working, governing King, a King with a policy' (F.W. Maitland, in Wiseman, 1966, p. 5).

The position has been exacerbated by the growth of party. The rise of party in the nineteenth century heralded the consolidation of policy-initiating power in the hands of the executive. Increasing demands on government by organized interests resulted in more public legislation and an increasing domination by government of the parliamentary timetable.

This development has not been peculiar to Britain. In the typology of Table 4.1, Parliament is a policy-influencing legislature. So too are most legislatures of Western Europe (Norton, 1990c, 1998a) and of the Commonwealth. The category, in fact, is the most crowded of the three. The number has been swelled by the new legislatures of central and eastern Europe (Olson and Norton, 1996), but even prior to their emergence it was the most populous category. What is noteworthy, but not altogether surprising given the effects detailed in Chapter 1, is that the first category – that of policy-making legislatures – is almost empty. The only major national legislature to have occupied the category on any consistent basis is the US Congress. It is joined by the state legislatures of the USA (see Mezey, 1979, ch. 2). The separation of powers in the USA, combined with an ideological consensus that has militated against the emergence of strong parties (Norton, 1993a), has resulted in a legislative system that stands apart from others.

The policy-making process

The process by which a proposal is translated into public policy is often a complex and lengthy one. Four principal stages in the process can be identified: initiation; formulation; deliberation and approval; and implementation.

Initiation is the first stage of a formal process. Within the policy process in the UK, it embraces two elements. The first is generating a particular policy proposal, and the second is agreeing that it should be brought before Parliament for approval. The decision to bring something before Parliament rests principally with the government, a role it shares with private members – any MP or peer can put forward a bill – but for constitutional and political reasons, the government is the principal generator of bills. Only ministers can propose bills making a charge on the public revenue and, as we have seen, Parliament looks to the executive to bring measures forward. The government's position is enhanced by its political hegemony.

In terms of *formulation,* we mean putting the flesh on the bones of a particular proposal. There are two elements to this stage as well. Those responsible for introducing the measure have to agree the detail. In the case of a government bill, for example, that would be the ministers in the relevant department and, subsequently, the appropriate cabinet committee. Second, there is the formal construction of the document. In the case of legislation, that means drawing up a bill. For government (and some private members') bills, this task is undertaken by trained lawyers known as parliamentary counsel. Where the proposal does not involve primary legislation, such as a document to be placed before an international body, the formal construction will usually be undertaken by departmental civil servants.

The stages of initiation and formulation may thus be taken to form the essential stages of policy-making. They involve the putting together – the crafting – of a coherent proposal that is intended to be applied in a particular community. Once a measure has been agreed, it is then laid before Parliament. Parliament is rarely involved prior to the formal introduction of the measure. However, there are exceptions, and these are growing in number. Parliament is involved increasingly at the stage between formulation and the formal introduction of the bill before Parliament. This stage is essentially discretionary – not all bills go through it – and it involves the publication of bills in draft, offering Parliament the opportunity for pre-legislative scrutiny.

The remaining stages complete the process from making to application. *Deliberation and approval* entail consideration of the full and published measure by Parliament and the formal giving of assent to it by the Queen-in-Parliament. Without that assent, it cannot constitute an Act of Parliament and be enforced as the law of the land.

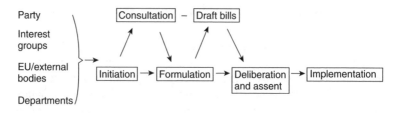

Figure 4.1   The policy-making process

Implementation constitutes the carrying into effect of the policy. The nature of the implementation will vary depending on the nature of the policy. Some measures can be implemented through administrative action by officials, such as the payment of a new kind of benefit, while some are implemented through police action, as with the enforcing of a ban on a particular activity.

The stages of the policy-making process are shown in simple diagrammatic form in Figure 4.1. The purpose of this chapter is to focus on the first two stages of the process. What role does Parliament play in policy-making? Our initial assumption, based on history and comparative observation, is that it is a minor one; however, recent empirical evidence points to it being somewhat less minor than before.

Initiation

Bills do not suddenly emerge from the ether. They are the product of a perceived need for a change in the law. Most bills that achieve passage, as we shall see, are introduced by government, in responding to demands that it deems are legitimate and sufficient to justify legislative action. The demands to which it responds derive from a variety of sources.

A major source is the party. The political parties contest elections on the basis of increasingly bulky and detailed election manifestos. Both parties have processes for discussing party policy. The Labour Party operates through policy commissions reporting to a national policy forum, and a joint policy forum, chaired by the prime minister, drawing members from among ministers, the party's national executive, and the national policy forum. The party conference has responsibility for determining what form the party's programme takes (see Seyd and Whiteley,

2001, pp. 78–82). In the Conservative Party, the party leader is formally the fount of all policy. In practice, however, various party bodies have been created – especially under William Hague's leadership in 1998 – to discuss policy, though policy documents usually emanate from bodies established by or operating under the leadership of members of the cabinet or shadow cabinet (Norton, 2002b, pp. 73–7). Both parties have provision now for consulting party members; the draft Labour manifesto for 1997, for example, was put to party members for endorsement. However, despite the reforms of recent years, the process is essentially determined at an elite level (Beetham *et al.*, 2002, pp. 116–17). The party's MPs are not involved in the process collectively; those having any significant impact do so because they occupy leadership positions within the party.

The party manifesto provides the basis for the government's flagship legislation during a Parliament. Winning parties have a very good record of implementing manifesto promises (Hofferbert and Budge, 1992, pp. 151–82). However, a party manifesto is no guarantee of success. Ministers may decide not to pursue particular proposals: there may not be time, the proposals may have been overtaken by events, or they may not be translatable into legislative form. They may encounter opposition within government itself.

Furthermore, bills derived from manifesto commitments constitute only a minority – about a tenth – of the legislation introduced by government (Rose, 1980, p. 70). Government will also introduce legislation as a response to particular crises; for example, to deal with international terrorism, or in order to give effect to international agreements it has negotiated. Some will emanate from EU commitments, especially EU directives. Certain bills, such as the Finance Bill, are brought forward as a matter of course. Most, though, derive from government departments as a result of pressure from and discussion with interest groups and other bodies (Rose, 1984, pp. 70–2). Road safety groups and families that have lost loved ones in road accidents may press for a tightening of the laws on reckless and careless driving. Employees whose pensions are under threat because of depleting pensions funds or because their companies have become insolvent may demand legislation to protect their pension rights. Divorced fathers who have limited access to their children may press for a change in the law to allow them equal access with the mothers. If ministers find their cases persuasive, they may agree to bring forward appropriate legislation.

Bodies seeking to change public policy may lobby parties to try to influence the party manifestos, but the main – indeed, usually, the first, and often *only* – port of call is a government department. A survey of business association and unions found that meeting civil servants was rated the most effective of seven types of pressure group activity (Mitchell, 1997, reported in Grant, 2000, p. 64). As Wyn Grant noted, when figures were aggregated, 'over 90 per cent of respondents selected a channel of influence involving the executive branch as the most effective' (Grant, 2000, p. 64). Another study found that in order to influence ministers, groups place as much emphasis on the mass media as they do on Parliament (Rush 1990). MPs may play a limited role as facilitators, helping to introduce representatives of a group or company to a minister, but their intervention is neither essential nor, consequentially, always sought. As one group in a 1986 survey of interest groups commented: 'We usually go to the minister direct without MPs' assistance .... Our comments do bear fruit, there are lots of examples where they have' (Rush, 1990, p. 272).

The essential link for organized interests is thus government departments. The links, as we have noted (see Chapter 1), have become extensive and institutionalized. The policy style involved in negotiations between civil servants and representatives of outside groups has been characterized by Jordan and Richardson (1982) as one of 'bureaucratic accommodation'. It is in the interests of both sides to produce a mutually agreeable proposal, which is then passed upwards for ministerial assent. Such negotiations are geared essentially to achieving incremental change: an adjustment, for example, to some existing regulation. For more substantial change, especially that involving major legislation, the principal figure is the minister.

A minister is the key figure in the legislative process. Once ministers are appointed to head departments, they normally like to generate some flagship bill that will help to make their name. However, most of the bills that emanate from their departments are the product of negotiation between their officials and outside groups. These bills are likely to have been brought forward regardless of which party is in power, and indeed are likely to be resurrected if they fall because of a general election and a new party takes office. The important role of the minister here is as gatekeeper. Even though most measures percolate up to a minister, rather than originating in the minister's office, it is up to the minister to agree to the proposal going forward.

If a minister agrees that change is necessary, this is no guarantee that a bill will be brought forward. It is now common for proposals to be put out for consultation, governed by a clear set of guidelines; interested bodies usually have twelve weeks to respond. Consultation tends to be extensive – all interested bodies are normally sent copies of the consultation paper – and invited to comment. It may take the form of a Green Paper, where different legislative proposals are canvassed. The Government may issue a White Paper, which embodies a statement of what it intends to do. In the 2002–3 session, for example, no fewer than 160 Green Papers were published, and sixteen White Papers (excluding the expenditure plans for each department). Though now more extensive than before, not all proposals will be subject to consultation; there may not be time, or the proposal may be a manifesto commitment to which the government is strongly committed.

The next stage is for the minister to persuade colleagues of the need for legislation. The proposal goes to the relevant cabinet committee. Much of the deliberation takes the form of the circulation of papers, the minister setting out the proposal and members of the committee responding. Getting clearance from the committee is a necessary but not sufficient condition for introducing a bill. Legislative proposals then have to go to the Legislative Programme Committee, chaired by the Leader of the House of Commons, which decides which bills will be included in the government's programme for the next parliamentary session. Bids from departments always exceed the slots available: 'There is no shortage of candidates. There never is' (Cook, 2003, p. 76). There is limited time available and so the committee has to be selective in its choice of bills to be brought forward. Departments may find that their bills, especially if of a minor, technical nature, may have to wait to a later session.

Bills approved by the Committee are then prepared for introduction. Ministers may be responsible for bringing bills forward, but they are not responsible for writing them.

Formulation

Once a bill has been approved for introduction, the relevant department draws up instructions as to what should go in the bill. The officials in the department who engage in this task are lawyers. This constitutes the first leg of this stage of the process. However, it is the second leg that is the most important. Though departments draw up instructions as to what they want to include, they are not responsible for drawing up properly formulated bills.

Drafting bills is a highly specialized art, undertaken, as we have noted, by lawyers known parliamentary counsel. They form the Office of Parliamentary Counsel; housed in an office in Whitehall, they are formally part of the Cabinet Office but operate as a distinct entity. They are highly trained, principally through on-the-job training; it takes about seven years to become qualified to draft a bill, even longer to take on a major complex measure (Bowman, 2004, p. 96). They work under considerable pressure – Robin Cook as Leader of the House of Commons referred to their 'Stakhanovite commitment to their job' (Cook 2003: p. 210) – and, to cope with the demands made on them, their number has been significantly expanded in recent years. In 1997 there were thirty-six parliamentary counsel; following reviews in 1999 and 2002 the number was increased and at the time of writing there are sixty-two. (Of these, ten are normally seconded to assist the Law Commission and the Inland Revenue.) Normally, they work in teams, a team of two or three usually dealing with each bill, though a slightly larger number will work on measures such as the annual Finance Bill. At one stage in 2004, twenty were working on the Finance Bill.

Counsel are important figures in that they have the power to tell departments that a particular principle cannot be embodied in legal form. A principle, however acceptable, cannot always be translated into the detail of legislation, amenable to interpretation and application by the courts. They will also advise on the best way to achieve a particular intention (Bowman, 2004; Engle, 1983). They also try increasingly to ensure that the language of bills is clear and accessible, without sacrificing the need to render them in sufficiently precise form for legal application. In drafting bills, they will bear in mind the parliamentary rules governing such matters as scope and hybridity (a hybrid bill is a public bill affecting private interests). If in doubt, discussions take place with the clerks in both Houses, with whom they have a close working relationship.

Parliamentary counsel have traditionally prepared bills ready for their introduction to Parliament. However, in recent years, there has been a growing practice of publishing bills in draft. The terminology is misleading; 'drafting a bill' refers to drawing up a bill in properly constituted form ready for formal parliamentary consideration (see Chapter 5), whereas a 'draft bill' refers to a bill drawn up, sometimes but not always in properly constituted form, in advance of its introduction to Parliament. (A better way to think of a draft bill is as a preliminary, or rough, bill.) The Conservative government of John Major (1992–7) published several bills in draft, and the Labour government returned in 1997 has extended the practice. The rationale for this is to enable consultation to take place on the particular provisions of a bill. Through such consultation it is possible to see if the provisions meet the purpose of the bill, if the provisions are too broadly drawn or may have unintended effects, or if they suffer from other defects.

Publication of bills in draft is especially important for Parliament. A draft bill provides the opportunity for parliamentary involvement at the formulation stage. Parliamentarians get to comment on it *prior* to it being laid officially before Parliament for approval. Involvement at this formative stage has the potential to be more productive than at later stages, when the government has determined precisely the provisions it wishes to be embodied and to which it is publicly committed.

There is thus a much greater opportunity than before for Parliament to engage in pre-legislative scrutiny. Draft bills may be considered by a departmental select committee in the House of Commons or by a joint committee of both Houses. Though government has conceded that bills should normally be published in draft (see Kennon, 2004, p. 477), not all can be – and most still are not. In the first session of a new government, there will not be time for the principal bills to be considered in draft: the government will need to introduce several bills at the start of the session, and measures introduced as a response to crises may need to be enacted swiftly. Certain bills, such as the Finance Bill, do not permit of such scrutiny.

None the less, the increase in the number of bills published in draft has, as we shall see, provided scope for parliamentary involvement at the second stage of the legislative process – in effect, Parliament operating at the interface between the stages of formulation and formal deliberation – and given it a capacity to influence the content of legislation to a greater extent, arguably, than has been witnessed since the advent of party government.

The impact of Parliament: decision-making

The different definitions of power enable us to view Parliament from three distinct perspectives. Viewed from a pluralist perspective, Parliament is essentially a marginal body. As we have seen, MPs and peers are not involved centrally in the initiation and formulation of legislation. It is overwhelmingly a government-centred activity. However, though Parliament may be a marginal actor in the process, it is not a non-existent one. And its involvement in recent years has grown rather than diminished. That involvement can be considered under three headings, each corresponding to a particular part of the policy-making process: agenda setting; initiating legislation; and pre-legislative scrutiny.

Agenda setting	Parliament may play a role as one of the bodies putting pressure on government to introduce measures. In marketing terms, government departments are targets for bodies seeking a change in the law. However, Parliament can serve as a channel for reaching the target. MPs enjoy proximity to ministers. They can raise issues and ensure a ministerial response in a way that the ordinary citizen cannot.

There are various mechanisms available to MPs and peers to bring issues on to the political agenda. We shall explore these in more detail in later chapters. They may write to ministers, they may (individually or in groups) arrange meetings with a minister (or arrange for representatives of affected bodies to meet ministers), or they may utilize structures or procedures within Parliament itself. On the floor of each House, members may employ questions and motions. Away from the floor, there are two unofficial routes, those of party groups and all-party groups, and one official route, that of select committees. There is also the opportunity to table early day motions. These means are not mutually exclusive, and several or all may be utilized to achieve consideration of a particular policy.

We shall be exploring these means of ensuring that the voices of different bodies in society are heard by government in later chapters. They serve an important role – some of them an increasingly important one – in ensuring that government is aware of particular problems and concerns. By bringing an issue on to the agenda, it is possible that it may prompt action – including legislative action – by government. An often-cited early example is reform of the law on homosexual relations – prompted by a debate initiated in the House of Lords by Lord Arran (Richards, 1970, p. 76).

However, what MPs and peers are doing more frequently through using these devices is not setting the agenda but rather reinforcing demands already voiced by different bodies – in effect, emphasizing the case for, and often against, issues already on the agenda, and trying to ensure that they achieve sympathetic treatment by ministers.

Initiating legislation	The principal focus under this heading is private members' legislation. Any MP or peer can introduce a bill. In the Lords, the convention is that the government does not oppose such a bill, so most pass through all their stages in the House. They rarely get any further, though, because there is no time for them in the Commons. In the Commons, MPs can introduce bills through one of three routes: the ballot; the ten-minute rule procedure; and the presentation bill – or unballoted – procedure.

Each session, a ballot is held for MPs wishing to introduce private members' bills; most MPs put their names in. The top twenty names drawn have an opportunity to nominate when their bills should be considered on one of the Fridays set aside each session for such bills; the top six or seven are normally assured of their bills having a full debate on second reading. This constitutes the main route for the introduction of bills likely to have some chance of enactment.

A ballot is also held for bills introduced under the ten-minute rule. Taken after Question Time on Tuesdays and Wednesdays, a member has ten minutes to make the case for the bill. Another member may then speak against it, also for ten minutes, and the motion is then put for the member to have leave to introduce the bill. If it is opposed, a vote takes place. If leave is given, the bill still stands little chance of becoming law as there is no time allotted to debate it.

The final method is simply to introduce a presentation bill. No ballot is involved. The member simply gives notice of the intention to introduce the bill; it is put on the order paper and then given a formal first reading – there is no debate – and it is printed (though some members do not even bother to go this far, bills remaining in name but not in substance). There is no time in the parliamentary timetable to debate these bills. Their titles are read out at the end of business on Friday. A single objection is sufficient to block a bill from progressing any further. A government whip will usually be present to ensure that a bill's passage is blocked. A short, widely supported and non-contentious bill may get through, but most fail to escape a cry of 'object'.

There are two views of private members' legislation that appear to be widely held. One is that they represent the exception to the rule in respect of the reactive role of Parliament. They represent the means, albeit a limited one, by which legislation can be initiated within Parliament. The second, related to the limited capacity, is that very few private members' bills are passed. MPs can initiate legislation, but they rarely do so successfully.

Both views are open to challenge. Although MPs and peers can introduce private members' bills, only a small number originate effectively from the sponsor. A great many, if not most, originate from interest groups, official reports or government departments. Indeed, private members' legislation provides a useful means through which some of the bills favoured by departments, but which were not included in the government's legislative programme for the session, may make it to the statute book. They are known as 'hand-out bills', ready to hand out to any MPs who are successful in the ballot and who would be interested in taking them through. The attraction of such bills to backbenchers is that they come properly drafted – by parliamentary counsel – and have government support; they are therefore likely to make it to the statute book. The government achieves its legislation and the private members in whose names the bills are introduced are able to claim the measures as 'theirs'. Marsh and Read (1988, pp. 45–6) found that 18 per cent of bills introduced in the sessions from 1979–80 to 1985–6 originated in departments, a larger proportion than in any previous post-war period. The practice is, if anything, a growing one.

If not originating from a department, a private member's bill stands a good chance of having originated from an interest group. Not only will groups lobby MPs to introduce particular measures, they may even draft them as well. Many organizations, such as the Consumers' Association, have become adept at drafting bills. If the bill finds favour with the government, it will be reviewed by parliamentary counsel. Failing that, it will be up to the members to make their own arrangements. Those members who rely on their own skills or those of sympathetic bodies run a high risk of finding that the bill is technically flawed. Where drafting is deficient, sponsors will often agree to accepting amendments to remedy the problem.

There are thus incentives to bring forward bills prepared and proffered by outside bodies. The fact that a number are hand-out bills may also explain the other caveat to the generally held view of private members' bills. Far more are passed than is popularly realized, with the figure sometimes reaching a dozen or more in a session. The number dipped somewhat in the years from 1997 to 2002, but in the twenty-five year period from 1977 to 2002, no fewer than 300 became law (Rogers and Walters, 2004, p. 209). The bills passed in the 2002–3 session were on a par with pre-1997 figures and are listed in Table 4.2. What is noteworthy about them is that all were passed under the ballot procedure.

However, what Table 4.2 does not reveal is the number of private members' bills that were unsuccessful. For every private member's bill that passes, there are usually about eight or nine others that do not make it. Table 4.3 presents the figures for the 2002–3 session. This provides a

Table 4.2　Private members' bills passed, 2002–3 session

Title of bill	Bill's sponsor
Aviation (Offences)	Frank Roy (Lab)
Co-operatives and Community Benefit Societies	Mark Todd (Lab)
Dealing in Cultural Objects (Offences)	Richard Allan (Lib Dem)
Female Genital Mutilation	Ann Clwyd (Lab)
Fireworks	Bill Tynan (Lab)
Household Waste Recycling	Joan Ruddock (Lab)
Human Fertilisation and Embryology (Deceased Fathers)	Stephen McCabe (Lab)
Legal Deposit Libraries	Chris Mole (Lab)
Marine Safety	Dr Brian Iddon (Lab)
National Lottery (Funding of Endowments)	Keith Simpson (Con)
Ragwort Control	John Greenway (Con)
Sunday Working (Scotland)	David Cairns (Lab)
Sustainable Energy	Brian White (Lab)

somewhat different perspective from that shown in Table 4.2. On the face of it, MPs and peers appear to devote time to introducing bills which stand little or no chance of success. It is extremely rare for a bill introduced under the ten-minute rule to make it to the statute book; not impossible (one was enacted in the 2001–2 session), but very rare.

Some private members' bills introduce important changes in the law – the 1997 Knives Act, for example, made it an offence to carry knives as offensive weapons – but most are modest in their effects. Unless government agrees, bills cannot make a charge on the public revenue (other than incidentally). There is limited time available, and government nowadays rarely makes extra time available in its own parliamentary schedule. Most, therefore, focus on adjustments to existing laws or introduce small changes that enjoy broad support. One may conclude therefore that private members' legislation makes relatively minor changes to the law and that MPs and peers are generally devoting their energies unnecessarily to bills that will never make it to the statute book.

Such a conclusion, though, would be misleading. Private members' bills, as we have seen, can result in some changes to the law. Only MPs

Table 4.3   Private's member's bills introduced, 2002–3

Type of bill	Number introduced	Passed	Failed
Ballot	20	13	7
Ten-minute rule	55	0	55
Presentation	18	0	18
Lords	17*	0	17
Total	**110**	**13**	**97**

Note: * Of these, only 5 had completed all their stages in the Lords.
Source: Compiled from House of Commons Information Office (2003)

and peers can introduce such bills and these individuals thus serve as gatekeepers; they can decide what is brought forward. There is thus a very limited initiating role, even if the measures are prepared by others. (Bills introduced by ministers are, after all, also prepared by other people.) However, the most important role fulfilled by private members' legislation is not that of initiating legislation but rather agenda setting and reinforcing the case for change. Private members' legislation takes up little time in the Commons – usually less than 5 per cent – but it is valuable time for raising issues. What is noteworthy about Table 4.3 is the number of bills introduced under the ten-minute rule: no less than fifty-five, none of which made it to the statute book. Why do MPs bother? Principally, because ten-minute rule bills are discussed in prime parliamentary time. It is a way of raising an issue, not only verbally but also by vote; if the motion is contested, a high vote in favour can demonstrate parliamentary support for action. Speaking after Question Time is early enough to attract media attention; there will be ministers on the treasury bench, usually waiting for the next business.

Private members' bills may rarely become law, but a number serve to prompt pressure for a later change in the law. Private members' bills to ban hunting with hounds helped to put pressure on the Blair Government to introduce a bill of its own in 2002. The previous Tory government blocked a disability discrimination bill introduced by a Labour backbencher but later, after attracting widespread criticism, introduced its own Disability Discrimination Bill (Berry, 1996). The fact that a bill is not passed does not mean that it has not had an effect. The fact of debate is valuable for making views known and getting them on the record, a point of relevance to discussion in later chapters. There may be a result in future years when government decides that it should act on the issue. Private members' legislation may be put under the heading of initiation, but more often than not debate of such legislation forms a sub-set of our previous category. As the sponsor of the disability discrimination bill, Roger Berry, put it, reflecting on his experience: 'the final lesson must surely be that even failed private members' bills can have an impact. Or, more correctly, campaigns can be mounted around such bills that can ultimately bring about change' (Berry, 1996, p. 144).

Pre-legislative scrutiny   The opportunity for Parliament to scrutinize bills before they have been formally introduced – while they are still, in effect, at their formative stage – has become a significant one since 1997. Ministers are now more willing than before to publish bills in draft and to submit them for parliamentary attention. Indeed, some of the bills are brought forward as very rough drafts: sometimes the clauses are not even formally drafted and the government instead makes available statements of what it intends to include. When the Legislative Programme Committee of the cabinet considers the legislative programme for the session, this will now encompass not only the bills to be laid before Parliament but also those that will be published in draft. They are then announced in the Queen's Speech.

Draft bills provide Parliament with an opportunity to influence government before it decides for certain what will be in the measure. During the period 1992–7, eighteen bills were published in draft, though not subject to systematic parliamentary scrutiny. In the seven sessions from 1997–8 to 2003–4, forty-two bills were published in draft. Not all were given parliamentary scrutiny, either because they were published too late or the relevant departmental select committee was too busy. However, twenty-nine bills were considered by parliamentary committees, including all ten draft bills published in the 2002–3 session. Those considered in 2002–3 are shown in Table 4.4. The bills are normally considered by the relevant departmental select committees in the Commons. These committees specialize in the relevant area and are already in place. Seventeen of the twenty-nine bills went to these committees. Eight, however, were considered by joint committees of both houses. Establishing a joint committee takes time; potential members have to be approached and then both Houses have to

Table 4.4   Draft bills subject to parliamentary scrutiny, 2002–3 session

Draft bill	*Committee considering the bill*
Police (Northern Ireland)	Select Committee on Northern Ireland Affairs
British Electricity (Trading and Transmission)	Select Committee on Trade and Industry
Nuclear Liabilities	Select Committee on Trade and Industry
Corruption	Joint Committee
Housing	Select Committee on the Office of the Deputy Prime Minister
Public Audit (Wales)	Select Committee on Welsh Affairs
Civil Contingencies	Joint Committee
Mental Incapacity	Joint Committee
Gender Recognition	Joint Committee on Human Rights
Gambling	Joint Committee

Source: Extracted from Kennon (2004).

agree motions establishing the committee. (There is also the problem of establishing party strength; the government has an overall majority in the Commons but not in the Lords.) Joint committees, though, are especially appropriate for bills that cut across sectors, involve particularly large and complex subjects, or where there is particular expertise on the subject in the House of Lords. They can also serve to relieve the pressure on departmental select committees, some of which are under particular pressure because of the number of bills in their sector. The remaining four bills of the session were considered by other forms of committee. As can be seen from Table 4.4, the draft Gender Recognition Bill was considered by a permanent joint committee, the Joint Committee on Human Rights.

The committees have to move quickly to scrutinize the draft bills. In doing so, though, they can, and do, summon evidence and by so doing put a lot of useful information in the public domain. They can draw on outside expertise in a way that – as we shall see (Chapter 5) – is often not possible once the bill is introduced. Evidence from those who have chaired or served on the joint committees has been that they have fulfilled a valuable role, resulting in effective scrutiny at a formative stage, enabling the government to accept many of the recommendations made by the committees (see Moonie, 2004; Greenway, 2004). Indeed, as Kennon (2004, p. 490) has noted, 'there is considerable evidence from recent replies that the government does accept many of the recommendations'.

The experience of the joint committee on the Communications Bill in 2002 illustrates the capacity of Parliament to influence outcomes. Of the 148 recommendations made in its report, no less than 120 were accepted. The report was also influential in the subsequent debates on the bill, especially in the House of Lords. (The committee had been chaired by a peer: the film director, Lord Puttnam.) Another joint committee having a significant impact was that established in the 2002–3 session to consider the draft Civil Contingencies Bill, a major measure designed to provide for extraordinary executive powers in times of emergency. The committee took written evidence, including from other parliamentary committees, before publishing its extensive report; in its response, the government accepted in full or in part most of the committee's fifty recommendations, including that of narrowing the scope of what constituted an emergency. As the government conceded, pre-legislative scrutiny had 'assisted the development of the bill significantly' (Cabinet Office, 2004, p. 3). The bill was ultimately in a very different form from the one the government had originally intended.

Pre-legislative scrutiny is a new and growing area of parliamentary activity, one that gives Parliament a valuable opportunity to scrutinize, in a structured manner, government proposals for law. By being able to have some input at the formulation stage, parliamentary influence is maximized. It also provides the House with valuable information for when the bill is introduced, including from external bodies who submitted evidence to the committee. It also ensures that there are members – those who served on the committee – who are already knowledgeable about the bill. There remain major limitations, however, Parliament remains a reactive body. The government decides which bills are published in draft and whether committees will have time to scrutinize them (see Hansard Society, 2004, p. 5). Pre-legislative scrutiny also imposes burdens, in terms of time, resources and members' commitments. However, the benefit to Parliament through engaging in such scrutiny is considerable.

The impact of Parliament: anticipated reaction

When we look at the capacity of Parliament to keep things off the agenda – as opposed to trying to get them on – we see its impact from another perspective. The impact is limited and difficult to observe and quantify, but what evidence we have suggests that Parliament is at least considered before measures are introduced.

There are two points at which anticipated reaction is salient. The first is when a minister is working up a proposal. Ministers do not want to alienate their own supporters and would prefer to take through Parliament a bill that earns them plaudits rather than condemnation from these allies. An ambitious minister may thus be influenced, sometimes certainly consciously, by anticipation of parliamentary reaction, and sometimes possibly subconsciously. The minister will discuss the proposal within the department. MPs and peers, as such, have no formal involvement, though ministers' parliamentary private secretaries (see Chapter 3) may participate in the preliminary discussions and, along with the relevant whip, give some advice on what back bench reaction is likely to be. Anticipated reaction may thus prove to be important. Given the privacy of discussions, and the fact that anticipated reaction may lead to a provision being deleted rather than inserted, it is difficult to quantify or even to generalize about the extent of such anticipation. There is little empirical evidence of it having a significant impact, though there is anecdotal evidence of ministers being especially concerned about reactions in the House of Lords. The support of back bench MPs could usually be assumed, but the support of peers could not.

The second point is after a minister has decided to put forward a proposal and it has gone through the relevant cabinet committee. The cabinet considers likely parliamentary reaction. In evidence to the House of Lords Constitution Committee in 2004, the Leader of the House of Commons, Peter Hain, revealed that, as chairman of the Legislative Programme Committee, he asked what consultation had taken place on each proposed bill, especially in respect of whether it was controversial or not: 'Is it likely to create difficulties for the Government in the House?' (Hain, 2004, p. 2). Ministers had to say to what extent difficulties or areas of controversy had been addressed.

When the government's proposed legislative programme is being considered in cabinet, the chief whips are especially important in indicating likely parliamentary reaction. The chief whip in the Commons now sits in the cabinet as a full member. The chief whip in the Lords is not a member, but attends. One newly-appointed Commons chief whip recalled that, on appointment, 'the decisions regarding the treatment of parliamentary business, the cajoling of ministers to think not only of their departments but also of the reaction of other MPs to what they had planned, and the persuading of colleagues to attend or not to rebel lay with me' (Renton, 2004, p. 22). If a hostile reception is anticipated, then the bill may not be proceeded with, or time will be given either to persuading members of the value of the measure or addressing their particular concerns. In practice, it is more likely to be the last two courses rather than not proceeding with the measure, but anticipated reaction none the less is a factor of cabinet deliberations.

The impact of Parliament: institutional constraints

The final perspective is institutional: concerned not so much with the constraints deriving from behaviour but rather from procedures. This in many respects is the most powerful constraint. There is only so much time available in a parliamentary session. Every bill, as we shall see (Chapter 5), has to go through several stages in each House. The government can impose timetable motions to expedite the passage of bills in the Commons, but even so there is a finite number of MPs available to serve on standing committees, and bills are normally sent to committee around the same time in the session. This is a consequence of another feature of the parliamentary process: the fact that bills (though now with some exceptions) fall unless passed by the end of the session. This creates what Robin Cook (2003, p. 11) has termed the 'tidal wave principle', with the bulk of the government's bills having to be introduced at the start of the session, in order to complete their passage in time.

The government is also constrained by the procedures of the Upper House. The government cannot impose timetable motions in the Lords; the Upper House is a self-regulating chamber and the government lacks a majority. The House guards its procedures jealously, and the government has therefore to work within established procedures and, indeed, resources.

Working within these procedures restricts the number of bills the government can introduce. In an ideal world, it may want to get its whole programme through within the session. But it cannot. This is not because its own supporters won't vote for it, but because of the procedural hurdles. Hence the government limits the number of bills it brings forward each session. The Legislative Programme Committee of the cabinet serves as a gatekeeper, deciding which bills deserve priority for introduction (see Cook, 2003, p. 76). More bills will be turned down because they cannot be accommodated during the session than because a negative reaction is anticipated from backbenchers.

The government's business managers play an especially important role in determining how many measures can be accommodated within the session. As one chief whip recalled, 'If I were asked in Cabinet or committee whether I thought a bill we were discussing would get through Parliament by Easter, in the way the Secretary of State presenting the legislation wanted, I only had to say that I thought it would be very difficult to achieve such a target date, and that would be the last word' (Renton, 2004, p. 23). This reflects not only the power of the whips in dealing with business, but also the constraints of parliamentary time and procedures.

There are also constraints imposed by limited resources available to government. This is notably the case with parliamentary counsel. Their number, as we have noted, has been expanded to cope with demand, but they remain fully stretched (Cook, 2003, pp. 210–11, 261; Bowman, 2004). However, this particular limitation may itself be the product of limited parliamentary time and the tidal wave principle. Hence the size of the Parliamentary Counsel Office is linked to the number of bills that can be accommodated by the parliamentary process. If there was a great deal more time, more parliamentary counsel would doubtless be recruited.

There is also a significant constraint deriving not only from parliamentary procedures as such, but also the form in which measures have to be laid before Parliament. Bills have to be drawn up in a very precise form – they are not simply broad statements of principle. The rules governing the form are detailed and precise (see Gifford and Salter, 1996). Bills have not increased significantly in number since the nineteenth century (Drewry, 1985), but their length has. They have become more complex. This places demands on parliamentary counsel and on the parliamentary timetable. There is little scope for more time – bills have increasingly to be levered into the process – and the government thus finds itself constrained by what is manageable in terms of the parliamentary process. It may seek to change some of the rules governing that process, but the changes are not likely to affect the overall body of rules and procedures that constrain it (Norton, 2001b).

The constraints imposed by the parliamentary process limit the flow of bills. They may also have served to trigger the downfall of a prime minister. At a cabinet meeting in 1990, Prime Minister Margaret

Thatcher berated the Leader of the House of Commons, Sir Geoffrey Howe, for his failure to have certain bills ready for the new session. A few hours later, Howe decided to resign, the incident in cabinet being the final straw that broke the camel's back. In so doing, he triggered a series of events culminating in Margaret Thatcher being challenged for leadership of the Conservative Party, and her resignation as party leader and subsequently prime minister.

Conclusion

Parliament does not figure largely as a significant influence in the introduction and content of bills, but it may contribute to the pressure that induces government to introduce a bill. Increasingly, it plays a role in the formulation stage of legislation through engaging in pre-legislative scrutiny, an activity that continues to expand. The initiative continues to rest – almost wholly, and compellingly – with government, which remains the generator of public policy. In so far as Parliament has an impact on government, it is principally as a constraint rather than a prompt. Its practices and procedures limit what government can bring forward. Anticipated reaction may be a constraint, but the most important question for ministers is not 'Will our side cause trouble?' but rather 'Do we have the time?'

5

Legislation

The third stage of the policy-making process – that of deliberation and assent – is undertaken, at least for UK legislation, by the Queen-in-Parliament. The two Houses of Parliament are responsible for the deliberation, and the two Houses plus the Crown are responsible for giving assent. The assent of the monarch is governed by convention (see Chapter 2). A bill has to go through several parliamentary stages before it can be submitted to the Queen for signature and hence become an Act of Parliament. The essential stages are listed in Table 5.1.

Table 5.1   Legislative stages in Parliament

House of Commons

First reading	Formal introduction. Title is read out. The bill is then published. At least two weekends are meant to elapse before moving to the next stage.
Second reading	Debate on the principle of the bill.
Committee	Consideration of clauses and amendments proposed. This normally takes place in a standing committee, though some bills are taken in committee of the whole house (or sent to a special standing committee, which can take evidence).
Report	Bill considered again in the House, when further amendments are possible.
Third reading	Final approval of the bill, usually taken immediately after the report stage.
Lords' amendments	After the bill has been approved, it is sent to the House of Lords. If the House of Lords makes amendments, these have to be considered by the Commons.

Table 5.1   Legislative stages in Parliament *continued*

House of Lords	
First reading	Formal introduction of the bill. At least two weekends elapse before the next stage is taken.
Second reading	Debate on principle. The House by convention does not vote on a bill that has appeared in the government's programme. Fourteen days elapse before the next stage is taken.
Committee	Committee stage is normally taken in committee of the whole house, though some bills are sent to grand committees, which any peer can attend but in which votes do not take place. On bills of considerable length and complexity, there is a fourteen day gap before the next stage.
Report	Further consideration of amendments, especially covering issues not resolved in committee. Three days then elapse before the third reading can be taken.
Third Reading	Unlike the Commons, the Lords can and does consider amendments after the formal motion for third reading and before considering the motion 'That the bill do now pass'.
Commons' amendments	If the bill originates in the Lords and the Commons makes amendments, the Lords considers the amendments.

If the two Houses cannot agree an amendment, it may 'bounce' between the two Houses until one gives way; otherwise the bill falls. Only when both Houses have agreed the text of the bill can it be sent for Royal Assent. Exceptionally, a bill may be sent for Royal Assent under the provisions of the Parliament Act 1949, under which a bill may be enacted without the consent of the Lords if the Lords has rejected the bill in one session and the Commons has passed the same bill in the second session.

Legislative process

All bills dealing with finance begin their passage in the Commons, but given the pre-eminence of the Commons, so do most other bills. However, a number each session are introduced first in the House of Lords. This avoids an excessive imbalance in the legislative workload during the parliamentary session. If the Lords only considered bills after they had first been through the Commons, it would have a light work-load in the first half of a session and an impossible one in the second half. In the 2002–3 session, twenty-seven government bills were intro-duced in the Commons (the figure includes five bills dealing with finance) and nine in the Lords. Among the bills starting in the Lords were the Courts Bill, the Licensing Bill and the Police (Northern Ireland) Bill.

As can be seen from Table 5.1, the stages in both houses are analogous. However, the way in which the two houses deal with bills is not identical.

The House of Commons

Most legislation considered by the House is government legislation. Government bills enjoy priority, other than on the Fridays set aside for private members' bills. About a third of the time the chamber is occupied by the consideration of government bills, but considerably more time is taken up in the standing committees established to consider the bills.

First and second readings

When a bill is introduced, it is given a first reading. This is a purely for-mal stage: the title of the bill is read out and a date for the second read-ing given; the bill – at this stage in dummy form, merely a long and short title on a piece of paper, with the names of the bill's sponsors – is also ordered to be printed. If the bill is not starting in the Commons, but coming from the Lords, these formal proceedings are dispensed with; the bill is scheduled for second reading with no prior proceedings on the floor of the House.

The bill is normally printed within days of its first reading and, indeed, in the case of most government bills, within a day. Second reading normally takes place about two weeks later. It is considered desirable for at least two weekends to elapse between first and second readings, though this is not an established rule and is not always adhered to. Second reading constitutes the first occasion the House has to discuss the measure. If it is a non-contentious bill, it may exception-ally be referred for its second reading debate to a committee, but other-wise – the usual practice – it is taken on the floor of the House.

Second reading constitutes the debate on principle. Some uncontro-versial bills are given a second reading without debate. Others will be subject usually to a half-day or full-day debate – in effect, roughly a three-hour or a six-hour debate. Bills of constitutional importance may be given two or more days. In the 1997–8 session, the three bills dealing with devolution – the Government of Wales Bill, the Scotland Bill and the Referendums (Scotland and Wales) Bill – each had two days for second reading. (Just over twenty years earlier, the ill-fated predecessor to these measures – the 1976 Scotland and Wales Bill – was given four days.) The Greater London Authority Bill in 1998 and the House of Lords Bill in 1999 were also each accorded two days.

Second reading debates are wide ranging. Taken on the floor, any member can seek to catch the Speaker's eye. The minister moves second reading and explains the contents and case for the bill, the minister's shadow on the opposition front bench outlines the opposition's stance, the spokesperson for the Liberal Democrats normally follows, and members from both sides are then called alternately before winding-up speeches from the front benches. At the end of the debate, opponents may divide the House – that is, force a vote. If it is a government bill, approval – as we shall see – is usually assured.

Committee stage

Once the House has approved the principle, the bill is sent to committee for detailed consideration. Unless the House votes otherwise, this will be a standing committee. Despite its name, a standing committee is permanent only in terms of its name, not its membership. The committees are designated by letters of the alphabet – standing committee A, standing committee B and so on – and usually no more than five will be sitting at any one time, though on occasion the number rises to as high as seven or eight. Private members' bills enjoy precedence only in one committee, standing committee C.

A bill is referred to one of the committees and MPs are appointed to serve on it for that particular bill. Once they have finished their task, and reported the bill to the house, another bill is sent to the committee and a new membership appointed for that bill. A committee can comprise between sixteen and fifty members, though the usual practice is to appoint at the lower end of the range, usually between sixteen and twenty-five. For major bills such as the annual Finance Bill, the committees are larger: the 2004 Finance Bill, for example, was referred to a committee of thirty-three members.

The composition of each committee will reflect the party strength on the floor of the House and, indeed, will take the form of the House in miniature, with ministers, a whip and back bench supporters on one side, and opposition front-benchers, a whip and backbenchers – plus usually a member or members from one of the smaller parties – on the other. As in the chamber, the two sides sit opposite one another, presided over impartially by an MP drawn from the chairmen's panel – a panel of senior MPs chosen for their ability to undertake such a task.

Each bill is considered on a clause by clause basis. Amendments are debated before a clause is approved on a 'stand part' motion ('that the clause stand part of the bill'). The committee is constrained by the decision taken by the House on second reading. It cannot reject the principle of the bill nor consider an amendment that goes against the principle. It is also precluded from considering any amendment that does not fall within the scope of the bill's long title.

Uncontentious bills that are likely to pass without discussion, bills for which immediate passage is sought, and bills of major constitutional significance will usually be taken for committee stage on the floor of the House – that is, in committee of the whole house (CWH). The first type is taken on the floor for convenience: there is little point in assembling a committee. The second is taken to expedite proceedings, avoiding a committee having to be appointed and assembled, and then reporting back to the House. The third is taken in order that all members may have an opportunity to deliberate on a matter of great import. The first category comprises about half-a-dozen bills a year. The scope of such measures in recent sessions has ranged from the Plant Varieties Bill in 1997 through to the Electricity (Miscellaneous Provisions) Bill in 2003. An example of the second, where time is considered of the essence, is the Northern Ireland Assembly Elections Bill, given a first reading on 13 March 2003 and then passed through all its stages, on the floor of the House, four days later. A similar urgency attached to the passage, two months later, of the Northern Ireland Assembly (Elections and Periods of Suspension) Bill. The third category does not involve a large number of measures, but the bills involved – the government's main constitutional bills – often take up a considerable amount of parliamentary time. Bills introduced by the Blair government falling in this category, and concentrated in the 1997–2001 Parliament, include the bills providing for devolution, referendums, the incorporation of the European Convention on Human Rights into UK law, the removal of hereditary peers from the House of Lords, and bills dealing with EU treaties and elections.

On rare occasions, the House has used its power to refer a bill not to a standing committee, or Committee of the Whole House, but rather to a select committee. This allows for a more detailed consideration of the merits of the bill, and for witnesses to be examined. The bill is then committed to a committee of the whole house. This procedure is used for the regular renewal of the Armed Forces Bill (most recently renewed in 2001) and has been used for consideration in recent years of three other bills, the Adoption and Children Bill 2001, Capital Allowances Bill 2001 and the Income Tax (Earnings and Pensions) Bill 2002. Since 1980, the House has also had the power to refer a bill to a special standing committee. This allows evidence-taking sessions to be held before the committee reverts to a normal standing committee format. The procedure has been used extremely sparingly; it was employed most recently for the Immigration and Asylum Bill in 1999.

Report and third reading

When a bill has completed its committee stage, the committee having gone through it, considered (and approved or rejected) amendments, and approved each clause and any new clauses proposed by members, the bill is then reported to the House.

This stage provides an opportunity for all members to consider the bill, and further amendments can be, and usually are, made. There is no consideration of each clause, and amendments that essentially repeat amendments that failed in committee are not usually selected for consideration. Though the report stage usually occupies only one or two sittings, they can prove to be long ones because of the number of amendments tabled. About 10 per cent of the time of the House – and sometimes more – is taken up with the report stage of government bills. In the 2002–3 session, when the House sat for a total of 1,287 hours, 134 hours were taken up with the consideration of bills on report.

After the report stage, a bill is given a third reading. This is the final debate on the measure, limited to its contents, and more often than not is taken immediately following report. Debate is usually short and does not figure prominently as a drain on the time of the House. Opponents may force a division. Once passed this hurdle, the bill then goes to the other chamber.

House of Lords

Whereas the Commons devotes about a third of its time to considering legislation, the Lords usually devotes most of its time to discussing the bills placed before it (see Walters, 2004, p. 216). In some years this can amount to over 600 hours; in 2000–1 it was 760 hours (60.9 per cent of the time the House was sitting). Usually, it occupies more than half the time of the House; in 2002–3 it was 53.2 per cent, and in 2003–4, 56.7 per cent (House of Lords, 2004, utilizing financial years). In the Lords, a bill has to pass through the same stages as in the Commons. However, Lords procedure differs from that of the Commons. The House is more rigorous in its rules governing the intervals between stages. Practice in those stages also differs from those of the Commons.

It is possible for a debate to take place on first reading, and on very rare occasions that has happened. Second reading is the debate on principle. This may take a whole day; sometimes, as in the Commons, two days may be devoted to it, as happened with the House of Lords Bill in 1999. Committee stage is normally taken on the floor of the House. This enables those peers with an interest in particular parts of the bill to participate. Proceedings are also less formal than at other stages, so members may intervene more than once during discussion of an amendment. Committee stage may take several days.

Though the majority of bills continue to be taken on the floor of the House, greater use is now made of committees away from the chamber. The House has provision for several types of committee. These include the special public bill procedure, which is not dissimilar to that for special standing committees in the Commons. The committees are empowered to take evidence. This committee has not been employed in recent years. The House may also refer a bill to a select committee. This is rarely employed, though in 2004 the House sent the Constitutional Reform Bill (to abolish the office of Lord Chancellor and create a supreme court) to a select committee. However, the committee that the House has started to employ with some regularity in recent years is the grand committee. This is not an evidence-taking committee, but essentially one that adopts the procedure as if the bill were being taken on the floor of the House. The principal exception is that no votes are taken. Hence, if someone opposes an amendment, it cannot be included, and the supporters of the amendment will need to return to it at report stage. The grand committee is used for bills that are not particularly contentious between the parties, and several are now sent to grand committee each session. In the 2003–4 session, for example, bills committed to grand committee included the Armed Forces (Pensions and Compensation) Bill; Civil Partnerships Bill; Domestic Violence, Crime and Victims Bill; Pensions Bill; European Parliamentary and Local Elections (Pilots) Bill; and Public Audit (Wales) Bill. There is then the report stage, when issues unresolved in committee can be considered again.

There is a major difference with procedures in the Commons in that all amendments tabled by peers are considered. In the Commons, the chairman makes the selection in standing committee and the Speaker makes the selection at report stage. The Lords are not so restricted. Again in sharp contrast with the Commons, there are no means of curtailing proceedings. In the Commons, proceedings can be timetabled through the use of programme motions which stipulate how much time is provided to consider particular parts of a bill, but no such facility to restrict proceedings exists in the Lords. The principal limitation at report stage is that no amendment can be considered if it has been voted on at committee stage.

Following the report stage, the bill moves to its third reading. Again, in contrast with the Commons, there is a stipulated interval between the two stages. Furthermore, amendments can be, and frequently are, tabled at third reading, though significantly fewer in number than at the report stage. The motion for third reading is usually agreed formally and the House then moves to amendments. Once those are dealt with, the House approves the bill on the motion 'That the bill do now pass.' The provision for amendments at this stage allows an issue to be considered thoroughly. The government may agree to bring forward an amendment at report stage in response to debate in committee; if there is a problem with the government's amendment, there is the opportunity to return to the issue at its third reading.

Once a bill has been considered and passed by the Lords, it then goes back to the Commons (if it originated there) so that it can consider any amendments made by the second chamber. (If a bill originates in the Lords, the reverse applies, and any Commons amendments are sent to the Lords.) In the event of an amendment proving unacceptable to the Commons, it goes back to the Lords. The process has the potential to be a lengthy one if the second chamber insists on its amendment. If this happens, the process is known as 'ping pong'. In practice, most amendments prove acceptable to the Commons and, in the event of a clash, the House of Lords usually defers – though not always immediately – to the elected chamber. Ultimately, if the bill originates in the Commons, the Commons can get its way under the provisions of the Parliament Act 1949 (see Chapter 2). The Act has only been invoked four times since its passage in 1949, the most recent occasion being in November 2004 on the Hunting Bill to ban foxhunting in England and Wales.

Private members' bills

Private members' bills have to go through the same stages as government bills listed in Figure 5.1. Both categories of bill constitute public legislation. However, the time for consideration of private members' bills is limited, confined principally to ten (or sometimes more) Fridays and taking up less than 5 per cent of the time of the House in each session. Most bills introduced are not debated (see Chapter 4), and those that are face considerable hurdles.

Opposition to the bill by government is usually fatal. No bill that has been the subject of a division on second reading has subsequently made it to the statute book without government time being provided (Marsh and Read, 1988, p. 49). Even government support does not guarantee its passage. Opponents may try to talk the bill out. On a Friday, the House sits at 9.30 am, and if debate is still continuing at 2.30 pm the bill under consideration falls to the back of the queue on subsequent Fridays, where it can easily be blocked (see Chapter 4). To prevent that happening, a bill's sponsor may move a closure motion: a motion that requires the question to be put immediately. However, for a closure motion to be carried, there must not only be a majority but also at least a hundred members voting in favour. Achieving that figure on a Friday is notoriously difficult. And if the bill has not been debated for very long, the Speaker will not even allow a closure motion to be moved. Hence, as we recorded in Chapter 4, there is a preference on the part of members successful in the ballot to opt for measures that enjoy government or widespread support, thus maximizing the chances of getting them on to the statute book.

Private legislation

There are essentially two types of legislation. The first, and most important, is public legislation, which enacts measures that apply to the whole community. This category includes both government bills and private members' bills. The second category is that of private legislation, which gives specified powers to particular individuals or bodies – for example, to give legal authority to Network Rail to acquire and build a railway track on a particular piece of land, or to a local authority to undertake a particular activity. There is also a category of bill that falls between the two, known as a hybrid bill: this embodies a public policy that affects the particular interests of some individuals or bodies in a way that does not apply to all individuals and groups within the category.

A private bill has to go through analogous stages to public bills, but the purposes of the stages differ and the bill itself is not initiated by government or by private members, but by petition from the body sponsoring it. At second reading, the House affirms the principle conditionally.

At committee stage, proceedings are quasi-judicial, with counsel representing petitioners. Witnesses are heard under oath. Government sometimes takes an interest in such measures, but normally leaves it for the House to decide. The majority of private bills have no political or, for most MPs, constituency implications. It is therefore a form of legislation that does not impinge much upon the consciousness of MPs and peers. (There are occasional exceptions, such as the Mersey Tunnels Bill in 2004, which provided, among other things for an increase in the bridge tolls.) Where members do take an interest, they can have a powerful influence: a single cry of 'object' is sufficient to force a debate. Nowadays relatively few such bills are introduced – in recent years the number in each session has been in single figures – and most are not debated, with the result that they occupy little time: in 2002–3, for example, the Commons devoted just over six hours – less than 1 per cent of its time – to private business.

Secondary legislation

There is one other category of legislation, and that is secondary legislation. Acts of Parliament frequently confer powers on ministers (and sometimes other bodies) to make orders; for example, to change the level of fees set for a particular service or to say how many governors may serve on the governing bodies of state schools. These powers comprise what is known as secondary, or delegated, legislation. They are now extensive in number, both in the total that now exist and in terms of the number brought in each year. They are extensive in number because they are attractive to government: they provide flexibility and enable changes to be made without having to bring in a new bill.

Orders are usually promulgated as statutory instruments (SIs). The act incorporating the power to make orders will stipulate what parliamentary approval, if any, is required. Important orders are normally subject to what is known as the affirmative resolution procedure; that is, they require parliamentary approval in order to take effect. Others are subject to the negative resolution procedure; that is, they take effect unless Parliament votes them down. Other, less significant, orders are not subject to any parliamentary consent at all; some simply have to be laid before Parliament and others are not even subject to that requirement. Before the 1970s, the number of statutory instruments laid before Parliament in each session was usually several hundred. Since 1970, the number has usually been well over a thousand, and in some sessions more than 1,500.

Given the number, there is not sufficient parliamentary time available to consider every statutory instrument. Once brought forward, they are considered by the Joint Committee on Statutory Instruments. (If they require only the approval of the Commons, the MPs on the committee sit as a Commons committee.) The committee checks the SIs to ensure that they are properly drawn; that is, within the powers granted and are not deficient in terms of drafting. The committee reports and it is up to government to decide whether to take any action. The committee has no formal powers and it is possible that an instrument may be approved by the House before the committee has reported. However, it is possible for adverse reports to influence the withdrawal of an instrument, though that rarely happens. The work of the committee is seen as worthwhile but largely unexciting.

Statutory instruments that require parliamentary approval under the affirmative resolution procedure are considered by the House, but usually in a standing committee on delegated legislation. Only a small number – nowadays usually between ten and twenty – are debated in the chamber. In 2002–3, the House devoted eighteen hours – just over 1 per cent of the time in the session – to debating such orders. Those subject to the negative resolution procedure are considered only if members table a motion (known as a prayer) to annul them, and even then time is usually found to debate them only if the motion is tabled by the Opposition front bench. Very few are debated on the floor. In 2002–3, no time was devoted in the chamber to such orders.

The House of Lords has a somewhat more extensive method of scrutiny. In 1993 it created a Delegated Powers Committee – now titled the Delegated Powers and Regulatory Reform Committee – to consider whether the delegated powers embodied in a bill, and the provisions for their parliamentary scrutiny, are appropriate. It variously recommends, for example, that an order-making power should be subject to the affirmative resolution, rather than the negative resolution, procedure. Its recommendations are normally accepted by government. The committee, however, only deals with what may be termed the input end of delegated legislation; that is, the inclusion of the powers in bills. In December 2003, the House appointed a committee – the Select Committee on the Merits of Statutory Instruments – to consider the output end, that is, the orders laid before Parliament. This committee examines all SIs subject to either the affirmative or negative resolution procedure and is empowered to draw to the attention of the House any instruments that have important political or legal implications; are inappropriate because of changes since the parent Act was passed; implement EU legislation inappropriately; or achieve their policy objectives imperfectly. By the summer recess of 2004, the committee had published fifteen reports, the fifteenth reporting on SIs on the date of referendums in different regions on elected regional assemblies.

For SIs requiring approval, the Lords usually takes them on the floor of the House rather than in committee (though some, primarily Northern Ireland orders, are now taken in Grand Committee). They are variously taken at the end of business or in what is known as the 'dinner hour'; that is, when the House adjourns the business for at least an hour, usually around 7.30 pm, to enable those taking part in debate to have dinner. The hour is occupied by other business, either an unstarred question (see Chapter 6) or orders. Most debates are on SIs subject to the affirmative resolution procedure, but on occasion the opposition moves a motion to annul an instrument subject to the negative resolution procedure in order to force a debate. Before 1999, the practice had developed of the House not voting against SIs, but there are now occasions when peers will force a vote.

The effect of Parliament?

Viewed from a pluralist perspective, what impact does Parliament have on legislation? Jean Blondel and others (1970) referred to the concept of Parliament's 'viscosity' – that is, the capacity to impede the flow of a stream: in effect, Parliament's capacity to constrain or to change the bills placed before it. Does Parliament exercise an independent capacity to alter a bill, resulting in it leaving Parliament substantially different in content from when it was introduced?

The answer is that it does so only at the margins. The impact of Parliament on government bills, similar to its impact on the initiation of measures, is sporadic. In the Commons, the investment of considerable time and effort does not result in a significant viscosity. Government is normally assured of having its measures passed. Moreover, it is normally assured not only of the principle of the bills being accepted but also the detail. In the Lords, the outcome is somewhat less certain.

Saying no to government

Parliament rarely exercises its coercive capacity (see Chapter 1). As can be seen from Table 5.2, the government will almost always succeed in

Table 5.2   Government bills introduced, 1997–2003

Session	Government bills		
	Passed	*Failed*	*Carried over*
1997–8	52	1	0
1998–9	31	3	1
1999–2000	39	1	0
2000–1	21	5	0
2001–2	39	0	0
2002–3	33	1	2

Source: Derived from House of Commons, *Sessional Information Digests*, 1997–2003.

having its bills passed by Parliament. Government, for the reasons discussed in preceding chapters, normally enjoys an overall majority in the House of Commons, with that majority ready to ensure its measures are passed. As explained in Chapter 2, the House of Lords abides by the Salisbury convention and does not vote on the second reading of bills that are in the government's programme. Whatever it may do to the detail, the House does not vote against the principle.

The years in which governments are most likely to fail with bills are election years. The government does not wish to signal that it plans to hold a general election during the session, so usually introduces a full legislative programme. When it calls the election, not all of its bills will have completed their passage through Parliament, so some are sacrificed. As can be seen from Table 5.2, the largest number of bills lost by the Labour government of Tony Blair was in the short session of 2000–1, cut short because of the calling of the general election. In other sessions, the government may lose a bill because it finds it does not have the time available to get it through, or decides not to proceed with it. However, a bill listed as having failed in one session may still make it to the statute book by being reintroduced in a subsequent session.

Government, then, is in greater danger of losing bills because of the calling of a general election than because of deliberate action by MPs or peers. The chances of government being defeated on second reading are rare. It occurred only three times in the Commons in the twentieth century (in 1924, 1977 and 1986) and only one of these was when the government had an overall working majority (on the Shops Bill 1986; see Chapter 2). The chances of losing a vote at third reading are similarly slim. It happened, exceptionally, in 1977 on the Local Authority Works (Scotland) Bill, when the government did not anticipate a vote taking place.

In the Commons, the party majority that ensures the passing of bills on second and third reading is also deployed to ensure that government gets its way on the detail of bills. Even if government backbenchers were tempted to go against their own leaders, various constraints operate other than merely political ones. One is structural. The *ad hoc* formation of standing committees militates against the development of a body of expertise and a corporate, possibly bi-partisan, feeling. Another factor is time. Given the size of bills, there is often little time to consider the detail adequately. This is compounded by partisanship. If a bill is strongly opposed, the government is likely to introduce a programme motion to ensure its expeditious passage. This then results in some clauses not in fact being the subject of debate. Furthermore, committee members are limited in the information they have at their disposal. Standing committees are not empowered to receive evidence. That is, they cannot interview witnesses or receive formal submissions. Individual members may receive material from outside bodies, but the committee may not do so collectively. And individual members have limited resources with which to commission research on a particular provision.

As a result, standing committees are in a weak position and are characterized by the partisanship that exists in the chamber. For MPs, serving on a standing committee is often frustrating. Government backbenchers have traditionally been encouraged to remain silent in order not to delay proceedings; so some have used the opportunity to read and reply to correspondence, only half-listening to committee proceedings. There is often little expectation by other members that their activities will have any tangible effect.

Most time in standing committee is spent agreeing government amendments and rejecting opposition ones. Usually about 90 per cent of amendments accepted in committee are moved by the government. Very few amendments are carried against the wishes of the government. We have touched upon the fact that there were various defeats during the period of Labour government in the 1970s (see Chapter 2). The period under Conservative government from 1992 to 1997 also saw various defeats in standing committee. There were sixty-seven in the period 1979–92; this figure, though, represented only just over 1 per cent of all votes held in committee (Melhuish and Cowley, 1995, p. 54). The large majorities achieved by Labour in the 1997 and 2001 general elections provided it with a generally defeat-proof majority in committees. Even were government to be defeated in standing committee, it would still have the option of seeking to reverse the defeat, in practice, at report stage.

The chances of MPs saying no to government are thus relatively slim. The position differs in the House of Lords, however. The House may not divide on second reading of a bill, but it is willing to say no to government when it comes to the detail. As we noted in Chapter 2, the government suffers defeats in the Lords; of these, virtually all are on amendments to bills. Prior to the passage of the 1999 House of Lords Act, a chamber with a preponderance of Conservative peers was more liable to defeat Labour governments than Conservative governments (though both suffered at the hands of the House). The position changed in 1999 (see Chapter 2). Since then, the government has faced a House in which no single party has a majority and is therefore vulnerable to other parties – or the main opposition party and cross-bench peers – combining against it. Opposition parties have proved willing to vote against the government in support of particular amendments. As reported in Chapter 2, the government suffered no less than 283 defeats in the Lords from the start of the new session in 1999 through to the end of the 2004–5 session. The figures per session are given in Table 5.3. The House appears more willing to defeat the government than was the case preceding the removal of the hereditary peers. In the first session of the Labour government (1997–8), there were thirty-nine defeats, and in the second session, thirty-one.

The government is thus more vulnerable to defeat in the Lords than in the Commons. However, the defeats in the Lords are not necessarily

Table 5.3   Government defeats in the House of Lords, 1999–2005

Session	Number of defeats
1999–2000	36
2000–1	2
2001–2	56
2002–3	88
2003–4	64
2004–5	37

Source: House of Lords website:
www.parliament.uk/faq/lords_govtdefeats.c/n

definitive. The House is not able, except in particular circumstances, to be a veto player (see Chapter 1). When the House amends a bill against the wishes of the government, those amendments require the approval of the Commons. If the Commons disagrees with the Lords, the Upper House usually does not insist on its amendments. If it does persist, the amendments shuttle between the two Houses until one side gives way. It is rare for the Lords to persist with an amendment. In 2004, it sent an amendment – to limit the number of regions in which all-postal voting could take place in the 2004 local government and European Parliament elections – back to the Commons three times before eventually conceding to the wish of the Commons. The government may accept defeats imposed by the Lords, either on their merits or because the Lords amendment finds some support among the government's own supporters, but acceptance is at the discretion of government. Only if proceedings on a bill are close to the end of the session, or if the government is keen to ensure the quick passage of a measure, is the Lords able to act as a veto player and, as such, ensure that the government accepts its amendments.

Persuading the government

Parliament, then, rarely says no to government. The Lords may require it to think again, but the government can use its Commons majority if necessary to overturn a defeat in the Lords. Where Parliament has somewhat more effect (though, again, the impact is limited) is in persuading government (see Chapter 1) to change its mind.

In the Commons, MPs can lobby ministers to accept a particular amendment and may threaten to vote against a proposal of which they disapprove. The threat may be sufficient to induce ministers to act. (Voting against the government is usually a sign that earlier attempts at persuasion have failed.) The government survived the vote in January 2004 on the second reading of the Higher Education Bill by a majority of five votes. This was seen as a narrow government victory, but it was achieved by making concessions to MPs who were threatening to vote against the government. A similar approach had been adopted on a number of bills where there has been significant opposition from government backbenchers. In 1998, Home Secretary Jack Straw made a number of concessions to backbenchers in order to smooth the passage of the Criminal Justice (Terrorism and Conspiracy) Bill; a plan to include incitement to commit offences abroad, for example, was withdrawn (Cowley, 2002a, p. 32). Straw also made concessions during the passage of the Immigration and Asylum Bill in 1999 (Cowley, 2002a, pp. 52–4). Other ministers sought to pacify dissenters. When one back bench opponent of the government's proposals regarding incapacity benefit, part of the Welfare Reform and Pensions Bill in 1999, went to see the Social Security Secretary, Alistair Darling, he was asked: 'What's your price?' (Cowley, 2002a, p. 47). The government ran into opposition from Labour MPs to its provision to establish foundation hospital trusts in the 2003 Health and Social Care (Community Health and Standards) Bill. Fearing not just back bench dissent, but possible defeat, the government made various concessions:

> It introduced a cap on the income that the new foundation hospitals could earn from private patients; it ensured that NHS pay arrangements applied to foundation hospitals ... it promised to make all hospitals foundation trusts within five years; and it improved the arrangements for local consultations. When John Reid, the Secretary of State for Health, faced the Commons before the crucial vote in November, he was quite open (indeed, almost boastful) about the extent to which the bill had been amended as a result of back bench pressure. He then added another major concession, agreeing to a review of the operation of the first wave of trusts after twelve months. (Cowley and Stuart, 2004b, p. 309)

MPs are thus able to put pressure on ministers to persuade them to amend bills as they go through Parliament. On rare occasions, the government has decided not to proceed with a bill. We have already made mention (see Chapter 2) of the bill in 1968 to reform the House of Lords. In 1980, an Iran (Temporary Provisions) Bill was not brought before the House when it looked as if up to 100 Conservative MPs might have voted with Labour MPs against it. In the 1984–5 session a Civil Aviation Bill also ran into opposition from Conservative MPs and was dropped; an Education (Corporal Punishment) Bill ran into trouble in both Houses, especially the Lords, and suffered a similar fate (Silk, 1987, pp. 113–14). In 2004, the government decided not to proceed with a bill to remove the remaining hereditary peers from the House of Lords. Ministers were not only worried by the possible reaction in the Lords but also by how their own backbenchers might behave in the Commons; there was the possibility that Labour MPs, supported by MPs from other parties, might seek to amend it to introduce more radical changes. As the government were unable to find ways of making the bill 'amendment proof', they dropped it.

By a variety of means, backbenchers may thus persuade ministers to amend bills. As a result, some measures are enacted in a form very different from that in which they entered the House; very occasionally, a bill might not even be proceeded with. MPs can thus make a difference. However, the occasions when MPs do achieve changes to bills are relatively rare. Though rebellions are more frequent than in the past, more often than not government backbenchers are united (see Chapter 2). Some changes may be achieved by force of argument, but again this appear to be relatively rare. Most government bills will leave the Commons in the form that ministers want them. Even when government makes concessions, they are often marginal or cosmetic. In the 1997–2001 Parliament, it was noted that 'concessions were often small. The accusation about certain ministers was that although they may give ground, in policy terms, it was always "the minimum they can get away with"... Negotiations with ministers rarely yielded anything that discontented backbenchers wanted' (Cowley, 2002a, p. 180). When concessions were offered, even though they did not meet the full demands of the rebels, a sufficient number of rebel MPs were prepared to go along with the government to ensure that it had a majority.

The government may thus be persuaded by MPs to make changes, but such occasions are very much the exception rather than the rule. Again, there is a contrast with the House of Lords. Government does not enjoy a majority in the Lords. The House sees itself as a House of experience and expertise (see Chapter 2). Although there is a high level of party cohesion in the Lords (Norton, 2003a), ministers cannot necessarily rely on their own supporters to back them. They remain vulnerable to opposition parties and the cross-bench peers combining against them. These conditions induce ministers to listen to what is said in debate and, on occasion, concede to the force of argument and/or the potential of losing a vote. Ministers have to assume that well-informed members will be taking part in a debate. They will normally therefore be well briefed and engage in a discourse with members, often in an environment that lacks the partisanship of the Commons. Also, debate tends to attract little media coverage, so ministers feel less of a need to become defensive. It is also usually on the detail of the bill, so no great principles are at stake. Ministers may thus find the environment more conducive to accepting amendments from opposition parties and individual members than is the case with their counterparts in the Commons.

The number of amendments made to bills in the Lords each year is substantial. It is not unusual for 2,000 to 3,000 amendments to be made each session in the Lords. The 1999–2000 session was remarkable in that no less than 4,761 amendments were made. On the surface this seems an impressive number. Most, however, emanate from the government itself. One study of the 1988–9 session found that non-government amendments accounted for well under 10 per cent of the amendments accepted by the House (Miers and Brock, 1993, p. 103). Some of these were not on substantive issues. This thus provides something of a corrective to the impression that members are responsible for persuading government to accept most of the amendments; more often, it is the government persuading the House. However, the figure underestimates the persuasive impact of the House. As Miers and Brock (1993, pp. 121–8) noted in their study of the 1988–9 session, various amendments were moved by government at the report stage in response to points made by opposition front-benchers or back bench peers. The number was not large, but some of these were substantive issues. The extent to which peers persuade government may also have increased following 1999. Miers and Brock were studying a House in which Conservative peers predominated during a period of Conservative government. After 1999, no party predominates. Ministers spend time engaging in dialogue with members, sometimes accepting points – and promising to introduce amendments at report stage – or sometimes being persuaded, through the threat of defeat, to make concessions. If the government is defeated and the amendments go to the Commons, negotiation remains a feature of proceedings; ministers may be willing to accept some defeats, but not others. The Lords is more likely to pursue an issue if it is one on which government supporters in the Commons are not united.

The Lords can thus make some difference to legislation, more so than the Commons, since the government cannot rely on a majority in the Lords. By argument, threat of defeat or actual defeat – forcing the Commons to think again – the Lords may persuade the government to accept changes to its bills. There have been some notable cases in recent years, including that of the Anti-terrorism, Crime and Security Bill, introduced in November 2001 following the terrorist attacks in the USA on 11 September. The government was keen for the expeditious passage of the bill. The Lords made amendments and then insisted on some of them; some found support among Labour MPs in the Commons. As a result of Lords pressure, changes were made covering the proportionality in disclosure of information, appeals, the confinement of new police powers to anti-terrorism and national security, and the removal of an offence of inciting religious hatred. Such high-profile cases are rare but they demonstrate the capacity of the Upper House to pursue an issue and, without a capacity to say a definitive 'no' to government, to persuade government to accept changes.

Institutional constraints

How useful are the other views of power in analysing Parliament in the legislative process? That of agenda-setting does not apply, since we are concerned here with measures once they are on the agenda. Once there, anticipation may be relevant, since a bill may run into opposition from government backbenchers and, anticipating defeat or bad publicity, the government may amend the measure or not pursue it. However, this involves events once an issue has been brought forward, and the opposition is usually observable.

The institutional view has a continuing utility; this is apparent from Table 5.1. A bill has to go through several stages in each House. Not only that; the bill also has to be considered by the two Houses on a consecutive basis, not a concurrent one – that is, one House has to finish with it before the other considers it. As we have seen, there are also intervals between the stages. These stages are not always followed in the Commons, but they are adhered to in the Lords, unless the House is persuaded not to impose them; for example, because the measure is accepted as urgent. Government therefore has to anticipate these stages and ensure that bills are passed within the time available.

The session itself provides a constraint on government. Bills not passed by the end of the session fail. Both Houses have introduced provisions enabling some bills to carry over from one session to the next. In the Lords, for example, a bill may be considered for carry-over if it has been subject to pre-legislative scrutiny. (In the 2003–4 session, the House also agreed to carry over the Constitutional Reform Bill after it had been subjected to scrutiny by a select committee.) However, as is apparent from Table 5.2, very few bills are carried over. The government's legislative programme is thus based on limited time and what Robin Cook has referred to, as we have seen (see Chapter 4), as the 'tidal wave' principle, most bills being introduced at the beginning of the session and then cascading down to standing committees later in the session. Government has to get its planning right. If it miscalculates, it may not get its bills through; mostly it does, but not always. Though it can employ programme motions in the Commons, it has no means of curtailing discussion in the Lords. The existence of established rules and procedures may also be exploited by MPs and peers to put pressure on government to accept amendments. The Lords tends to be in a position to persuade government to accept changes at the very end of a session if one or more bills have not yet got through all their stages. In order to get them through and on to the statute book, ministers will do various deals with the opposition parties in the Lords to ensure that they get through. Even if the government has a united Commons majority in support of the measure, they cannot put that majority to good effect if they have miscalculated the time needed to get the measure through.

Conclusion

We have drawn attention to Blondel's concept of viscosity: that is, the capacity to constrain a stream. The terminology has a particular utility. If we see legislation as the stream, then the institutional arrangements constitute the river bed. The government may be able to change the rules – in effect, widen the river bed – but doing that on an extensive basis is difficult. It therefore has to ensure that it gets its flow of bills largely within the existing institutional framework.

It is in seeking to constrain the legislative stream that Parliament can be seen to be at its weakest. Once bills have been introduced by government, they are almost certain to be passed. The weakest part of the process is to be found at committee stage in the Commons. This weakness has led to many calls for reform. However, though there have been changes at the pre-legislative stage (see Chapter 4), there has been no fundamental change to the legislative process within Parliament. Clearly, as we have seen, Parliament has *some* impact, and sufficient to make it a relevant target for pressure-group attention – more so in the twenty-first century than ever before – but it remains, at best, a proximate actor and, at worst, a marginal one in determining the content of measures of public policy.

6

The Administration of Government

The final stage of the policy-making process is that of implementation. If we were to look at Parliament's role solely in terms of systematic scrutiny of measures once they have been enacted – that is, become Acts of Parliament – then it would be a very short chapter. The extension of parliamentary scrutiny at the pre-legislative stage (see Chapter 4) has not been complemented by a similar development at the post-legislative stage. Royal assent to a measure is announced in Parliament, and this announcement marks the end of any formal parliamentary involvement. On occasion, a specific measure may be reviewed within a year or so of being implemented, but such cases are isolated. There is no formal mechanism to trigger parliamentary scrutiny. The 2001 Anti-terrorism, Crime and Security Act is unusual in that it embodies a provision that, within two years of its enactment, the secretary of state shall appoint a committee to conduct a review of the Act. There was thus a review, under the chairmanship of a former Conservative Cabinet minister, Lord Newton of Braintree (Privy Counsellor Review Committee, 2003), but it was – as required by the Act – a committee of privy counsellors and not a committee of Parliament. When the Constitution Committee of the House of Lords examined the legislative process in 2004, it found that at this post-legislative stage parliamentary scrutiny was at its most unsystematic and deficient (Constitution Committee, 2004b, pp. 42–6).

In so far as there is any study by Parliament of the effect of legislation, it is embodied within its scrutiny of executive actions. This is the function identified by Packenham (1970) (see Chapter 1) as 'administrative oversight'. This encompasses scrutinizing decisions taken by government that do not require legislative sanction, as well as the conduct – the actual administration – of departments. Much administration carried out is routine, but ministers have to act within their powers. They may act under the royal prerogative – that is, carrying out powers that still reside in the Crown, but are exercised by ministers in the name of the monarch – or under powers granted by statute. The royal prerogative remains important, since it encompasses powers such as that of declaring war. As we have seen, powers granted by statute usually take the form of delegated legislation.

As we have noted already (see Chapter 2), the terms of reference of departmental select committees in the House of Commons are to examine 'the administration, expenditure and policy' of the related government departments. These terms can encompass the workings of particular legislative measures. If a policy enacted through legislation does not appear to be having the desired effect, it may be the subject of parliamentary scrutiny. A good example is the Child Support Act 1991, establishing the Child Support Agency. The Agency began working in 1993 but did not work as intended; subsequently it has been the subject of parliamentary investigation and debate. It is thus possible for particular Acts to be subjected to parliamentary scrutiny, but – as we have noted – such scrutiny is not systematic and is just one element of administrative oversight.

By what means, then, does Parliament engage in administrative oversight, and what impact does it have? The means available can be grouped under two general headings: those available in the chamber, and those available outside the chamber. The latter category, as we shall see, can be sub-divided into formal and informal means.

Inside the chamber

The principal means of scrutiny inside the chamber are debates and question time. Both suffer from a range of limitations.

Debates

Debates are the oldest method by which the two Houses subject the actions of the executive to critical scrutiny. There are several types of debate, other than those – covered in Chapter 5 – on the second and third readings of bills. In the Commons, there is the annual debate on the address – usually five days devoted to debates on the Queen's Speech outlining the government's programme for the year. There are also debates in which the topics are selected by the opposition, by a committee of the House, and by private members, as well as by government itself.

Opposition

There are twenty *opposition days* each session. These are days on which the subject for debate is chosen by opposition parties. The Leader of the

Opposition chooses the topic on seventeen and the leader of the third largest party in the House selects the subject on the other three. (The government now also provides some time for debate on topics selected by the minor parties.) Each day may be utilized for one full-day or two half-day debates. Subjects chosen during the 2002–3 session are listed in Table 6.1. If the Opposition is dissatisfied with the conduct of

Table 6.1   Opposition days, 2002–3

Date	Subject(s) of debate
2 Dec. 2002	Policing in Northern Ireland*
8 Jan. 2003	Foundation hospitals
13 Jan. 2003	Criminal justice system/drugs policy
14 Jan. 2003	Future of education in Northern Ireland*
25 Jan. 2003	Occupational pensions/Food Supplements Directive
30 Jan./12 Feb. 2003	Iraq: humanitarian contingency plan/economy and public services
29 Apr. 2003	Community services
15 May/5 Nov. 2003	School funding/decommissioning in Northern Ireland
4 June 2003	Iraq/pensions
11 June 2003	European treaty referendums/Post Office card accounts
17 June 2003	Government reshuffle/Community pharmacies
23 June/25 June 2003	Student finance/government responsibilities for transport (LD)
25 June 2003	Tuition fees/fair trade
2 July 2003	Road and rail transport/small businesses
7 July 2003	Government targets/tax credits
16 July 2003	Iraq/vulnerable children
9 Sept. 2003	Military situation in Iraq/teacher shortages
10 Sept. 2003	Fairness and security in old age/role of UN in Iraq (LD)
16 Sept. 2003	Electricity supply/EU constitution
15 Oct. 2003	State pension reform/neighbourhood policing
22 Oct. 2003	Iraq – call for judicial inquiry
27 Oct. 2003	NATO and EU defence policy/health care targets

Notes: (LD) = Liberal Democrat day.
* Debates not allotted as opposition days; used for debate by Northern Ireland Unionist parties.
Source: House of Commons Information Office (2003).

government, it may also table a motion of no confidence in the government. Such motions are tabled very sparingly, but when tabled, time is found to debate them as a matter of urgency. The last speech of Margaret Thatcher as prime minister in 1990 was in a debate on a motion of no confidence.

Committee of the House

There are also now three *estimates days* in each session. Introduced in the 1982–3 session – the first debate was in March 1983 – these provide for debates on estimates selected by the Liaison Select Committee, a committee comprising the chairmen of select committees. Previously, estimates were not usually subject to debate. It is not unusual for two subjects to be debated on each estimate day. Table 6.2 lists the estimate day topics in the 2002–3 session. As is apparent from the table, the Liaison Committee tends to opt for subjects of topical interest. Though only three days are involved, covering only a minute proportion of the annual estimates, the significance of the days lies as much in who selects the topic of debate as in the topics themselves. They are selected not by government, by opposition parties, or by private members, but by a committee of the House. On the one hand, that is a remarkable advance for the House, but on the other, compared to other legislatures, it is remarkable that so little of the parliamentary timetable is in the hands of the House itself or its committees.

Backbenchers

There are also debates initiated by backbenchers. The House used to allocate Fridays for debates of private members' bills and private members' motions. Fridays tend now to be divided between private members' bills and non-sitting days; in each session, the House has ten

Table 6.2   Estimates days, 2002–3

Date	Principal subject
5 Dec. 2002	Government drugs policy
11 Mar. 2003	War against terrorism
19 June 2003	Children's home investigations/waste management

Source: House of Commons Information Office (2003).

non-sitting Fridays, allowing MPs to devote time to their constituencies. (In practice, most members spend time in their constituencies on Fridays, regardless of whether the House is sitting.) The opportunity for backbenchers to raise issues has shifted not only to other days of the week but also to a different venue: Westminster Hall. Debates in Westminster Hall (see Chapter 2) allow backbenchers to raise issues of concern. Though not held in the Commons chamber, proceedings are the equivalent of proceedings in the chamber: they are televised and are published in *Hansard,* the official report of Commons debates.

Sittings are held in Westminster Hall on Tuesdays and Wednesdays from 9.30 am to 11.30 am, and from 2.00 pm to 4.30 pm, and on Thursdays from 2.30 pm to 5.30 pm, presided over by a deputy speaker or senior member of the chairmen's panel. The Tuesday and Wednesday sittings provide an opportunity for a series of short debates. Back-benchers wanting to initiate debates send their names to the Speaker and a ballot is held. The first debate lasts for ninety minutes and is followed by a thirty-minute debate. In the afternoon sessions, a ninety-minute debate is followed by two half-hour debates. (Thursday sittings are dedicated to discussing Select Committee reports and general debates.) Examples of debates on a single sitting day are shown in Table 6.3. Each debate not only gives the initiating backbencher the opportunity to make a short speech, but it also provides an opportunity for a number of other MPs to speak – especially in the ninety-minute debates – before a minister replies. (This is normally a junior minister, but exceptionally a

Table 6.3   Sittings in Westminster Hall, 8 September 2004

Time	MP initiating debate	Subject of debate
9.30–11.00 am	John Lyons (Lab)	MRSA in hospitals
11.00–11.30 am	Brian White (Lab)	Planning Inspectorate interim report on the Milton Keynes Local Plan
2.00–3.30 pm	Alex Salmond (SNP)	Electricity market in Scotland
3.30–4.00 pm	Angela Browning (Con)	Asperger Syndrome and adults
4.00–4.30 pm	Joyce Quin (Lab)	Survival of the red squirrel in North East England

senior minister has replied.) Members are thus able to have their views recorded, and to ensure that there is a response by the government. As can be gleaned from Table 6.3, the debates provide an opportunity to raise issues of constituency or regional concern, and issues of social concern outside the normal context of party debate.

Although debates in Westminster Hall were treated warily by some members when first introduced, they are now generally accepted as a useful complement to the chamber itself. Attendance is usually small – sometimes fewer than a dozen members – but numbers are not particularly pertinent in the context of what MPs wish to achieve. The debates allow backbenchers to raise issues they would otherwise not generally have the opportunity to raise in the chamber, and certainly not for the length of time afforded by Westminster Hall. The opportunity afforded can be shown in terms of the number of hours that sittings occupy. In the 2002–3 session, the sitting hours in Westminster Hall totalled just over 431, a substantial number in absolute terms and the equivalent of more than a third of the hours that the House itself sat. This thus constitutes a substantial amount of additional time available to back bench MPs.

Back bench members also have the opportunity to raise a topic in the *half-hour adjournment debate* at the end of each day's sitting in the chamber. Each such 'debate' is confined to half an hour (unless preceding business finishes early), with the member initiating the debate speaking for ten to fifteen minutes, perhaps allowing another member to intervene for a few minutes, and the remaining time being occupied by the minister responding. No vote is taken. As with debates in Westminster Hall, the attendance is small (sometimes no more than the member initiating the debate, the junior minister who is replying, and the duty whip) but again is considered a useful opportunity to raise an issue. The occasion is used most frequently to raise specific constituency matters, but may also be utilized to discuss more general issues of policy and administration such as, for example, problems of solvent abuse and water fluoridation.

Government

The other main type of debate is that on *government motions*. These may take the form of substantive motions, inviting the House to approve or take note of some action or proposal, or they may take the form of adjournment motions, allowing the House to discuss a particular topic but without having to reach a particular decision on it. These adjournment debates are distinct from the half-hour adjournment debates just discussed, and are usually employed when the government itself has no fixed position and/or when it wishes to invite a wide-ranging discussion.

Most substantive motions tabled by the government will tend to be of a procedural or 'domestic' nature – proposing, for example, the creation of a new select committee, an amendment to existing pensions arrangements for members, or a vote of thanks to a retiring Speaker or Clerk of the House. Some, however, will be on items of public policy. In the period since 2001, for example, there have been several debates relating to the international situation. Table 6.4 lists the twenty-three substantive motions discussed in the 2002–3 session, and shows the mix of procedural and substantive motions that characterize the list each session.

In combination, then, these different types of debate provide the House with opportunities to discuss myriad aspects of policy and executive actions. Tables 6.1–6.4 are noteworthy for the diversity of issues covered. They are also notable for the amount of time they occupy.

About a third of the time spent on the floor of the House is occupied by these various types of debate, including the annual debate on the address. In the 2002–3 session, the House sat for just over 1,287 hours, and just over 400 of them were taken up by these various debates. As we have already recorded, a slightly greater number of hours were occupied by debates in Westminster Hall. The aggregated number of hours is thus substantial and could not be matched in the period prior to the introduction of debates in Westminster Hall.

In the House of Lords, the variety is not quite so great. In Chapter 5 it was mentioned that almost two-thirds of the time of the House is now occupied by legislation. Debates occupy just over 20 per cent of the time of the House. The principal debates are held on dedicated debate days (previously Wednesdays, but Thursdays in the 2005–6 session) (see Chapter 4), accounting for about 15 per cent of the time of the House. The topics for debate are selected by each of the parties, plus the cross-bench peers, and there are a number of days where the topics are selected by ballot. There are usually two debates on each debate day. The total time allotted for both debates is five hours. These debates provide an opportunity for all peers who are interested in speaking; unlike in the Commons, there is no need to catch the Speaker's eye for permission to speak, as there is no authority figure to make such a choice. Instead, peers sign up on a speakers' list in advance of the debate and their names are published shortly before the debate. Peers speak in the order they appear on the list, which is agreed by the whips earlier in the day. (The names are usually listed to ensure that there is some alternation between the different parties.) The time is then divided between the number of speakers, and peers are advised of how long they each have

Table 6.4   Government substantive motions, 2002–3

Date	Subject
13 Nov. 2002	Sessional Orders
21 Nov. 2002	Commons Fisheries Policy
21 Nov. 2002	Committee of Selection
25 Nov. 2002	UN Security Council Resolution
2 Dec. 2002	Convention on the Future of Europe
11 Dec. 2002	On the retirement of Sir William McKay KCB (Clerk of the House)
12 Dec. 2002	Environment, Food and Rural Affairs
9 Jan. 2003	House of Lords Bills
27 Jan. 2003	Lord Chancellor's Department Select Committee
28 Jan. 2003	Membership of the Lord Chancellor's Department Committee
29 Jan. 2003	Public Accounts Committee reports 2001-02
4 Feb. 2003	House of Lords reform
12 Feb. 2003	Mid-term review of the Common Agriculture Policy
26 Feb. 2003	Iraq
27 Feb. 2003	Standards and Privileges (2nd Report 2002–3)
3 Mar. 2003	Intelligence and Security Committee Report on the Bali bombings
18 Mar. 2003	Iraq
30 Apr. 2003	Membership of Modernisation Committee
26 June 2003	Standards and Privileges (3rd Report 2002–3)
9 July 2003	Convention on the Future of Europe
11 Sept. 2003	Standards and Privileges (4th report 2002–3)
30 Oct. 2003	Pay for chairmen of Select Committees
6 Nov. 2003	Modernisation measures

Source: Extracted from House of Commons Information Office 2003 (some errors in dates in the Digest corrected).

available to speak. If many peers sign up, each may only have a few minutes to speak.

The process of debate in the Lords may seem artificial, but it has proved to be effective. Peers who wish to speak do so; and knowing that they have a limited time to speak, they choose their words carefully. Because speeches are short, no member is able to go on for too long or to dominate proceedings. (If they attempt to, they are reminded of the time limit.) Given that in most (though not all) debates, the majority of speakers will have some experience or expertise relevant to the subject, the result often is a well-informed, and informative, debate. The topics themselves, especially those chosen by ballot or selected by the cross-benchers, often tend to fall outside the framework of partisan conflict. Peers are thus able to raise issues of concern to groups outside Parliament and to ensure that there is a government response; each debate is replied to by a minister.

About 5 per cent of the time in the House is taken up with 'unstarred' questions, which are dealt with under this heading because each question is debatable and results, in effect, in a mini-debate. They are the equivalent of the half-hour adjournment debates in the Commons, but take up more time. If they are held in the dinner hour (see above) they last for sixty minutes. If they are taken as the last business of the day, they last for up to ninety minutes. In this time, it is possible for several peers to contribute. (As with other debates, they sign up in advance.) On occasion, more than half-a-dozen peers may speak before a minister replies to the question. On occasion, as with debate days, so many peers decide to speak that they have only a few minutes each.

Towards the end of the session, the demands of legislative scrutiny are such that debate days are devoted to dealing with bills and there are few unstarred questions. However, for most of the session, these debates provide valuable opportunities for backbenchers, often specialists in the field, to raise issues of current concern. They are not the only debates, however. Some time is given to debating, similar to that occupied in the Commons on government motions. There is the same mix of procedural motions and debate of substantive issues, such as the war in Iraq and the European Union constitution. Time is also found to debate reports from select committees. In the Commons, some committee reports are debated, especially now in Westminster Hall, but there is a problem with finding time to debate all those that may merit discussion. In the Lords, if a select committee recommends that a report it has issued be debated, then time is found to discuss it. The House has resolved that time should normally be found in prime time but this is often not possible and some are debated during Friday sittings (the House sits on some Fridays to deal with such debates as well as to approve SIs). The number of committees (see below) is now such is that there is sometimes a list of between half-a-dozen and a dozen reports awaiting debate. The advantage of debating the reports is that there is a ministerial reply. The government cannot get by simply by responding in writing.

Both Houses thus have a range of means available to raise and debate issues that are of concern to citizens, and where the topic of debate is not necessarily in the gift of the government.

Question Time

The House of Commons sits at 2.30 pm on Mondays and Tuesdays; 11.30 am on Wednesdays and 10.30 am on Thursdays. (If it sits on a Friday, it meets at 9.30 am, but there is no Question Time and it is therefore excluded from this discussion.) After prayers, any formal announcements by the Speaker (such as of the death of a member) and any private business (taken formally), Question Time commences. It lasts until one hour from the commencement of the sitting (that is, 3.30 pm on Mondays and Tuesdays, 12.30 pm on Wednesday and 11.30 am on Thursday). Departments answer questions on a rota basis, each one coming up every four weeks. All questions are tabled to the appropriate secretary of state, but all ministers in a department will be involved, dealing with those questions that fall within their particular remit. During questions to the Secretary of State for Education, for example, questions dealing specifically with universities will normally be answered by the junior minister with responsibility for higher education.

Small departments, and ministers without departmental portfolios, such as the Chancellor of the Duchy of Lancaster, are given slots towards the end of Question Time. The prime minister makes an appearance each Wednesday, from noon to 12.30 pm Prior to 1997, Prime Minister's Question Time occupied two fifteen-minute slots, one on a Tuesday and one on a Thursday. When Tony Blair became prime minister, he aggregated the time and moved the session to Wednesday.

MPs can table questions up to three sitting days in advance (five days for questions to the Secretaries of State for Northern Ireland, Scotland, and Wales) – until 2003 it was ten sitting days – and are limited to one question per department on any day and no more than two in total on the day (it is thus possible to ask a question of the minister preceding Prime Minister's Question Time as well as of the prime minister). Because of the large number of questions tabled – which may run into three figures for the larger and more popular departments, such as the Treasury – there is a random computer shuffle to determine the order in which they are taken. Only the top twenty-five are published (fewer if a department is not taking up the whole of question time) and the rest are treated as lost. Not all of the twenty-five will necessarily be dealt with in the time available; those that are not reached receive a written answer.

Question Time begins with the Speaker calling the member in whose name the first question stands. The member stands and simply announces the number of the question. (Given that the question is on the order paper, time is saved by not reading it out.) The relevant minister then rises and reads out a prepared answer. The member is then called again in order to ask a supplementary question and, at the discretion of the Speaker, one or two other members may also be called to ask supplementaries. If a member of the opposition front bench rises after the first supplementary, he or she takes precedence. The process is then repeated for subsequent questions on the order paper.

Questions must be confined to matters for which the answering minister has responsibility. This creates a problem at Prime Minister's Question Time, as there is no prime minister's Department. Consequently, questions are usually 'open' questions, asking the prime minister if he will pay an official visit to a particular place or – what is now the standard question – to list his official engagements for that day. The MPs lucky enough to have come high in the ballot then have an opportunity to put the questions they really wanted to ask in the form of supplementaries.

Though questions are required to be precisely that – questioners may not make statements or advance arguments – they are not necessarily information-seeking but rather means of raising issues and criticizing (or praising) ministers. Ministers may well know the content of supplementary questions from their own supporters – who brief the minister so that a response demonstrating the government's strengths can be given – whereas supplementaries from opposition members have to be guessed at; the opposition members will often try to catch the minister out with an unexpected (but in order) supplementary.

Prime Minister's Question Time is seen as the cut-and-thrust of political conflict between the two sides of the House, and in particular between the prime minister and the leader of the opposition. It is a focus of media attention. However, it presents an exaggerated picture of Question Time. Questions to departmental ministers will not necessarily be as sharply partisan and are characterized at times by informed questioning by members pursuing issues of concern to constituents and others in society.

Members also have the option of tabling questions for a written answer. These are printed, along with the minister's reply, in *Hansard*. Written questions allow members to obtain information in a form that may not be possible on the floor (in tabular form, for example), or to receive answers to questions that may not be reached in Question Time. There is no limit on the number of written questions that may be tabled. It is perhaps not surprising, therefore, that the use of these is popular among MPs. The number tabled each session is at the time of writing usually in excess of 50,000. (In the long session of 2001–2 it exceeded 70,000.) In the 2002–3 session, 45,940 questions were tabled for a non-priority written answer, and 9,486 for a priority written answer. The former are normally answered within a week and the latter on the date stipulated by the member. Because of the number of priority questions that began to be tabled – becoming in the 1990s as popular as the non-priority questions – a limit has been imposed and each member is restricted to a maximum of five priority questions a day. There is no limit to the number of non-priority questions that can be tabled. Some MPs are avid users of written questions.

Written questions are an important part of MPs' activity. Data for the 2001–2 session revealed that the average MP received answers to 103 written questions and asked ten (substantive or supplementary) oral questions (Young *et al.*, 2003, p. 5). (Each made an average of twenty-three debate contributions in the chamber and Westminster Hall.) However, these averages mask some wide disparities. In that session, seventeen MPs each tabled in excess of 500 written questions; these MPs are listed in Table 6.5. What is noteworthy is not only the number

Table 6.5 MPs tabling the most written questions, session 2001–2

MP	Number of written questions tabled
John Bercow (Con)	4,206
Andrew Turner (Con)	1,337
Chris Grayling (Con)	1,160
Paul Burstow (Lib Dem)	897
Tim Loughton (Con)	833
Theresa May (Con)	833
Matthew Taylor (Lib Dem)	761
Mike Hancock (Lib Dem)	754
David Liddington (Con)	690
Dr Vincent Cable (Lib Dem)	681
Norman Baker (Lib Dem)	652
Oliver Heald (Con)	599
Angus Robertson (SNP)	594
Dr Liam Fox (Con)	579
Peter Ainsworth (Con)	573
Ann McIntosh (Con)	558
Bernard Jenkin (Con)	556

Source: Data from Young *et al.* (2003).

of questions asked but also the aggregate – between them they account for 16,263 questions, almost a quarter of all written questions (24 per cent) – and the parties of the questioners. All listed in Table 6.5 belong to opposition parties.

A further revealing feature of Table 6.5 is that most of the members listed are members of the opposition front bench or are Liberal Democrat spokespersons. Written questions are thus employed as a significant weapon in the armoury of opposition front-benchers in questioning ministers. The data for both oral and written questions reveal that usage is greater among opposition MPs. In 2001–2, the average Labour backbencher tabled 180 questions (oral and written), the average Conservative MP, 193; and the average Liberal Democrat MP 252. The figure for the Scottish National Party (SNP) was no fewer than 417 (Young *et al.*, 2003, p. 17).

Questions are seen, not least by MPs themselves, as an important means of subjecting ministers and departments to critical scrutiny. One survey of MPs on both sides of the House in the early 1990s found there was general agreement that questions were important for holding ministers to account (Franklin and Norton, 1993; ch. 4). Oral questions were seen as being marginally more important than written questions in this context. Written questions were deemed to be more important than oral questions for obtaining information that would otherwise be difficult to acquire.

In the Lords, Question Time is also taken at the start of a sitting from Mondays to Thursdays, but differs notably from that in the Commons, in four respects. The first is in terms of time: Question Time occupies 30 minutes. The second is in terms of scope: whereas the Commons goes for breadth, trying to get through as many questions as possible, the Lords go for depth. No more than four questions are taken. This allows for about eight minutes per question, thus giving time for a number of supplementaries, enabling a particular subject to be pursued in some detail. Consequently, ministers have to be well briefed, not least given the expertise of those who may be asking the questions. The third is in terms of ministers who reply: there is no rota system for departments. Questions are not tabled to particular departments but instead are addressed to Her Majesty's Government. Questions can be tabled up to a month in advance (though the final question on Tuesdays, Wednesdays and Thursdays is a 'topical question' chosen by ballot two sitting days in advance), and on any particular day one may deal with social security, another with foreign affairs and so on. In this case, the relevant social security minister will be in attendance to answer, as will the relevant foreign office minister. A minister may thus make a number of appearances at the despatch box in a week. The fourth difference is that there is less partisanship than in the Commons: questions can be tabled to seek information and in order to pursue an issue outside the context of party politics. Some are very specific to the interest of the questioner, which may cover a matter of general public concern, such as the international situation, and others may be more parochial, such as responsibility for digging up roads in London.

There is also another notable difference between the two Houses. Peers are less likely to table questions than are MPs. Even so, there are limits in order to prevent any peer dominating Question Time. No peer should have more than two questions on the order paper at any one time, or have more than one question on any one day. In an average session, about 700 questions will be asked. There are other procedural differences. The peer with the question rises and says 'I beg leave to put the question standing in my name on the order paper', and, after the supplementary to the minister, other peers intervene to put supplementaries. As there is no Speaker with powers to call people to put questions, the House must decide who should ask a supplementary if two peers persist and neither gives way; in practice, the Leader of the House normally comes to the dispatch box to suggest that peer X should perhaps be heard, and then peer Y. The normal convention is to give way to another peer, and a question coming from one side of the House, should be followed by a question from the other side.

Peers may also table questions for a written answer, though the number tabled each session – usually between 4,000 and 5,000 – is, again, small relative to the number in the Commons, though it is growing. Some peers are regular questioners, but most will tend to ask questions when they in fact want information. Some will pursue issues central to their area of expertise; the leading lawyer, Lord Lester of Herne Hill, for example, frequently tables questions on issues of human rights. The questions should be answered within a fortnight. Questions which have not been answered within the deadline are reprinted on the order paper.

Outside the chamber

There are various means available to MPs to raise issues other than through debates and questions. Indeed, these means have expanded noticeably in recent decades. The most prominent of these comprise select committees and represent the formal means of engaging in administrative oversight. At the informal level – informal in that they are not officially-designated agencies of the House – there are back bench groups and all-party groups. Members also have the option of pursuing matters individually, for example, through a meeting with or writing to a minister.

Select committees

Select committees are appointed to consider a particular issue. They were used frequently in earlier times, such as during the Tudor era, but were largely, though not wholly, squeezed out by the advent of party government in the nineteenth century. They can be divided into two types: domestic committees and investigative committees. Domestic committees cover such matters as catering and management functions. Each House has several such committees. They are intrinsic to the smooth running of each House, but they need not concern us here as they are not tools of administrative oversight.

Investigative select committees in the Commons fall into one of two categories. There are the departmental select committees and there are other investigative committees, of which the oldest and most important is the Public Accounts Committee.

Departmental select committees

The creation of departmental select committees in 1979 added a major new dimension to the work of the Commons (see Chapter 2). As we have noted, their creation constituted the most important reform of the latter half of the twentieth century. At the end of the 2001–5 Parliament, there were eighteen of them; see Table 6.6. The committees are multifunctional. Formally, as we have seen, they exist to consider the administration as well as the policy and expenditure of departments. Finding out what departments have done, why and with what effect, constitutes a central part of their activities.

The committees are responsible for determining their own agenda and they have significant advantages over the use of the floor of the House to subject departments to sustained scrutiny. Debates and questions can be deployed only for sporadic scrutiny of particular programmes and activities. Committees can pursue a particular issue at some length. They can do so by questioning not only the appropriate minister but also the relevant civil servants. They can also call witnesses from other bodies to offer their knowledge and advice, and they do so frequently; the majority of witnesses are not drawn from government

Table 6.6 Departmental select committees, 2004

Committee	Chairman
Constitutional Affairs	The Rt Hon. Alan Beith (Lib Dem)
Culture, Media and Sport	The Rt Hon. Sir Gerald Kaufman (Lab)
Defence	The Rt Hon. Bruce George (Lab)
Education and Skills	Barry Sheerman (Lab)
Environment, Food and Rural Affairs	The Rt Hon. Michael Jack (Con)
Foreign Affairs	Donald Anderson (Lab)
Health	David Hinchcliffe (Lab)
Home Affairs	The Rt Hon. John Denham (Lab)
International Development	Tony Baldry (Con)
Northern Ireland Affairs	Michael Mates (Con)
Office of the Deputy Prime Minister: Housing, Planning, Local Government and the Regions	Andrew Bennett (Lab)
Science and Technology	Dr Ian Gibson (Lab)
Scottish Affairs	Irene Adams (Lab)
Trade and Industry	Martin O'Neill (Lab)
Transport	Gwyneth Dunwoody (Lab)
Treasury	The Rt. Hon. John McFall (Lab)
Welsh Affairs	Martyn Jones (Lab)
Work and Pensions	Sir Archy Kirkwood (Lib Dem)

departments. Oral evidence is supplemented by the submission of written evidence, both solicited and unsolicited. The committees are also empowered to appoint, and most do appoint, one or more specialist advisers – outside experts paid on a daily basis – to assist them throughout a Parliament or for particular enquiries, as well as appointing specialist assistants – usually highly-qualified graduates in the field, employed on a fixed-term contract for two or three years.

Each committee normally meets every week while the House is sitting, with meetings lasting between sixty and ninety minutes. They may undertake extensive, long-term enquiries or short, rapid ones. Some will have single sessions on a particular subject or an annual meeting with the minister; for example, the Treasury Committee has a session with the Chancellor of the Exchequer each year. The topics chosen may reflect a committee in a proactive or a reactive mode. That is, a committee may seek to influence an issue just as it is coming on to the

Table 6.7   Subjects covered by selected select committees, 2003–4

Select Committee on Education and Skills
• Secondary Education: School Admissions
• UK eUniversity
• Public Expenditure
• Draft School Transport Bill
• Prison Education
• National Skills Strategy: 14–19 Education
• The work of OFSTED
• Higher Education Bill

Select Committee on Foreign Affairs
• Foreign Policy Aspects of the War against Terrorism
• South Africa
• Strategic Export Controls – Annual Report for 2002, Licensing Policy and Parliamentary Scrutiny
• Human Rights, Annual Report 2003
• Iran
• Implications for the Work of the House and its Committees of the Government's Lack of Co-operation with the Foreign Affairs Committee's Inquiry into the Decision to go to War in Iraq
• Foreign Policy Aspects of the War against Terrorism
• Foreign Affairs Committee Annual Report 2003
• The Decision to Go to War in Iraq

Select Committee on the Treasury
• Restoring confidence in long-term savings
• The 2004 Budget
• The Administrative Costs of Tax Compliance
• Annual Report for 2003
• The 2003 Pre-Budget Report
• Transparency of Credit Card Charges
• Child Trust Funds
• Appointment Hearing: The Chief Executive of the Office of Government Commerce
• Bank of England February 2004 Inflation Report

Source: Derived from House of Common website: committee section.

political agenda, or it may decide an issue already clearly on the agenda and one generating concern. As we have seen (Chapter 4), select committees may also play a role in pre-legislative scrutiny, enabling them to influence legislation at an early stage. The range of subjects on which

Table 6.8   Number of departmental select committee reports, 1979–2001

Parliament	Number of reports published
1979–83 (4)	193
1983–87 (4)	306
1987–92 (5)	403
1992–97 (5)	453
1997–2001 (4)	430

Note: Number of sessions in parentheses.
Source: Data calculated from *Sessional Information Digest*, 1979–2001.

the committees undertake enquiries, and subsequently issue reports, is diverse. Examples of that diversity are shown in Table 6.7, which lists subjects covered by three committees – Education and Skills, Foreign Affairs, and Treasury – in one session, that of 2003–4.

The committees take evidence, both oral and written, before drawing up and agreeing a report. The reports are published in paper form and are also available on the internet. The committees are prolific in output. Table 6.8 lists the number of reports published in the five full Parliaments since the committees were formed. In the first two sessions of the 2001 Parliament, the committees issued 147 reports, and in the period from their appointment in 1979 through to the summer recess of 2004, they were responsible for publishing 1,932 reports. Significantly, some committees have also taken to reviewing previous reports to see what action was subsequently taken.

The committees have thus invested considerable time and energy in reviewing government action in the different sectors of public policy. By their questioning of ministers and civil servants, they have required the occupants of government departments to explain and justify particular policies and particular actions. They have been able to do so by virtue of their special status. Though the committees cannot force the attendance of ministers and civil servants, there has usually been no problem in achieving the attendance of the witnesses sought. Ministers do not wish to attract the parliamentary opprobrium that would result from a refusal to attend. Civil servants cannot make comments to the media. Appearing before committees, they can speak only in the name of their ministers, but none the less, by appearing they are in a position to provide information and explanations that would probably not otherwise be put in the public domain.

Committees are thus able to ensure that ministers and civil servants are subjected to scrutiny in a public authoritative forum, eking out explanations and data that otherwise might not be forthcoming. In so doing, they have ensured what, in Judge's terminology (1990, p. 167), is a greater transparency of departments, ensuring that their actions are more visible to Parliament as well as to the public and outside groups. Through issuing reports and recommendations they also have some impact on departmental thinking. This impact does not usually extend to initiating significant new policies, but it can affect the implementation of existing policies and administrative practices. By taking evidence from interested bodies, the committees have the potential also to look at policies from different perspectives and by so doing may influence government to re-examine and re-appraise existing policy positions (Judge, 1990, p. 198).

Other committees

The Commons also has four investigative committees that cut across departmental boundaries – the Public Accounts Committee (PAC), the Environmental Audit Committee, the European Scrutiny Committee, and the Public Administration Committee – as well as three committees that straddle the categories of domestic and investigative: the Liaison Committee; the Modernisation Committee; and the Procedure Committee.

First appointed in 1861, the PAC primarily undertakes value-for-money audits of government programmes. The audits themselves are undertaken by, and on the initiative of, the Comptroller and Auditor General, who heads the National Audit Office, a body with a staff of approximately 800. The Comptroller and Auditor General presents reports to the committee, reports that are often short but generally numerous: about thirty or forty per session, focusing on how money is spent and whether it is used most efficiently to achieve its intended purpose. Given the number of reports, the PAC cannot spend too much time on any particular one, and tends to hold one hearing, rather than several, on any given report. The Permanent Secretary of the relevant department will normally appear as the witness in the capacity of accounting officer. If not satisfied with the responses, the committee can issue a critical report. By virtue of the nature of the enquiry by the National Audit Office and the status of the PAC, such reports are treated seriously in Whitehall. Committee recommendations are considered by the Treasury in consultation with the relevant department and, if accepted, put into effect according to Treasury instructions. If not accepted, a reasoned reply has to be given to the committee. The committee, traditionally chaired by a senior opposition MP, may then choose to return to the matter at a later stage. PAC reports and enquiries contribute substantially to the scrutiny of the administration undertaken by the house, forcing departments to justify their actions in spending monies in the way that they do.

The Environmental Audit Committee is of more recent origin. It was formed in 1997 to consider to what extent the policies and programmes of departments and non-departmental public bodies 'contribute to environmental protection and sustainable development', and to audit their performance against such targets as may be set for them by ministers. Whereas the PAC conducts a financial audit, this committee – as its name implies – undertakes a 'green' audit. (Both committees are unusual in that each also has a minister serving on it – a Treasury minister in the case of the PAC and the Minister for the Environment on this committee – but each sits ex officio and does not attend.) The Committee has been extremely active and in the 2003–4 session issued thirteen reports. These covered such topics as GM Foods – Evaluating the Farm Scale Trials; Water: The Periodic Review 2004 and the Environmental Programme; Environmental Crime and the Courts; Environmental Crime: Fly-tipping, Fly-posting, Litter, Graffiti and Noise; and Budget 2004 and energy.

The European Scrutiny Committee was previously the Select Committee on European Legislation and had a fairly narrow remit in terms of considering proposals and other documents presented by the European Commission to the Council of Ministers. It was responsible for reporting to the House documents that were of legal and political significance and whether such documents merited debate. It fulfilled a worthwhile role but it was essentially reactive. Its terms of reference were later expanded, providing it with an opportunity to address wider issues of concern (see Chapter 7). It has utilized the opportunity to report on such issues as the role of national parliaments in the EU and successive European treaties.

The Public Administration Committee is another committee that has evolved. It was created in 1997, bringing together two existing committees: the Select Committee on the Parliamentary Commissioner for Administration (the Ombudsman) and the Public Service Committee, which was concerned especially with the civil service. The Committee thus has responsibility for receiving reports from the Ombudsman, who investigates complaints of maladministration (see Giddings, 1998), and 'to consider matters relating to the quality and standards of administration provided by civil service departments, and other matters relating to the civil service'. The committee has tended to range more widely than its terms of reference suggest, and has looked more at the whole sphere of public administration. (It has even been known to go beyond that – in looking, for example, at House of Lords reform.) It has proved to be a prolific committee, frequently examining issues that are of topical concern. In the 2003–4 session, for example, it examined the honours system, ministerial accountability to Parliament, the holding of government inquiries, and government communications, in addition to reports from the Ombudsman.

The Liaison Committee is the body that draws together all the chairmen of the select committees of the House. (This includes domestic committees, so it is a large body.) It has various administrative functions, not least in relation to the budget and activities of select committees. As we have seen, it chooses the subjects for estimate day debates. However, it also has an investigative role, and has pursued the issue of the role of select committees. In 2000, for the first time, it took evidence in public, when it called the then Leader of the House, Margaret Beckett, to give evidence. It has also acquired a new role as a result of the prime minister agreeing to appear twice a year to answer questions from members. The first such session took place in July 2002. Given the size of the committee, specific themes are selected for the sessions, a particular committee chairman leading each one. Even within the time available – each session lasts the whole morning – the session has to flit from one subject to another.

The Modernisation Committee was established in 1997 to look at ways in which the Commons could be modernized. Chaired by the Leader of the House, it examines a range of possible reforms, and has issued reports on different aspects of the legislative process as well as issues such as electronic voting for MPs and the sitting hours. The Procedure Committee is a more long-standing committee and, as it name shows, is concerned with examining the procedures of the House. It has reported on such matters as the committee structure – its 1978 report led to the creation of the departmental select committees – as well as private members' legislation and Question Time. Both committees are essentially conduits for reform proposals.

The House of Commons, which for much of the twentieth century had very few permanent investigative select committees, is now a much more committee-orientated House, in essence changing the very nature of the institution. There is extensive activity taking place in committee rooms in the different parts of the parliamentary estate, especially on Tuesdays and Wednesdays. The committees themselves do not necessarily confine themselves to Westminster and have power to meet elsewhere to take evidence. This power is sometimes employed to take evidence abroad as well as in different parts of the United Kingdom.

House of Lords

The House of Lords is not dissimilar to the Commons in that it has seen a notable expansion of committee activity in recent years. Until the 1970s, it was very much a chamber-orientated institution. That changed with the creation of the European Communities Committee in 1974. The committee worked through sub-committees, and the House developed a reputation for its thorough and informed inquiries in the field of European legislation. It was facilitated by terms of reference that enabled it to look at the merits of documents. The committee – now the European Union Committee – works through seven sub-committees (the number was increased from six to seven in 2004) and we shall be examining its work in more detail in Chapter 7.

The European Communities Committee was joined in 1979 by another permanent committee – the Science and Technology Committee. These two comprised the main investigative committees of the House, supplemented on occasion by *ad hoc* investigative committees. A further committee was added in 1993, when the Delegated Powers Committee came into being. The committee – now the Delegated Powers and Regulatory Reform Committee – has responsibility, as we have seen (see Chapter 5) – for examining order-making powers that are included in bills. The largest addition to the committees of the House came in 2001, when two new committees – the Constitution Committee and the Economic Affairs Committee – were created, along with a Joint Committee of both Houses – the Joint Committee on Human Rights. Another committee – the Select Committee on the Merits of Statutory Instruments – was appointed in December 2003. As we have seen (in Chapter 5), its role is to report to the House on statutory instruments that are of political or legal significance, or are inappropriate or imperfectly drawn to achieve their objectives.

The number of committees has thus grown and they are listed in Table 6.9. They are designed to complement those in the Commons by covering topics that transcend particular policy sectors and are not confined to particular departments. There is some overlap. The Science and Technology Committee was appointed in 1979 when the Commons abolished its committee on Science and Technology. When the Commons brought it back into existence, the Lords decided to maintain

Table 6.9   Investigative select committees in the House of Lords, 2004

Committee	Chairman
Constitution Committee	Lord Norton of Louth (Con)
Delegated Powers and Regulatory Reform	Lord Dahrendorf (Lib Dem)
Economic Affairs	Lord Peston (Lab)
European Union	Lord Grenfell (Cross-bench)
Merits of Statutory Instruments	Lord Hunt of King's Heath (Lab)
Science and Technology	Lord Oxburgh (Cross-bench)

its committee. The Lord Chancellor's Committee in the Commons was renamed the Constitutional Affairs Committee in 2003, thus overlapping with the Lords Constitution Committee, but it focuses on the responsibilities of the department, which cover primarily the administration of the courts and reform of civil law. The Constitution Committee in the Lords addresses wider issues, having a remit to keep the operation of the constitution under review.

The committees are also designed to play to the strengths of the House, with members appointed because of their expertise in the field. The chairman of the Science and Technology Committee is usually a distinguished scientist. When the new committees were established in 2001, the House appointed Lord Peston, a former professor of economics at the London School of Economics to chair the Economic Affairs Committee; and a professor of government – the writer of this volume – to chair the Constitution Committee.

The Committees, like their Commons counterparts, tend to be prolific. The European Union Committee, working through its subcommittees, has been especially productive, notably so in 2003–4, during the examination of the proposed EU constitution.

Back bench and all-party groups

MPs and peers can also examine what government is doing through informal processes; that is, processes that are not formally established by either House and do not form part of parliamentary proceedings, but are created by parliamentarians and operate within the Palace of Westminster.

Back bench groups

The twentieth century saw a notable institutionalization of the parties in Parliament (see Norton, 1979). The main parties developed an infrastructure that provided the means for backbenchers to discuss issues of common concern and to convey their views to party leaders. Parliamentary parties retain their own organization, independent of the party whips. Each parliamentary party holds a weekly meeting; these tend to be held to announce future business and often to listen to speakers, who may be leading front-benchers or outside speakers. The two largest parties have a sufficient number of members to sustain various committees, or groups, to cover particular areas of policy. These used to be especially numerous and influential on the Conservative benches (Norton, 1979, 1994a) but other pressures on MPs' time, and the reduction in the size of the parliamentary party, have led to a reduction in numbers. Instead of committees covering virtually every government department, four policy groups were created in the 2001–5 Parliament – covering home, foreign, economic, and environmental affairs – which took it in turn to meet on Tuesdays at 5.00 pm. Meetings are open to all Conservative MPs as well as Conservative peers and MEPs.

The Parliamentary Labour Party now looks more like the Conservative parliamentary party used to look in terms of infrastructure. It has a series of subject groups, usually one for each government department. The groups meet regularly to discuss issues of concern within the policy area. (There are also regional groups to discuss issues of concern to each region.) The groups usually meet fortnightly to discuss forthcoming business relevant to the sector, and on occasion to hear from outside speakers as well as ministers. Some groups are especially active, and some ministers – but by no means all – make use of the groups to keep in touch with interested backbenchers and to brief them on issues within the sector. Each Labour MP can be a voting member of no more than three groups but is able to attend any group he or she wishes. Attendance fluctuates depending on the topic under discussion. A crisis, and a briefing on it by a minister, can swell numbers.

The party infrastructure is important to enable MPs to make their views heard by party leaders (Norton, 1979) and to do so within the closed confines of the parliamentary party; they are not engaging in a public dialogue (though reports of meetings may be leaked). It is less easy for a minister to shrug off criticism in a crowded party meeting – confined to party supporters – than is possible in the chamber where the criticism is coming from one's political opponents. Critical comments in a party meeting may serve to alert the whips, and ministers, to the fact that there is a problem with a policy.

All-party groups

MPs (and peers) increasingly have the opportunity to join with members of other parties on issues that cut across party lines. All-party groups have grown in number in recent years, covering not only policy areas but also cultural and sporting interests. The first all-party group was the Parliamentary Science Committee in 1933, which was re-formed as the Parliamentary and Scientific Committee (PASC) in 1939 (Powell, 1980), providing 'a unique forum for the exchange of ideas between the parliamentary and scientific worlds' (Wakefield of Kendal, 1980, p. 5), and the number has grown since then. By 1988, there were 103 all-party subject groups and 113 country groups (Jones, 1990, p. 125). By 2004, there were 303 subject groups and 116 country groups. The country groups exist to foster links with the country concerned. The subject groups vary in their purpose. Some exist to enable members to meet and enjoy common interests, such as tennis or chess. Most, however, serve primarily to raise awareness of the topic they cover. This is especially so with those concerned with social issues – encompassing, for example, breast cancer, epilepsy, hospices, learning disabilities, mental health, motor neurone disease, pensioner incomes, and poverty. Some of the groups exist in name only. Others are active, holding meetings regularly with outside speakers, and lobbying ministers and civil servants. Some also arrange photo opportunities for publicity to raise public awareness. An illustration of the work of an all-party group concerned with disability is provided in Whiteley and Winyard's study of the poverty lobby:

> The all-party group had a large number of meetings with voluntary organizations ... This took up about 80 per cent of its time, the rest being devoted to meeting civil servants and ministers. All the MPs in the group were generally sympathetic to the disabled, and the meetings helped them to choose priorities as well as to understand the operation of the welfare state as it applied to the disabled. (Whiteley and Winyard, 1987, p. 96)

The all-party groups provide a means of contact between outside organizations and MPs, and serve also as a means of reaching ministers through parliamentarians. All-party groups are especially attractive to interest groups as they operate outside the context of party – the groups cannot be accused of siding with any particular party – and are a means of identifying and keeping in touch with sympathetic MPs and peers. As a result, many all-party groups receive support from outside organizations, especially in the form of administrative support. One study in 2004 found that 202 all-party groups received support from an interest group, with administrative and secretarial support being the most prominent (Moyes, 2004, p. 53).

For MPs and peers, membership of all-party groups enables them to keep informed of subjects of particular interest to them. In the words of one MP, 'all-party groups allow MPs to band together over a common interest' (Barbara Follet, quoted in Moyes, 204, p. 21). Ministers are also likely to be sympathetic to such groups, given that the members cannot usually be seen to be acting in a partisan way or out of self-interest.

All-party groups constitute an important and increasingly pervasive part of the parliamentary landscape. Each party MP (and peer) receives with the weekly party whip an all-party whip, listing the forthcoming meetings of all-party groups. There is usually a long list for each week. Some, as we have said, are more active than others. Some have proved to be influential. Their attraction to outside groups is a particular feature, which is both a strength – in terms of the information it produces – and a weakness. As one lobbyist noted in identifying the strengths and weaknesses of different parliamentary bodies, all-party groups 'can mobilize support on occasions (e.g. VAT on books)' but, as a weakness, are seen as 'too influenced by pressure groups' (Miller, 1990, p. 55).

Meetings and correspondence

MPs and peers can also operate at an individual level in scrutinizing what government is doing. They meet ministers and correspond with them. Writing to ministers is usually in pursuit of constituency casework (see Chapter 9) but it is also a device for obtaining information from ministers and ensuring that they are aware of particular issues that concern members. As such, it can be seen as supplementary to parliamentary questions, requiring ministers to respond to particular points, but to do so less publicly and usually at greater length. A parliamentary question may elicit a short response, but a letter to a minister can result in a reply two or three A4 pages in length, explaining in some detail why a particular policy has been pursued or what plans government has made to deal with an issue. A letter also enables the member to develop a query, or make a point, in a way that is not possible in a parliamentary question.

Correspondence may be supplemented by personal contact. A member may arrange a private meeting with ministers to pursue particular points about the conduct of their departments. Such contact may be through a scheduled meeting, at the department or in the minister's room in the Palace of Westminster, or through a chance – or, indeed, planned – meeting in the division lobby, corridor or tea room. Such contact is a regular feature of activity in the division lobbies, being popular with members for the reason already noted in Chapter 3: it is difficult for a minister to give a negative response when face to face with a member making a particular request.

The important point about these informal means is that they supplement the formal means available. In combination – and it is the combination that is important – these various devices result in both Houses of Parliament, and the Commons in particular, devoting considerable time and attention – both on and off the floor – to the actions and administration of government.

Impact?

But what impact does all the time and energy devoted to the conduct of government in fact have? Looked at from a pluralist perspective, Parliament's capacity to affect decisions through administrative oversight is extremely limited. However, by drawing on the other perspectives of power, we are able to develop a more subtle understanding of Parliament's impact on the administration of government.

Limitations

Parliament exercises very little coercion in undertaking administrative oversight. The activities we have outlined are very rarely subject to a vote. There is virtually no opportunity for Parliament to say no definitively to government. Even when votes take place, as may happen on opposition days, they are declaratory; they have no legal force. The one occasion when the House of Commons can be extremely powerful is in passing a vote of no confidence in government. That, though, has no legal force. It is a convention that, when defeated on a vote of confidence, the government resigns or requests a dissolution of Parliament (Norton, 1978b). That is does so points to the strength of conventions. Generally, in engaging in administrative oversight, Parliament is operating in persuasive rather than coercive mode.

To what extent, then, is Parliament able to influence government? From a pluralist perspective, there are obvious problems in attempting such an evaluation. For one thing, there is the problem of disentangling the scrutiny of administration from the other tasks fulfilled by

Parliament. The scrutiny itself, as we have seen, takes different forms and embodies a range of consequences. For another, there is the problem of generating criteria for measuring Parliament's impact (Nixon, 1986; Judge, 1990). Even if the contours were clear, generating measurable objectives offers a virtually insurmountable obstacle.

Taken purely in terms of observable decision making, there is little evidence of Parliament affecting policy outcomes regularly and significantly. There are, for example, occasions when select committees have recommended a certain action and the government has then taken the action recommended. It is plausible to assume cause and effect, though that cannot be proved: the government may have intended to take the action anyway. Conversely, the government may reject a report, only for its recommendations to find their way on to a ministerial agenda a few years later (what is known as the 'delayed drop' effect), though again one cannot prove cause and effect. When an MP tabled a question in the 1980s asking for a list of all the recommendations emanating from select committees in the 1985–6 session that the government had accepted, the answer ran to several pages of *Hansard* and encompassed 150 recommendations. (Such data have not been available for more recent years, the government deciding that it could only be researched at disproportionate cost.) However, even this information, while indicating a large number of actions by government that are unlikely to have been undertaken had it not been for the committee reports, masks some limitations. First, the recommendations were generally on small items – detail rather than policy – and, second, they constituted a minority of the recommendations made by committees. As Peter Riddell has noted, committees have influenced various policy changes on the part of government, but these are the exception and not the rule (Riddell, 2000, p. 213). Furthermore, 'ministers can, and frequently do, disregard or ignore findings with which they disagree without much of a political stir' (Riddell, 2000, p. 213).

The committees are also limited in terms of what they can cover. They have limited resources – of which time is one – in which to scrutinize the whole gamut of government activity. They necessarily have to be selective, and policy tends to be more attractive than administration or estimates. Furthermore, 'witnesses do not always make it easy for committees to do their work' (Negrine, 1992, p. 406). Though committees normally get the witnesses they want, they do not always get the answers they want, civil servants being prohibited from giving information on internal discussions, interdepartmental negotiations, or anything that is commercially sensitive. Ministers and their officials can prove to be tight-lipped, offering nothing of substance.

There is little evidence that opposition day debates have affected government actions: they are simply part of the partisan conflict in the chamber and are rarely reported by the media. Debates themselves are a misnomer, in that there is rarely a 'debate', and members deliver set-piece orations, often – after the front bench speeches – to an almost empty chamber; and the outcomes of debates are usually predictable. Prime Minister's Question Time is regularly deemed to be newsworthy by the broadcast media, again because of its partisan content, but not the questioning of departmental ministers. At Question Time, there is limited opportunity to question the whole range of departmental activities. There is a substantial list of topics on which ministers will not answer questions, such as arms sales and budgetary forecasts. The randomness of question selection militates against pursuing an issue in a sustained manner.

The result is that Parliament cannot claim to subject the conduct of government to continuous and comprehensive scrutiny. Much, if not most, of what government does avoids parliamentary attention. When it *is* the subject of such attention, the attention is frequently sporadic and fleeting, affected by partisan considerations, time pressure and lack of knowledge. Ministers have various ways of deflecting probing by members, and to ignore recommendations for a change in practice or policy.

Strengths

Parliament's capacity to review government actions and administration is, then, clearly limited. However, it is not so limited as to be of no consequence. Indeed, it can be argued that Parliament, limitations notwithstanding, has the capacity to influence government. To tease out the capacity to persuade we can bring in the other perspectives of power.

The elitist, or agenda-setting, perspective is useful for drawing attention to what Parliament *can* do as much as to what it does do. Parliament may serve to keep certain matters off the agenda through the government anticipating reaction to parliamentary questioning or inquiry. In other words, it may have a deterrent effect. Knowing that an issue *may* be raised in the House, ministers and civil servants might be wary of pursuing a particular policy if they believe that it would attract adverse public reaction. Debates and questions may draw out something that government may not wish to be drawn out. The creation of the departmental select committees is especially important in this context. A committee may choose to investigate a particular policy. Committees choose their own agendas, usually after consultation with the department, but they may opt to pursue a subject government would prefer them not to. Ministers and civil servants may be more inclined than before to anticipate that their work might be subject to inquiry by a committee able to take evidence and to publish a report. As Peter Riddell (2000, p. 213) observed, 'ministers have to provide detailed replies to reports and that concentrates minds in Whitehall – as does the need to present evidence'.

The deterrent is likely to be greatest where there is consistency in scrutiny. This is notably the case with committees that examine every bill to ensure compliance with particular standards. The Joint Committee on Human Rights, for example, has chosen to consider every government bill (a practice now extended to *all* bills) to ensure that it is compliant with the provisions of the Human Rights Act. It has also started examining them to ensure that they also meet obligations embodied in other international human rights obligations (see Chapter 7). In its first three years of existence, the committee examined in excess of 300 bills. In the opinion of its founder chairman, Labour MP Jean Corston, the committee has affected outcomes, both directly and indirectly: 'Here it is the *threat* of parliamentary scrutiny, and an adverse opinion from us, that is the key factor. This threat, I believe, is much enhanced by the comprehensiveness of our coverage' [emphasis in original] (Corston, 2004, p. 165).

The deterrent capacity of committees has arguably also been enhanced by two independent developments. One has been the introduction of television cameras to the Palace of Westminster. A minister's appearance before a committee will attract the cameras if it looks as though the minister is in for a rough time. The other development is the growing link between the committees and the floor of the House. When first established, they operated largely in isolation, with few reports being debated by the House; over time, however, opportunities to debate reports has increased, first through estimates days and now debates in Westminster Hall. In the Lords, the opportunity to debate reports is better established; the change in the Lords has been the increase in the number of investigative committees.

Ministers and officials may thus decide, consciously or even subconsciously, not to pursue a particular policy for fear of parliamentary investigation. The extent to which this happens is impossible to determine, certainly not in any quantitative sense. Even if ministers claim they have been deterred from pursuing a particular line, one cannot prove that anticipated parliamentary reaction was the cause. One illustration of this, though focused on decision-making, was the claim by Margaret Thatcher when prime minister that 'I would like to be tougher on public spending. But I have to do what I think we can get through Parliament' (quoted in *The Times,* 11 January 1982). She may have been deterred by the prospect of being given a hard time in debate by Tory as well as Labour MPs. Then again, she may not have intended being tougher anyway, but none the less wished to assuage the criticism of those pressing for more radical action. All we can say is that Parliament has the potential to induce non-decision making on the part of government. Ministers remain within Parliament (see Chapter 3) and depend on the goodwill of their own supporters, not only for getting measures through but also to aid their own advancement. Given that, it would seem plausible to argue that ministers do not put parliamentary reaction totally out of their minds in the course of determining their policy and future actions.

There is also the positive side of agenda setting. That is, members may induce certain issues to be brought on to the agenda. This may be achieved through the obvious route of seeking to initiate a debate or it may be the result of tabling questions. Ministers devote considerable time to preparing for Question Time. This applies to the prime minister as well as to senior ministers. The prime minister will go over possible questions with a team of advisers, assisted by a small unit in 10 Downing Street, which draws together material from departments. Senior ministers will draw together junior ministers and senior officials in order to prepare. A parliamentary question ensures that the issue is brought before a minister; it may alert ministers to something of which they were not aware and which may merit further attention or action. Indeed, it can be argued that parliamentary questions assist administrative oversight through ensuring that ministers are briefed about a range of issues within their departments and which, without the prompt of members' questions, may otherwise not be put before them by civil servants. Again, the extent to which this contributes to agenda-setting in any significant sense is questionable, but there is a persuasive case that it helps to keep ministers abreast of developments for which their departments have a responsibility.

The institutional approach may be of even greater utility in assessing Parliament's capacity to engage in administrative oversight, and induce ministers and civil servants to act in a way that they would not otherwise. The relevance of the institutional approach is perhaps best illustrated by Peter Riddell's observation about select committees: 'Select committees are now part of ministers' lives and therefore part of the policy-making debate' (Riddell, 2000, p. 213). The same applies to debates and Question Time, as well as the other institutional means of administrative oversight. In other words, the behaviour of ministers is shaped by the institutional framework of Parliament.

The extent to which it shapes behaviour is illustrated by comparison with other legislatures. In some legislatures, ministers have the option of choosing which questions they wish to answer; and some may not even bother to turn up for Question Time. In Westminster, there is no question of departmental ministers not being on the Treasury bench for Question Time. They may sometimes be adept at side-stepping questions, but they offer some response and then have to contend with sometimes hostile supplementaries put to them. When major debates are held, either on opposition days or in government time, senior ministers will be present to argue and defend the government's case. In 2003, as we have seen, there were several debates on Iraq, both in opposition time (see Table 6.1) and government time (see Table 6.4). Both Prime Minister Tony Blair and Foreign Secretary Jack Straw were at the dispatch box to argue the government's case for war with Iraq.

The ministerial guidelines issued by the prime minister emphasize that ministers should make important policy announcements to the House of Commons. Ministers may be adept at handling the House, especially given a supportive majority, but the important point is that they present themselves to the House; it is part of the culture to which they have been socialized. They know the environment in which they will be operating. It is usually a supportive one, but on occasion may not be; a poor performance at the dispatch box may render the government's position vulnerable (see Chapter 3); on occasion, a minister may be fighting for his or her political life. In 2003, Prime Minister Tony Blair was arguing for the government's life in seeking parliamentary support for the war with Iraq. Also in 2003, Home Office minister Beverley Hughes resigned after admitting to having misled the House. Just as avoiding paying income tax is legal but evading it is not, so being economical with the truth at the dispatch box is permissible, but misleading or lying to the House is not. Ministers therefore have to be careful what they say. This has nothing to do with the size of the government's majority. It is one of the accepted rules of the game, and ministers play by the rules.

This institutional framework is important because it shapes ministers' behaviour and induces them to act in a way that otherwise they would not. That may sometime be in terms of decision-making, but more pervasively it is in terms of putting material in the public domain that otherwise would not be there. If MPs and peers did not ask questions or debate issues, then much of the material embodied in ministers' answers and speeches might not be revealed at all. Much of the material generated through the devices we have outlined may not be of great import, but some of it is. Select committees have contributed significantly to the process, extracting from ministers and civil servants information that is important, both quantitatively and qualitatively. Indeed, it can be argued that, prior to the passage of the Freedom of Information Act, the select committees were the most important contributors to open government in the United Kingdom. Indeed, given the limitations of the Freedom of Information Act, it is possible that the description may continue to apply for some time.

The structures and procedures we have detailed thus facilitate the release of information by government, and hence the means by which government can be judged; or at least judged more objectively than would be the case if these devices did not exist. They help to open up government, not only to Parliament itself but also to the media, interested organizations – who are the most frequent consumers of select committee reports – and the public. The public acquire information principally through television and the print media, though the internet provides expanding scope for direct access.

As Nevil Johnson (1988, p. 165), observed, the select committees were created under a government that adhered to a traditional view of parliamentary government: 'It is a view of the constitution which can accommodate strengthened select committees as critical organs of the House, but it has no place for committees with pretensions to the status of parallel governments.' The committees have therefore not served as decision-making bodies – they have no coercive capacity – but what they are able to engage in is a discourse with departments. They serve not simply as conduits for raw data, but rather engage in informed dialogue to enhance the understanding of government actions and intentions. They have expert advisers to assist in the process and thus engage in informed dialogue. Treasury officials know, for example, that the advisers to the Treasury Committee will run their economic forecasts through different economic models (Laugharne, 1994). In the Lords, the experts are themselves sometimes members of the committees.

As Johnson argues, the committees:

> are accepted by the departments as regular interlocutors, and can to some extent build on their accumulated experience of the sector of government entrusted to them. All this helps ensure that the House of Commons, ministers, and the departments all see the committees as regular elements in the processes of discussion, debate, and exchange of information through which public decisions are implemented. As a result organs of the House are latched on to the work of the executive in a more secure fashion than previously. (Johnson, 1988, p. 167)

The select committees thus add to the existing parliamentary means for prising out of government information and explanations. They contribute to a parliamentary framework for questioning and opening up of government, and are an established part of the parliamentary landscape. Regardless of the size of its parliamentary majority, government has to work within this framework of administrative oversight. Ministers accept that the framework and how it operates is legitimate. They are socialized to the process and accept it, on the grounds of both principle and self-interest. Ministers one day will cease to be ministers and the mechanisms now used to scrutinize them may prove to be useful tools in their own hands.

Conclusion

Parliament devotes a substantial amount of time to questioning the actions of government, including the implementation of policy goals (a decision to commit troops abroad, for example) and more mundane administration of public programmes (payment of benefits, for example). It has a range of devices at its disposal. However, even as devices for eking out information, each suffers from certain limitations. MPs are limited in what that may ask questions about. Partisanship in Question Time is tending to squeeze out genuine information-seeking (Norton, 1993b, pp. 201–3). The select committees will never be able to scrutinize more than a fraction of the policies and actions of government, and they are liable to focus on policy to the detriment of administration and expenditure. Their utility as scrutinizing bodies will vary considerably, depending in large part on the quality and commitment of the members, and in particular the chairman. Partisanship in the House of Commons will ensure that debates are characterized by high levels of generality rather than informed and forensic scrutiny.

Those devices, none the less, have considerable consequences for government. They provoke responses in the form of information, explanation and justification. They absorb the time and intellectual energy of ministers and senior civil servants. They shape behaviour. They create a critical environment for the discussion of particular programmes and actions. They ensure greater openness on the part of government. Use of these parliamentary tools may occasionally influence a change of policy or minister or, more frequently, some change in administrative techniques and departmental practices. And their very existence, and the occasional observable impact they sometimes have on policies and careers, may have a pervasive deterrent effect throughout the corridors of power.

7

Beyond Central Government: The European Union, Devolution and Human Rights

The history of Parliament, as we have seen (see Chapter 2), has in large part been the history of its relationship to the executive, and its capacity to affect public policy has been determined largely by changes in that relationship. It acquired the capacity to determine supply (the raising of money) and legislation; it other words, a coercive capacity. However, political pressures have largely curtailed the use of that capacity. Parliament has had to adapt to these pressures and, as we have seen, has done so through developing its persuasive capacity to affect outcomes.

Parliament has also had to adapt to other, significant developments. The period since 1970 has seen major constitutional change, on a scale largely unparalleled in modern British political history (Norton, 2003b; Stevens, 2002, p. xiii). As a result of policy decisions by government, assented to by Parliament, designated powers – coercive and persuasive – have been transferred to other bodies, both within the UK and beyond its shores. These developments have transformed the constitutional landscape and create particular challenges for Parliament.

The three principal changes are, in chronological order, membership of the European Community (now the European Union); the devolution of powers to elected bodies in different parts of the United Kingdom; and the passage of the Human Rights Act 1998, incorporating the European Convention on Human Rights into British law. They have had major consequences for Parliament, both individually and collectively.

The collective impact has been a judicialization of the British constitution. The courts, previously subordinate to Parliament – a position confirmed in 1688/9 under the judicially self-imposed doctrine of parliamentary sovereignty – have acquired a new role (Norton, 2004e).

They now determine any conflict between EU law and UK law and give precedence to that of the EU. As a consequence, UK law may be suspended while a final determination is made, as in the *Factortame* case in 1990–1, or struck down as conflicting with EU law, as has happened most notably in the *Ex Parte EOC* case in 1994 (Maxwell, 1999; Double, 2004). The courts are, in effect, constitutional courts for Scotland, Wales and Northern Ireland; they have to interpret the legislation stipulating the responsibilities of each devolved body. What are formally termed 'devolution issues' are dealt with by the Judicial Committee of the Privy Council (see, for example, O'Neill, 2001; Winetrobe, 2002). As a consequence of the Human Rights Act, the courts have to interpret Convention rights. If the courts deem them to conflict with other provisions of UK law, they can issue declarations of incompatibility. It is then up to Parliament to bring the law into line with the Convention, and it has established a fast-track procedure for doing so.

The changes have thus transformed the role of the courts, and judges have had to adapt to that role. Indeed, the main provisions of the Human Rights Act were not put in place until 2000, in order to give judges time to be trained in interpreting the Convention. The influence of the Convention on judges has extended beyond a simple interpretation of the Human Rights Act, extending to development of the common law (Klug and O'Brien, 2002). Parliament, too, has also had to adapt to a new role. It could be argued by some that it is a diminished role. In part, it has transferred a coercive capacity – not wholly, but in large part – and has had to adapt by developing its capacity to persuade. In this respect, it mirrors its changing relationship with British government.

The European Union

The UK became a member of the European Community (EC) on 1 January 1973. Membership of the Community resulted in the transfer of several policy-making competences to the institutions of the EC. These competences – the capacity to promulgate law in certain sectors – have been expanded with successive treaties. The Single European Act, which took effect in 1987, not only transferred more sectors to the EC domain, but it also strengthened the powers of the Community institutions at the expense of the national institutions of the member states. This was achieved principally through the extension of qualified majority voting in the Council of Ministers, the principal decision-making body of the Community, composed of ministers from each of the member states. Previously, unanimity had been the norm: each country had thus been a veto player. Later treaties – those of Maastricht, Amsterdam and Nice – further extended the fields of competence as well as instituting various institutional changes. (Under the Maastricht Treaty, the EC became the European Union, comprising the three pillars of: the European Community (EC), common foreign and security policy (CFSP), and justice and home affairs (JHA); it also strengthened the position of the European Parliament.) Other treaties provided for enlargement of the EU and in 2004 it expanded to twenty-five members. A Convention in 2003 on the Future of Europe also produced a draft treaty establishing a constitution for the EU, a document with potentially far-reaching consequences for the nature and operation of the Union. There has thus been a significant dynamic to EC/EU development. The challenge for Parliament has been to keep pace with this development.

After the UK became a member, Parliament decided to establish some means of scrutinizing EC activity. This was intended to give it a greater capacity to influence ministers prior to meetings of the Council of Ministers. As such, Parliament was developing the means to engage in a form of pre-legislative scrutiny. The difference between this and the pre-legislative scrutiny discussed in Chapter 4 is that, in the case of the EC, Parliament was operating at one remove from the decision-makers. Furthermore, there was nothing beyond pre-legislative scrutiny. There was no legislative stage for Parliament, and it was not called upon to give its assent to measures promulgated by Community institutions. That had been given in advance by the 1972 European Communities Act, which not only gave the force of law to existing Community law but also to future Community law. Parliament could determine how best to give effect to European directives, but it had no power to say no to them.

How, then, has this pre-legislative scrutiny developed? Both Houses have created a distinct process for dealing with European law.

The House of Commons

In the Commons, EU documents are deposited with the European Scrutiny Committee. The Committee began life in 1974 as the Select Committee on European Secondary Legislation. It considered legislative proposals emanating from the Commission but its terms of reference have been expanded to encompass 'EU documents', which includes consultation papers, proposed common positions and joint actions under the second and third pillars of the EU, and the draft of the annual budget. It is also empowered to consider 'related matters', thus giving it a wide focus. EU documents are deposited with the Committee within two days of their receipt by the Foreign Office. (Some minor documents are now listed rather than being deposited with the Committee.) Within ten days, the relevant government department submits a detailed explanatory memorandum, explaining – among other matters – the legal base under the treaty provisions, the government's position, the effect on existing UK law, and the financial implications. The memoranda tend to be detailed and informative, often helping to make sense of what otherwise may appear to be impenetrable documents.

The documents are considered by the European Scrutiny Committee and sifted into one of four categories:

(i)   those of sufficient legal or political importance to justify debate;
(ii) those of legal or political importance but not warranting debate;
(iii) those of no legal or political importance; and
(iv) those of legal or political importance in respect of which the committee is not yet in a position to decide whether debate would be justified.

The committee, aided by a professional staff of fourteen, has a substantial workload. It considers about 1,100 documents each year; in 2003 the number was 1,080. About half are usually technical and routine, raising no important political or legal questions. All those that are deemed to be significant politically or legally are discussed in the Committee's weekly reports. The committee will usually recommend about fifty to a hundred documents for debate.

Those recommended for debate are considered either in a European Standing Committee or, occasionally, on the floor of the House. While such consideration takes place, the documents are subject to what is known as the 'scrutiny reserve'. Under this, ministers are expected to withhold agreement in the Council of Ministers to any proposal 'which has not completed scrutiny or which awaits a resolution of the House'. The only exceptions are where the committee has indicated that agreement need not be withheld, or the minister concerned considers that 'for special reasons' agreement should not be withheld. Such special reasons have been taken by government to include the need to avoid a legal vacuum and the desirability of getting a measure of benefit to the UK into force as soon as possible. In practice, a small number of proposals are accepted each year by the Council prior to debate in the Commons, even though recommended by the committee for further consideration. Despite this, the scrutiny reserve is seen as a useful means available to Parliament – it applies to scrutiny in both Houses – to give it some leverage in discussing EU proposals with ministers.

Most of the time of the Scrutiny Committee is taken up with the EU documents sent to it, but under its terms of reference it now monitors the activities of UK Ministers in the Council, and keeps legal, procedural and institutional developments in the EU under review. As we have already noted (see Chapter 6), this has enabled it to undertake wider inquiries, including into the role of national parliaments in the EU.

European standing committees

Most documents recommended for further consideration are taken in one of three European Standing Committees. Before 1991, such committees were appointed on an *ad hoc* basis. Each committee considered a document on a motion moved by a minister, to which amendments could be moved, and sat for two-and-a-half hours. It then reported to the House. Such committees often suffered from poor attendance and were of only limited use in saving time on the floor of the House. Most documents recommended for consideration were taken on the floor. To try to improve scrutiny, and reduce some of the burden on the chamber, the Procedure Committee in 1989 recommended the appointment of European standing committees to consider EC documents in particular sectors, each committee having a membership nominated each session. This, it was felt, would allow for greater specialization and greater commitment by members. Following problems with recruiting members, the House approved the creation of two such committees early in 1991. The number has since been increased to three. European Standing Committee (ESC) A deals with environment, food and rural affairs, transport, local government, and the regions. ESC B covers finance, work and pensions, foreign affairs, home and legal affairs, and international development. ESC C encompasses trade, industry, education, culture, media, sport and health. Even with the increase in number, each covers a remarkably broad terrain.

Each committee has thirteen members appointed for the session. Chairmen are appointed for the consideration of individual documents. As with the previous *ad hoc* committees, any MP who is not a committee member can attend and seek to speak, though not to vote. However, they differ from the previous committees in that, prior to the usual debate on the documents, they can question the relevant minister for up to one hour. The questioning of the minister can be useful and influence the minister's thinking; preparation for it can help to concentrate the mind of the minister and officials. The meetings, though, are often not well attended. When the Minister for the Environment and Agri-environment, Elliot Morley, attended European Standing Committee A in June 2004 to discuss an EU document relating to the marketing of genetically modified maize, the meeting was delayed briefly by the absence of a quorum. During the hour-long meeting, only five members attended, though another five – not members of the committee – did turn up to put questions to the minister.

After the hour-long questioning, a motion is then put – usually a 'take note' motion – and debated for up to ninety minutes; amendments can be proposed. After the committee has completed its deliberations, and agreed a motion, the government moves a motion in the House; this is usually the same motion – though it need not be – as that agreed by the committee. (On one occasion, a committee agreed a motion different from that preferred by government; but the government moved its preferred motion in the House.) The motion is not debatable, though it can be voted on.

Floor of the House

The Scrutiny Committee can recommend that a document be debated in the chamber rather than in a European Standing Committee. However, it is at the government's discretion as to whether such a debate takes place. It rarely agrees to such debates (of five recommended in 2003, only one was taken on the floor), so the time taken by EU documents on the floor of the House is very small. In the 2002–3 session, for example, the time spent on EU documents was just over 4 hours (0.3 per cent of the time during that session). Apart from the discussion of EU documents, there are two debates each year prior to the six-monthly meetings of the European Council, the body comprising the heads of government of the member states. The time taken by the general debates far exceeds that taken by scrutiny of particular documents.

Select committees

Departmental select committees can examine European issues that impinge on departmental responsibilities, and the Scrutiny Committee may request comments from them. A weekly report on EU developments is circulated to them. In 1989, the Procedure Committee advised against the creation of a single committee to consider EC policy issues, preferring to leave the task with the existing departmental committees. However, the demands made on the time of select committees are such that very little time is devoted to EU matters. Some committees, such as that for environment, food and rural affairs, have given time to EU issues, including the common agricultural policy and the common fisheries policy, but no committee undertakes systematic scrutiny of EC legislation. Conflicting priorities are likely to ensure that this remains the case.

External links

Parliament has developed links with EU institutions. There is now a British Parliament Office in Brussels. Although the House has not accorded significant rights to UK Members of the European Parliament (MEPs), there are occasional meetings of members of the Scrutiny Committee (and the Lords EU Committee) with UK MEPs (European Scrutiny Committee, 2004, para. 18). The first such meeting took place in February 2003; at the second, in October 2003, the structural funds and the environment were discussed. Some members of the Scrutiny Committee attend the twice-yearly meeting of the Conference of European Affairs Committees – known by the French acronym COSAC – which draws together representatives from such committees to discuss matters affecting national parliaments and to share best practice (Tordoff, 2000). The chairman and officials of the Scrutiny Committee will visit Brussels, for meetings with EU officials, as well as the country holding the EU presidency. The Committee is also developing bilateral links with its counterpart committees in other legislatures. Scrutiny Committee reports, now easily accessible on the internet, are sent to EU institutions.

The House of Lords

Like the Commons, the Lords has a committee for the scrutiny of draft EU legislation. However, its work is more extensive than its equivalent in the Commons. It encompasses, in effect, the work done in the Commons by the Scrutiny Committee *and* the European Standing Committees. Its scrutiny is of a different nature. The two Houses seek to avoid duplicating the work of each other, and engage in complementary activities. Whereas the Commons goes for breadth, examining all documents, the Lords goes for depth, examining some documents in great detail (Norton, 1996). However, to draw on the strengths of both Houses, each agreed in 2004 to establish a Joint Committee to address EU issues.

The European Union Committee

In 1974, the House of Lords created a European Communities Committee (see Grantham and Moore Hodgson, 1985, pp. 118–32), renamed in 1999 as the European Union Committee. It is appointed to consider documents and report to the House on those that it considers raise matters of principle and policy, and questions to which the Committee believes the attention of the House should be drawn. As such, it can comment on the merits of proposals.

The committee has eighteen members, and meets fortnightly, operating principally through seven sub-committees. (The number has varied over the years between five and seven.) Each is known by a letter of the alphabet (Sub-Committee A and so on) and has responsibility for considering documents in a number of sectors (see Table 7.1). Each sub-committee comprises two or more members of the committee and usually between five and twelve co-opted members. As a result, about eighty peers – over 10 per cent of the membership of the House – are actively involved in committee work. Other peers may attend sub-committee meetings, thus allowing the sub-committees to benefit from members' expertise in particular areas.

Committee deliberations are notable for their lack of partisanship. The main committee is chosen to reflect the broad political balance

Table 7.1 Sub-committees of the House of Lords European Union Committee

Sub-committee	Sectors covered
A	Economic and financial affairs, trade and international relations
B	Internal market
C	Foreign affairs, defence and developmental policy
D	Environment and agriculture
E	Law and institutions
F	Home affairs
G	Social policy and consumer affairs

within the House, but interests and experience largely determine which peers are appointed to the committee or co-opted to the sub-committees, and which become chairmen. The chairman of Sub-Committee E, on law and institutions, is always a law lord. The sub-committee usually includes leading lawyers, former ministers with experience of the EU, and professors of politics. The chairman of the main committee, Lord Grenfell, is a former adviser to the World Bank. Members of the committee include peers who have held office as Secretary-General of the European Commission, Permanent Representative to the EC (and later UK Ambassador to the UN), and Chancellor of the Exchequer. A number of former Members of the European Parliament serve, or have served, on the committee and its sub-committees.

Whereas sub-committees cover particular sectors, the main committee looks instead at cross-cutting topics as well as taking evidence from every incoming EU presidency and from the UK minister for Europe after major meetings of the European Council.

EU documents are submitted to the Lords as well as the Commons. The chairman of the EU Committee undertakes a weekly 'sift', sorting out the more important documents that require further consideration, from the less important documents. In this, he is assisted by an expert legal adviser as well as by the clerk of the committee. Documents deemed to be important – generally about a quarter of the total – are then sent to the relevant sub-committees. It is then open to the sub-committees either to clear the proposals without subjecting them to further scrutiny, or to undertake inquiries.

If a sub-committee decides to undertake an inquiry, it can be a short one, with some evidence taken, and followed by a letter to the appropriate minister, or it can be a substantial inquiry, with oral and written evidence taken and a report made to the House. The inquiry need not be confined to a particular document. It may look at particular aspects of EU activity or even anticipate events. Typically, a sub-committee begins a meeting by considering documents referred to it – some of which may be revised versions of earlier proposals – before moving on to take evidence, in public, as part of a specific inquiry. When undertaking full-scale inquiries, a specialist adviser will normally be appointed, and bodies such as the EU Commission, professional and trade organizations, and other organized interests – including pressure groups – will be invited to submit evidence. Evidence from the government will be invited as a matter of course. Sub-committees have also variously invited Members of the European Parliament to give evidence. Some will also undertake occasional visits in order to obtain evidence.

When a sub-committee has completed an inquiry, a draft report is submitted to the main committee for approval, and the committee decides whether the report should be sent to the House for information or for debate. The reports themselves are often substantial documents and, though addressed to the House, copies are sent to the EU Commission, Parliament and the UK representative in Brussels.

The remit of the committee is such that its inquiries will often range widely. It has reported on such subjects as EU/US relations, the European Central Bank, the proposed second chamber for the European Parliament, the EU Charter of Fundamental Rights, the Working Time Directive, and in 2003 it issued several reports on the draft EU treaty establishing a constitution for Europe. It will scrutinize EU documents to get some idea of the direction in which the Union appears to be moving in particular sectors and may then undertake, through the appropriate sub-committee, what amounts to a forward-looking enquiry. Whether a report is recommended for debate or not, the government publishes a reply within two months of publication.

The floor of the House

The committee will usually make thirty or more reports a year to the House, with about half of these recommended for debate. When a report is recommended for debate, then it will be debated. However, pressure on time means that some reports are squeezed into inconvenient times, with some debates being held on Fridays. Debates on EU Committee reports occupy a relatively small part of the House's time – usually less than 3 per cent per session – but the debates serve a valuable purpose. When a report is debated, the issue gains a more public airing and a minister replies for the government. Some are not short debates; they can be substantial, lasting for several hours.

Given the need to move quickly to influence some EU decisions, the practice of undertaking short inquiries followed by letters to relevant ministers is frequently employed. The correspondence is regularly drawn together and published.

External links

The Lords, like the Commons, has developed links with EU institutions. Some members of the Committee attend the meetings of COSAC. The sub-committees have variously taken evidence from commission officials and from *rapporteurs* of European Parliament committees. The committee clerks attend the plenary sessions of the European

Parliament regularly and liaise with parliamentary and commission officials. The chairmen of the main and sub-committees visit Brussels every two or three years to meet the President of the Parliament and officers of relevant committees to discuss matters of common interest. Some contact also takes place through correspondence. Such links, though not necessarily substantial, are reasonably regular and have been developed over the years since the committee was appointed.

Devolution

Devolution is not dissimilar to EU membership in that Parliament has transferred specified powers to other bodies. In the case of Scotland and Northern Ireland, legislative and executive powers have been devolved. In the case of Wales, executive powers only have been devolved, with Westminster legislating for Wales as well as England. In the case of Scotland, the 129-member Scottish Parliament is able to legislate in all areas, other than those reserved to Westminster (such as foreign and defence policy, fiscal matters and social security policy). Devolution has thus seen Parliament transfer a substantial law-effecting capacity to other bodies, especially the Scottish Parliament.

The challenge for Parliament, and indeed for government (see Constitution Committee, 2003; Trench, 2004a), has been to adapt to the changed conditions. The Scottish Parliament has been an active body. In its first four-year session, from 1999 to 2003, it enacted 62 bills (Arter, 2004a, p. 72). It has developed an extensive committee system, with each committee combining both a legislative and an investigative role. The committees have even been empowered to initiate bills. It has sought to distinguish itself from the Westminster Parliament and to develop a more consensual style of policy-making. It has also sought to achieve input from the public, not least through the use of public petitions. However, though it operates in a way that is certainly different from Westminster (see Winetrobe, 2004), it has been heavily influenced by Westminster. Many of the Scottish politicians who were initially responsible for developing the Parliament were also Westminster MPs (see Constitution Committee, 2003). Party became a central feature of the institution, with party cohesion and party conflict characterizing proceedings (Arter, 2004a, 2004b). The committees became heavily involved in considering bills brought forward by the executive.

The effect of devolution has been to move Scottish matters largely off the parliamentary agenda at Westminster. By convention, the Secretary of State for Scotland cannot be asked about matters that are the responsibility of the devolved body. Though Parliament has the capacity to legislate for Scotland in devolved matters, it chooses not to do so, other than by invitation. If Westminster is considering a bill that the Scottish Parliament believes is also appropriate for Scotland, then – rather than passing a separate bill itself – the Scottish Parliament invites Westminster to extend the scope of the measure to Scotland. It does so through agreeing to what is known as a 'Sewel motion' (named after the Scottish Office minister, Lord Sewel, when the Scotland Bill was going through Parliament). In practice, Sewel motions have been far more extensive than was initially envisaged (see Page and Batey, 2002), but they have no effect on the capacity of Parliament at Westminster to exercise its own judgement in respect of matters effecting Scotland.

The House of Commons has retained the departmental select committees covering Scotland, Wales and Northern Ireland, and these variously report on matters affecting the part of the UK they cover, but there has been little linkage between Westminster and the devolved bodies. The House also has Grand Committees for Scotland, Wales and Northern Ireland. These committees comprise all the MPs holding seats in that part of the UK, though MPs drawn from other parts of the UK may be added. The committees may hear statements from ministers, question ministers, and discuss issues affecting that part of the UK; also some bills and delegated legislation may be sent to them for discussion. In practice, the effect of devolution has resulted in them meeting infrequently and then usually only for general debates. They are also permitted to meet away from Westminster, but now rarely do so.

When the Constitution Committee of the House of Lords investigated inter-institutional relations in the UK in 2002, it found that there was no effective mechanism for contact between the legislative bodies. There were particular problems with respect to Wales (Constitution Committee, 2003). Though powers to make secondary legislation had been conferred on the National Assembly for Wales, primary legislation was still passed at Westminster. There was no established procedure for the National Assembly making its views known on bills that affected Wales. As a result of the Committee's report, there were some improvements (there is now a section on the effect on Wales included in the explanatory notes that accompany bills), but there remains little structured contact between Westminster and the elected bodies in the different parts of the United Kingdom. Within Wales, there is pressure for the devolution of legislative powers (see Lambert and Navarro, 2004; Richard Commission, 2004), thus bringing Wales closer to the position in Scotland.

The transfer of law-effecting power to the Scottish Parliament has left the Westminster Parliament with little to do with respect to Scotland. It engages in no pre-legislative scrutiny of Scottish legislation. As such, it undertakes no role comparable to that for EU legislation. The distinction between the two is significant. EU law applies throughout the European Union, and hence is applicable throughout the United Kingdom, but the Scottish Parliament has no remit beyond the borders of Scotland.

The position is more complicated in relation to Northern Ireland and Wales. Power – shared among the parties – was devolved to the 108-member Northern Ireland Assembly but, as a result of political problems, the Assembly was suspended briefly in 2000 (from February to May) and then again from October 2002, and was dissolved in April 2003. During the periods when the Assembly has not been operating, power has been exercised by the UK government (as it was previously during direct rule) with law being made by Orders in Council, which are subject to assent by both Houses. This has created greater scope for using the Northern Ireland Grand Committee and the Select Committee on Northern Ireland Affairs, but these have neither the time nor the resources to substitute for the work of the Assembly. The National Assembly for Wales, as we have seen, operates in an unusual and far from settled situation, having limited powers and not yet having established a working relationship with the body that makes its primary laws.

Human Rights Act

The Human Rights Act 1998 enshrined the European Convention on Human Rights (ECHR) into British law. The UK was a signatory to the Convention and ratified it in 1951, but had not previously given it effect in domestic law. (The Convention pre-dates and is independent of the European Community/Union.) The Act, as we have seen, contributed significantly to the judicialization of the British constitution and makes it unlawful for public authorities to act in a way that is incompatible with convention rights. A public authority acting under statutory powers may be challenged because those powers contravene convention rights. The higher courts can issue declarations of incompatibility where UK law is deemed to be incompatible with the ECHR. Parliament can then act to rectify the position by bringing the law into line with the Convention, either by enacting a new law or through a remedial order (a statutory instrument subject to affirmative resolution in both Houses).

The first use of the remedial order – the fast-track route for bringing the law into line with the convention – came in 2001 to make amendments to sections of the Mental Health Act found to be incompatible with the convention. A further remedial order was introduced in 2004 to rectify an incompatibility between the Naval Discipline Act 1957 governing the composition of naval courts martial and convention rights to a fair hearing before an independent and impartial tribunal.

The courts have thus acquired a further and important role. By the end of 2003, declarations of incompatibility had been issued in fifteen cases, though five of these had been overturned on appeal (see Norton, 2004e). The consequence of judicial interpretation of the ECHR has been that various decisions taken by Parliament and enshrined in law have been overturned or modified by the courts. In 1999, for example, Parliament passed the Youth Justice and Criminal Evidence Act, incorporating a provision designed to prevent rape victims being cross-examined in court about their previous sexual history. The courts in 2001 modified this to permit some discretion to the judge in order to bring the provision into line with Article 6 of the convention (Woodhouse, 2002, p. 257). In 2003, in the case of *Bellinger* v. *Bellinger,* the courts held that a section of the Matrimonial Causes Act 1973 was incompatible with the convention. Parliament then passed the Gender Recognition Bill – conferring rights on those who changed gender, including the right to a new birth certificate – to bring the law into line with the court's interpretation. The courts, in particular, are concerned to ensure that powers granted by Parliament or exercised by ministers are 'proportionate'. A policy goal may be desirable, but the powers vested may be excessive in order to achieve it and may conflict with the provisions of the convention. The courts none the less recognize that Parliament is democratically elected and may give it the benefit of the doubt (see Edwards, 2002; Clayton, 2004).

For Parliament, the challenge has been to come to terms with the measure it has itself enacted. The principal means it has created is the Joint Committee on Human Rights (see Evans, 2004). The Committee was established at the beginning of 2001. It has twelve members, six from each House, and is aided by a legal adviser; it has the powers of a select committee, and can thus examine witnesses as well as meet at places outside Westminster. As a joint committee, it has been able to utilize the skills of members of both Houses. Its founder chairman was Jean Corston, a Labour MP who also chaired the Parliamentary Labour Party, and its members include a number of senior peers who are lawyers.

The joint committee was created in order to consider 'matters relating to human rights in the United Kingdom (but excluding consideration of individual cases)' and remedial orders introduced under the Human Rights Act. In practice, the committee has utilized its broad terms of reference to consider each government bill brought before Parliament for its compatibility with the Human Rights Act. It announced its intention so to do in its First Special Report: 'Where appropriate our Chairman will put written questions to the relevant Minister in charge of the bill and we may, in the light of the answers we receive, decide to conduct a detailed inquiry of the bill' (Human Rights Joint Committee, 2001, para. 1). Since then, it has extended its coverage to private members' bills and private bills, and begun to consider the extent to which bills comply with obligations and guarantees contained in international human rights instruments, other than the ECHR, to which the UK is a party (Corston, 2004, p. 164). The result has been a significant correspondence with ministers, all of which has been published. Each government bill is examined by the committee's legal adviser, who reports to the committee on whether it has implications for human rights. The committee normally, though not always, accepts that advice.

The joint committee has proved to be an active one. As was noted in Chapter 6, by mid-2004 it had considered in excess of 300 bills and drawn the attention of each House to around a hundred of them (Corston, 2004, p. 165). Its first report was on the implementation of the Human Rights Act. The committee examined the extent to which government departments had prepared for the implementation of the Act and begun to build a 'human rights culture'. It has been especially vigilant in reporting on anti-terrorism legislation, and in August 2004 issued a report reviewing counter-terrorist powers. In 2004, it also reported on matters such as deaths in custody and the meaning of 'public authority' under the Human Rights Act, as well as issuing reports on bills before the House. The Committee, after a two-year investigation, advocated the creation of a Human Rights Commission. In 2004, the government published a White Paper proposing the establishment of a Commission for Equality and Human Rights, largely in line with the committee's recommendation.

The committee represents Parliament's way of dealing with a situation that it has itself sanctioned. Parliament has enacted a measure to protect rights, in effect limiting its own capacity to determine rights, and then established a body to ensure that bills comply with those provisions. Despite occasional controversy – the committee attracted criticism in 2002 for arguing that an amendment to the Adoption and Children Bill, denying same-sex couples the power to adopt children, was incompatible with the convention – the committee has established itself as a significant element of Parliament's scrutiny powers. Apart from influencing particular decisions, it has persuaded departments to place more information in the public domain, especially material under-pinning claims that a bill is compliant with the ECHR (Corston, 2004; Hazell, 2004, p. 498). As a consequence, it has helped to build up in government what Jean Corston termed 'a culture of justification' rather than one of assertion (Corston, 2004).

Parliamentary adaptation

How successful has Parliament been in adapting to the changed consti-tutional landscape? In terms of the pluralist view of power, we can see that there has been a significant change. Parliament has transferred significant power – coercive and persuasive – to other bodies.

Formally, the transfer of coercive powers has not been complete. In terms of EU membership, Parliament retains a coercive capacity in rela-tion to new, or amendments to existing, European treaties. It is not called upon to ratify treaties (other than in respect of very specific pro-visions affecting the European Parliament), since treaty ratification remains a prerogative power. However, it has to enact any measures where the treaties require a change in domestic law. Given that the treaties normally do require a change in UK law, Parliament is thus in a position to refuse to make such changes. It has never done so, but the passage of the 1993 European Communities (Amendment) Act, giving effect to the provisions of the Maastricht Treaty, was politically fraught.

Ultimately, Parliament retains the power to repeal the 1972 European Communities Act, the effect of which would be to remove the UK from membership of the European Union. Were it to repeal the 1972 Act, the general view of constitutional experts is that the courts would enforce it under the doctrine of parliamentary sovereignty. The doctrine of parlia-mentary sovereignty is also retained in respect of devolution and the Human Rights Act. The doctrine finds explicit recognition in the devo-lution legislation. Though Parliament has devolved legislative and exec-utive powers, it has none the less retained the capacity, should it wish to exercise it, to enact legislation for Scotland. (It continues to enact leg-islation for Wales and, with the dissolution of the Northern Ireland Assembly, also does so currently for Northern Ireland.) Again, it retains the capacity to repeal the legislation creating the devolved bodies: what Parliament creates by statute it can also destroy by statute. The doctrine also led to the provisions of the Human Rights Act stipulating only that the courts can issue declarations of incompatibility. They cannot directly strike down legislation as being incompatible with the European Convention.

In reality, however, the chances of Parliament exercising its coercive capacity are very limited. The fact that it exists is important, but the political reality is that it is not going to be exercised other than in the most exceptional circumstances. What is important, therefore, is how Parliament has developed a persuasive capacity. As we have seen, it has done so principally through the creation of committees that exist to scrutinize EU documents and to scrutinize bills for their human rights implications. EU committees seek to exert influence prior to proposals being discussed in the Council of Ministers. The Joint Committee on Human Rights checks that a bill is compatible with the ECHR as soon as it is introduced into Parliament; there is therefore time for the government to propose changes.

The committees are limited by the extent to which they operate independently of the chamber. As we have seen, few EU documents are debated in the Commons. Furthermore, the committees have a persuasive capacity only. Unlike three other Parliaments of member states of the EU (Denmark, Finland and Austria), there is no capacity to mandate a minister in the Council of Ministers; that is, to stipulate what the minister may or may not agree to. However, as persuasive bodies, they are arguably as effective as they can be within the context of executive–legislative relations in the UK – that is, if a government does not wish to be persuaded, there is little a committee can do. However, in the context of the EU, the work of the European committees at least serves to focus the minds of ministers and officials; and it can at times influence the nature of the debate within the EU. The work of the European Union Committee in the Lords is seen as being particularly good at contributing to debate, both within government and in the institutions of the EU. Its examination in 2003 of proposals emanating from the Convention on the Future of Europe was possibly the most authoritative commentary on the work of the Convention.

There are also proposals to give national parliaments a greater role in the European law-making process (see, for example, Cygan, 2003). They have no formal role in determining the outcome of legislation, but successive treaties have recognized that they should be kept informed of proposals and play a part in influencing national governments. Indeed, one of the changes was influenced by recognition of the work of the Committee in the Lords. In 1991, it encouraged the government to obtain from heads of government at the Maastricht summit a declaration encouraging 'greater involvement of national Parliaments in the activities of the European Union' and calling for contacts between national Parliaments and the European Parliament to be stepped up. The draft treaty on a European Constitution in 2003 also proposed an enhanced role, incorporating what was termed the 'yellow card' procedure. Under this procedure, if national Parliaments make representations to the EU that a proposal breaches the principles of subsidiarity and proportionality, and the national Parliaments represent a third of all the votes allocated to national Parliaments, 'the Commission shall review the proposal'. (The proportion is a quarter for proposals regarding freedom, security and justice.) The Commission, after reviewing the proposal, may amend, withdraw or maintain the proposal; in other words, it is free to continue with the proposal. A 'red card' procedure, under which a proposal would have to be withdrawn, was not accepted for inclusion in the draft treaty. Hence the proposal is for national Parliaments to have a persuasive capacity only, but one that extends beyond the persuasive capacity exercised at present by national Parliaments in relation to their own governments; it helps to raise Parliaments collectively beyond the national level.

Given the constraints within which Parliament operates, it could be argued that it has adapted as well as it can in relation to both EU membership and the Human Rights Act. In relation to the EU, Parliament has a number of advantages that are not enjoyed by all other Parliaments of the member states. These include the scrutiny reserve and the explanatory memoranda that accompany European documents. The way in which the two Houses complement one another in exercising systematic scrutiny – the House of Commons, as we have mentioned, going for breadth, and the House of Lords for depth – is also a remarkable feature of the UK Parliament.

The persuasive capacity of Parliament is not, however, easily demonstrated in observable outcomes, as there are few changed decisions that can be attributed to the work of the scrutiny committees. However, the work of the committees is seen in a somewhat different light when viewed from the other perspectives of power. In terms of agenda-setting, or non-decision-making, then the deterrent effect becomes important. Ministers and officials know that EU documents will be considered. They know that all their bills will be checked for compatibility with the ECHR. Though ministers are required to certify that a bill is compatible with the ECHR, Parliament does not take that certificate to be conclusive, and the Joint Committee may take a different view. The result has been expressed well by the founder Chairman of the

Committee. We have already quoted (see Chapter 6) her evidence to the Constitution Committee in the Lords in 2004, when she identified 'the *threat* of parliamentary scrutiny' and an adverse opinion from the Joint Committee as the key to influencing ministers and officials. As she said:

> the growing awareness that within government departments that each and every bill will be examined by us means, I believe, that the human rights implications of proposed legislation are subject to specially anxious scrutiny by departmental lawyers and draftsmen, and where there are problems, it is more likely that they will be drawn to the attention of Ministers before bills are published. (Corston, 2004, p. 165)

This is a view reinforced by the legal adviser to the Joint Committee from 2001 to 2004, Professor David Feldman, who concluded that fewer government bills in the 2002–3 session gave rise to serious rights concerns than had been the case in the two preceding sessions: 'Fewer provisions are drafted in ways that leave rights subject, in my view, to inadequate safeguards' (quoted in Hazell, 2004, p. 498).

Viewed from the institutional perspective, we can see what has happened in two different lights. New institutional structures, or processes, have been created within and beyond the UK, and they have acquired legitimacy through an Act of Parliament. They exist independently of Parliament. On the other hand, Parliament has created its own institutional arrangements and the committee process in respect of EU documents and measures affecting human rights is well established and accepted by government. Hence, as we have seen, all EU documents are deposited with Parliament and it is up to the scrutiny committees, advised by legal experts, as to what action to recommend. The explanatory memoranda, as we have noted, help to focus the minds of ministers and civil servants. The scrutiny reserve serves as something of a constraint on government. It is a means of forcing a minister to think more deeply about a proposal and to justify it or the government's stance on it. The committees recognize that the scrutiny reserve should not be utilized unreasonably and so, in effect, a balance exists; the government complies with the scrutiny reserve knowing it is not being overly used.

The committees are not in a position to say no to government, but government accepts the institutional process: all documents flow through the European committees; all bills are considered by the Joint Committee on Human Rights. The *process* is important and limiting, especially in a deterrent sense. It may limit the flow of bills – government may decide not to bring a bill forward because of its implications for human rights. It may so decide (consciously or subconsciously) because it anticipates the reaction of the Joint Committee on Human Rights or, for that matter, the courts (or both). Government prefers to avoid a negative response from either.

Conclusion

Parliament has had to adapt to a changing constitutional landscape. The changes have seen it transfer some of its law-effecting powers elsewhere. However, given the dominance of the executive in its relationship to Parliament, the coercive capacity of Parliament is arguably not as great as, on the surface, it appears to be. Rather, Parliament has sought to adapt to the changed conditions by creating new mechanisms to scrutinize and influence government. The formality of coercion has, in effect, been replaced by a more politically realistic capacity to persuade. That capacity is arguably not as well developed as it might be – there is a problem in developing a relationship with devolved bodies in the UK and is constrained, as in other areas, by the executive dominance of the House of Commons. There are dangers in scrutiny being hived off to committees if those committees do not enjoy a clear link with the chamber – a particular problem in the Commons with EU documents. There is also the problem that the effectiveness of the procedures depends on members being willing to make them work. As we have seen, attendance at European Standing Committees in the Commons is problematic. The involvement of the Lords, characterized by a greater commitment by members, has offset this to some extent, but it remains a problem. The challenge for Parliament is trying to cope with the growing demands made of it.

Part II
Parliament and Citizen

8

Representing the People

The history of Parliament, as we suggested in Chapter 7, has largely been shaped by its relationship to the executive. Yet there is another relationship that is important, that of Parliament to the people. Each relationship has had an impact on the other, though the distinction between the two is especially important in the context of Parliament's longevity. Parliament is the national representative assembly. However, the nature of its relationship to the people, like its relationship to the executive, has changed substantially over time.

Fundamental to understanding Parliament is the concept of representation. The term itself post-dates the development of Parliament and has been accorded several meanings. The word itself has come into the English language through French derivatives of the Latin *repraesentare* (meaning 'to make present or manifest or to present again') and did not assume a political meaning until the sixteenth century (Beard and Lewis, 1959, pp. 22–3; Pitkin, 1967, pp. 241–52). The term has come to be used in different ways. It is possible to identify four separate usages (see Pitkin, 1967):

(i)   acting on behalf of some individual or group (that is, defending or promoting the interests of the person or body 'represented');
(ii) being freely elected;
(iii) replicating the typical characteristics of a group or class (as in socioeconomic background or, as in a survey, a sample group); and
(iv) acting as a symbol ('standing for' something: for example, a monarch or flag 'representing' the unity of the nation).

All four usages are relevant for analysing Parliament. However, because of Parliament's longevity, pre-dating the emergence of a mass electorate in the nineteenth century, none is problem free.

159

Acting on behalf of some individual or group

The use of the term as denoting acting on behalf of some individual or group has been common in Britain from at least the beginning of the seventeenth century (Beard and Lewis, 1959, p. 23) and is the key to understanding Parliament's contemporary role and its popular legitimacy. However, the way in which it has served as a representative body has changed fundamentally over time.

Parliament existed initially to fulfil a form of functional representation. Those summoned to give assent to the monarch's demand for more money attended in order to give assent on behalf of the clergy, barons and different communities (counties and boroughs). As we have seen (Chapter 2), what emerged over time were two Houses, with the Lords comprising the Lords spiritual (the senior clergy) and the Lords temporal (the senior barons). The Commons has its origins in the summoning of knights, and then burgesses, to the king's court. They were summoned from particular *communes,* or organized communities, hence the emergence of the name Commons.

There has thus been a long-standing link between particular communities and members of Parliament. The perception that MPs are 'representatives' of local communities, or constituencies, is well entrenched. However, what has changed over time has been the nature of that link. For most of Parliament's history, the nature of representation by MPs has been what Edmund Burke termed 'virtual representation' (Pitkin, 1967, ch. 8). By that, he meant that MPs could speak on behalf of particular interests (such as agriculture and trade), and that what was best for those interests could be discerned without the members necessarily being chosen by popular election. As long as there was at least one constituency defined by a particular interest (say, agriculture) returning an MP, then that member was able to represent the interest as a whole. Indeed, by not being dependent on a popular vote, it was possible to argue that MPs could act in their better interests rather than in response to their immediate opinions. The representative owed the people 'devotion to their interest' rather than 'submission to their will' (quoted in Pitkin, p. 176).

This interpretation thus justified a detachment of Members of Parliament from the people. MPs represented the interests of the people but they were neither elected by the people nor subservient to their views. There was a highly restricted franchise, dictated by custom and statute. From the fifteenth century to the seventeenth, the standard qualification to be an elector in a county seat was ownership of a freehold valued at 40 shillings a year. In the boroughs, the franchise was remarkably varied. The electorate comprised a small body of electors, normally amenable to patronage or bribery. Many seats were, in effect, owned by local landowners, often members of the House of Lords. Politics were largely conducted 'within parliamentary circles and the drawing rooms connected with them' (Ostrogorski, 1902, p. 15). There was a link between MPs and the shires and boroughs, but it was arguably no stronger than that of the landowning aristocrats who had a territorial base.

This Burkean view of representation gave way eventually to a liberal conception. Under this conception, which already held sway in the USA, representation was generally seen in terms of individuals rather than of interests or classes (Pitkin, 1967, pp. 190–1). With the country being too large to sustain a system of direct representation (citizens meeting to make decisions) then representatives have to be chosen to act on behalf of citizens. However, the general acceptance of a liberal view of representation did not equate initially to all the people having the vote. There were concerns that not everyone had the capacity to exercise an informed choice and act for the public good rather than for personal benefit. Hence, rather than extending the vote to all – seen in preceding centuries as a dangerously radical view (Birch, 1964, ch. 3) – a property franchise was employed, property owners being thought to be better able to exercise a sound judgement than those without property.

The move towards a view of representation encompassing all the adult population was a gradual one. The nineteenth century, as we have seen, was the crucial transitional period. Burkean and liberal views clashed over parliamentary reform. During debate on the 1832 Reform Bill, Sir Robert Peel stuck to the concept of virtual representation, arguing that 'we are here to consult the interests, not to obey the will of the people, if we honestly believe that will conflicts with those interests' (Birch, 1964, p. 49). However, the liberal view came to dominate (Birch, 1964, ch. 4), supported by the growing clamour for political reform.

The emergence of a mass, though not universal, franchise had major constitutional consequences. At the beginning of the nineteenth century, the government was chosen by the monarch, who was often able to use patronage and position to ensure a favourable House of Commons, but by the end of that century, the government was chosen by most of the adult male population. As we have seen (in Chapter 2), the 1832 and 1867 Reform Acts enlarged the electorate, and other measures ensured greater equity in constituency boundaries. By 1884, a majority of adult males, albeit a bare majority, had the vote (Butler, 2004, p. 737). Other

Acts, not least the Ballot Act of 1872, helped largely to eliminate corrupt practices.

The transformation was reflected not only in the transfer of the capacity to choose the government, but also in the relationship between the two Houses. The Commons could then claim to be the chamber elected by the people. We have already quoted the observation of Lord Shaftesbury on the effect of the change (see Chapter 2). It is worth recording his opening comments:

> So long as the other House of Parliament was elected upon a restricted principle, I can understand that it would submit to a check from a House such as this. But in the presence of this great democratic power and the advance of this great democratic wave ... it passes my comprehension to understand how a hereditary House like this can hold its own. (Quoted in Norton, 1981, p. 21)

As we have seen, it was not able to hold its own, and the country witnessed a shift from a form of co-equal bicameralism to one of asymmetrical bicameralism, a position confirmed in statute by the Parliament Act of 1911. The Commons thus came to be the dominant chamber by virtue of its claim to be the representative chamber, elected to act on behalf of the people.

The House of Commons has thus established its claim to be the representative chamber of the nation. It is popularly elected – a point to which we shall return – to defend and act on behalf of the people of the United Kingdom. However, a number of problems arise from the nature of Parliament's adjustment to the changing conceptions of representation. It is in this context that Parliament's longevity is crucial. Parliament existed long before the liberal view of representation took hold. Though Parliament has adapted to the political pressures resulting in a mass franchise, it has not necessarily discarded the views that predated the emergence and acceptance of this franchise. The liberal view has dominated but has not displaced other views of representation. As a result, we can identify certain tensions within the political system.

The first is between the role of government and the electorate. Anthony Birch has identified Tory and Whig attitudes to representation (Birch, 1964, ch. 2) which clashed in the seventeenth and eighteenth centuries. The former emphasized the need for government by the monarch; the latter saw the need for Parliament to have a greater role, limiting royal power. However, both saw government as an essentially elite activity. The Whig view embraced some concept of representation but it was essentially Burkean: that of virtual representation and with the Members of Parliament exercising their own judgement. These views gave way in the nineteenth century to the liberal view, but this view essentially married acceptance of popular election with existing views of the role of Parliament. Parliament had asserted its dominance over the monarch in the Glorious Revolution of 1688. The Glorious Revolution served to confirm the doctrine of parliamentary supremacy. The doctrine had been asserted before but not necessarily accepted by leading lawyers. Now that the monarch was subject to the will of Parliament, then so too were the monarch's courts; they were thus bound to accept the outputs of Parliament and could not set them aside as being contrary to some superior body of law. The doctrine of parliamentary supremacy thus pre-dated the emergence of popular election. However, the effect of popular election was not to displace but rather to sustain the doctrine. The House of Commons was now elected by the people. The leading nineteenth century law professor, A. V. Dicey, argued that the legal sovereignty of Parliament was underpinned by the political supremacy of the electorate (Dicey, 1959).

As Birch has noted, Dicey was expressing an idealized view: 'It assumed that the political power flowed exclusively in one direction, from the electors to Parliament and from Parliament to the government, and never in the opposite way' (Birch, 1964, p. 74). As Birch noted, the view did not take into account party management and the political reality that the cabinet could control Parliament. The view may have been idealized, but it is a view that has held sway and dictated the constitutional framework within which government operates. Parliamentary sovereignty may be a political fiction, but it continues to dictate the formal structures of the British constitution. Recent decades, as already discussed (see Chapter 7), have seen major constitutional changes. Yet, as David Judge (2004, p. 696) has noted: 'Each constitutional reform ... has been accompanied by a ritual reaffirmation of the continuing centrality of parliamentary sovereignty to the legitimation of the state and government.' The doctrine of parliamentary sovereignty has been written into the devolution legislation and the Human Rights Act. The outputs of Parliament remain supreme; Parliament can override the devolved bodies and is not bound by declarations of incompatibility made by the courts; it could repeal the 1972 European Communities Act. The result, paradoxically, as Judge (2004, pp. 696–7) observes, is that representative government in the UK continues to be conceived as a means of legitimating executive power. Through popular election, the people are, in effect, sustaining executive dominance.

A second tension is between party and constituency. One can identify two types of parliamentary representation: the general and the specific (Norton, 1981, pp. 56–62). The former, representing broad interests within the population, is fulfilled through the medium of political parties. Parties serve to aggregate opinions, to express them and seek to give effect to them in public policy. Party government is sustained by the doctrine of the mandate. This developed in the nineteenth century and has underpinned the political process since then. One can distinguish mandates as being permissive or prescriptive. A permissive mandate is one in which a party, by virtue of enjoying a majority of seats in the House of Commons, is deemed to have legitimacy to govern: 'we have the people's mandate'. The prescriptive mandate is one in which a party is elected to fulfil particular promises laid before the electorate in a general election. These promises are embodied in a party manifesto. A government can thus claim that in carrying out its manifesto promises it is carrying out its electoral mandate. Both forms of the mandate have currency, usually employed by the governing party as appropriate to justify its actions. The party in government can, and does, utilize the claim to have a mandate as the basis for requiring the loyal support of its MPs. The MPs were elected because of the party label and as such are expected to support the manifesto on which the party stood for election.

The other form, specific representation, constitutes acting on behalf of individuals or particular groups. It is fulfilled principally, though not exclusively, through MPs acting as constituency members. There is substantial empirical evidence for the claim that MPs are elected on the basis of the party label. There is some evidence of a personal vote (Norton and Wood, 1993) but it is not usually sufficient to affect the electoral outcome in a constituency. However, the long-standing link between an MP and a particular geographic constituency remains important. That link pre-dates the emergence of popular election and the mandate. The MP is elected as the member a particular constituency. In the Commons, MPs address one another not by name but by constituency (the Honourable Member for such-and-such a constituency). There are survey data to show that constituents expect the Member to accord priority to speaking and acting on behalf of the constituency over that of the collective function of calling government to account. Equally, MPs themselves accord priority to their constituency role (Norton, 2002a, pp. 29–34).

Normally, MPs perceive party policy as being congruent with the interests of their constituencies and vote accordingly. On occasion, however, a perceived constituency interest clashes with government policy. The government may decide that there is a need for cuts in the defence budget and – to take actual examples – earmark some dockyards for closure or merge army regiments based in constituencies represented by some of its MPs. Those MPs then have to resolve an apparent conflict between loyalty to party and standing up for the interests of constituents. Such occasions are infrequent but notable for the intensity of the tensions experienced by MPs. Bodies lobbying for a change in public policy sometimes encourage supporters to put pressure on MPs at the constituency level. The defeat of the Shops Bill in 1986 (see Chapter 2) is attributable in part to effective constituency lobbying. That was an exceptional event, but illustrates the clash that MPs sometimes face between party and constituency.

A third tension is between constituency (or party) and conscience. An MP, as we have just seen, represents both constituency *and* party. On some issues, though, the MP may be influenced by a personal philosophy or religious beliefs that clash with the preference of the party *or* of constituents. On occasion, a party may recognize that it is split on an issue and allow MPs a free vote, though justifying it on the moral high ground that it is an 'issue of conscience' (see Cowley, 1998a). However, if the party stands aside from an issue, constituents do not necessarily do so. An MP may decide to follow what is perceived as a constituency view – there is rarely any systematic polling of constituents in a specific seat to determine what in fact constituents *do* think – or decide to follow their own view. When they take their own line, this is usually justified in Burkean terms: that is, that they are trustees rather than delegates, offering constituents their judgement rather than a slavish capacity to follow whatever it is that constituents or the local party want. There are various instances of this in recent years, not least on the issue of capital punishment and European integration. Judge (1999b, p. 22) quotes Tony Blair arguing in 1994 against the restoration of the death penalty. He said he understood why a majority of his constituents favoured a return of the death penalty, but Parliament had at various times voted against it:

> Such a large majority of Members did not vote against the restoration of the death penalty on each occasion because they were unaware of their constituents' views but because, on reflection and after considered debate, they could not support those views ... I certainly do not believe that my understanding is superior to that of my constituents, but ... we are representatives, not delegates, and we must act according to our conscience.

In practice, MPs generally adhere to the party line, or vote along party lines even where there is a free vote (Cowley and Stuart, 1997; Cowley, 1998a). They none the less like to reserve to themselves the discretion to follow their consciences should a conflict occur, an approach that appears to have a wider resonance. Judge (1999b, pp. 31–2) quotes one observer as writing: 'We expect them [MPs] to exercise their own judgement, not simply to reflect ours'. As Judge notes, what is noteworthy about the statement is that it was made at the end of the twentieth century, not the end of the eighteenth: 'The ghost of Burke continues to haunt British parliamentary politics!' (Judge, 1999b, p. 32).

Freely elected

We have already seen how the House of Commons has moved from being elected by a narrow band of electors to being elected by the adult population. The nineteenth century saw the widening of the franchise and the introduction of the secret ballot. (Before 1872, an open ballot was employed: the list of how electors had voted was published.) The 1880s also saw single-member constituencies, and the first-past-the-post method of election (the candidate with a plurality of votes being declared elected), become the norm. Neither, however, became universal: some two-member constituencies survived, as did a system of proportional representation in university seats (seats where the constituencies were not geographic but functional: the electors were graduates). The 1918 Representation of the People Act provided for universal suffrage for men based on residence rather than rates, though a 'business vote' survived based on occupancy of business premises worth £10 a year. (Defence of the business vote reflected a residual attachment to the concept of functional representation.) The 1948 Representation of the People Act abolished two-member constituencies as well as university seats (and hence the only surviving use of a system of proportional representation) and the business vote (see Butler, 1963, pt II). The effects of the Act were seen for the first time in the general election of 1950.

The 1950 election thus saw the realization in large measure of the principle of 'one man, one vote', to which Jeremy Bentham had added 'one value' (Norton, 1981, p. 53). MPs were elected in single-member constituencies in which every adult (with very few exceptions, such as convicted criminals) had one vote and one vote only. They were able to cast their votes in general elections that were regulated by statute in order to ensure fairness and secrecy. Electors cast their ballots in the privacy of the polling booths. Only electoral officials were permitted in the room where voting took place. Accusations of fraud by individual electors or by party officials were rare.

Boundary Commissions had been established in 1944 to review regularly constituency boundaries in order to try to ensure equity. As a result of demographic changes, the size of constituencies varied substantially – there was no boundary review between 1918 and 1944 – and the Commissions (one for each part of the United Kingdom) were designed to make sure that the electoral quota (the average size of the electorate per constituency) did not deviate too dramatically. The greater the equity in the size of constituency electorates, the closer it was possible to achieve what Bentham meant by 'one value', since a vote cast in one constituency would carry the same weight, proportionately, as one cast in another.

The achievement of one person, one vote served to underpin the popular legitimacy of the political system. As Birch (1964, p. 65) observed, the liberal view of the constitution 'amounted to a theory of legitimate power'. It did not derive from some mythical social contract, as advocated by John Locke and Jean-Jacques Rousseau, and had the advantage that it was tied to existing institutions: 'Partly because it was a local rather than a universal theory, it could readily be accepted by the man-in-the-street' (Birch, 1964, p. 66). There was a willingness to accept the outputs of a Parliament freely elected by the people. Electors demonstrated a willingness to exercise the vote. In the 1950 election, 84 per cent of electors turned out to cast a ballot.

However, various criticisms have been levelled at the means by which MPs are elected. Three principal criticisms can be identified. The liberal view of the constitution has been challenged as being incomplete. The electoral system is undermined by the fact that 'one person, one vote' is not the same as saying that each vote is equal. The first-past-the-post system, it is pointed out, can produce 'wasted' votes (votes cast for losing candidates have no effect) and, given that it is difficult to ensure constituency electorates of precisely equal size, a vote in a constituency with a small electorate will count for more than one cast in a large constituency. Population movement (as well as tactical voting and differential turnout) can have a distorting effect. Since 1987, when there was a level playing field, '[T]he electoral system appears to have developed a spectacular bias in favour of Labour' (Butler and Butt, 2004, p. 169). In 2001, the Conservatives would have needed 42.7 per cent of the national vote to secure a parliamentary majority, whereas Labour only needed 35.6 per cent of the vote to achieve victory. Furthermore, the system is non-proportional, in that it can – and usually does – result in a party winning an absolute majority of seats on the basis of less than 50 per cent of the votes cast. In the 2005 general election, for example, the Labour government was returned to office with 356 seats – 56 per cent of the total – with just over 35 per cent of the votes cast nationally.

Critics of this situation argue the case for a new electoral system, claiming that a system of proportional representation (PR) – the percentage of seats equalling the percentage of votes cast – would be a fairer system and hence more legitimate, serving to bolster support for the political system (Norton, 1982a, pp. 231–2). They also claim that a consequence would be greater continuity in public policy, since a stable coalition government is likely to achieve enduring support and thus be able to engage in long-term planning, hence resulting in a more stable system.

Supporters of the existing arrangements counter that a system of proportional representation would be likely to break the link between MP and constituency (depending on the type of PR system chosen) as well as result in no overall majority for any one party, necessitating either coalition or minority government and thus jeopardizing the coherence of the existing system. There is also an allied argument based on the 'one value' argument, namely that 10 per cent of votes equalling 10 per cent of the seats will not then equal 10 per cent of the negotiating power in the House of Commons. Instead, a minority party or parties holding the balance of power will exercise disproportionate negotiating power (Norton, 1998b). There is also a likelihood that governments will be the product of post-election bargaining. That, it is argued, would constitute a greater threat to the legitimacy of the political system than any flaws in the existing arrangements.

The contending views reflect different perspectives of what elections are for. Supporters of PR tend to argue the case on grounds of equity, or fairness, while opponents tend to embrace the older view of elections as confirming a government in office in order to ensure that government is carried on. The conflict means that the legitimacy of the existing system is thus contested. In this, there is nothing particularly startling. The electoral system has frequently been the subject of political dispute (Norton, 1982a, p. 227). Nor is the United Kingdom exceptional in this regard. When a political system is under pressure, there are often demands for a change in the electoral system. The essential point, though, for our purposes is that the legitimacy of the existing system in the United Kingdom does not go unchallenged and the critical voices are much louder now than in post-war decades. The issue came on to the political agenda in 1997: the Labour party's election manifesto promised a review of the electoral system and a referendum on an alternative to the existing system. In the event, there was a review (chaired by Liberal Democrat peer, Lord Jenkins of Hillhead), published in 1998 and advocating the use of Alternative Vote with a variant of the additional member system (Independent Commission on the Voting System, 1998), but there was no referendum. However, the electoral system remains a subject of political dispute.

A second criticism of the electoral system is not only the disparity between constituency sizes but also the disproportionate distribution between the different parts of the United Kingdom. Both Scotland and Wales have had a larger number of seats than their population justifies. The electoral quota in both has been significantly lower than that for England. For the fifty years (1922–72) that Northern Ireland had its own Parliament at Stormont (on the outskirts of Belfast), the number of seats was lower than its population justified. After the Stormont Parliament was abolished, the number of Westminster seats was increased (in 1978) from twelve to seventeen. With devolution, it was argued that the smaller electoral quota in Scotland and Wales, relative to England, could not be justified (in so far as it ever was justified). The point was conceded by government in respect of Scotland. At the 2005 election the number of seats was reduced from 72 to 59 to bring the electoral quota into line with England. However, there are no proposals to reduce the number of seats in Wales. The issue is not as politically divisive as that of proportional representation but remains a contested one, especially given that one party (Labour) has benefited substantially from the over-representation of Scotland and Wales. Even with the number of seats in Scotland reduced, the electoral quota in Scotland is the same as that in England, even though Scotland has its own Parliament and England does not; hence there is the argument that the precedent of Northern Ireland should be followed, with the number of constituencies in Scotland being reduced even further to compensate for the existence of its own legislature.

A third criticism that has arisen is more recent. In the twenty-first century, there have been various experiments with all-postal voting in elections. Initially, these were confined to local elections, but in 2004 it was extended to four of the ten regional constituencies for elections to the European Parliament. The justification for all-postal voting was principally because of its potential to increase voter turnout: it was more convenient for electors to vote by post than to go to a polling booth on a specified day. There was an increase in voter turnout, by 5 per cent on average, but the elections were marred by some allegations of fraud. More pervasively, one of the criticisms was that the effect of all-postal voting undermined the Ballot Act of 1872. The Act introduced the secret ballot and helped to reduce the potential for fraud and undue influence. This was overturned by all-postal voting. Whereas the polling booth guarantees secrecy, the private home does not. The Electoral Commission, the official independent body created to advise on electoral matters, urged a change in the law to deal with issues of secrecy and undue influence (Electoral Commission, 2004, pp. 75–80). Criticism of all-postal voting led to plans for its wider use to be scaled back, though not abandoned completely. Instead of achieving a universal welcome, as expected, the practice proved to be contested.

The popular legitimacy of the electoral process thus underpins the acceptance of the political system and the outputs of Parliament. If the electoral process is contested, then it undermines the legitimacy of the parliamentary process. The most contested element is the first-past-the-post method of election.

Socially typical

Seen in terms of representation denoting a body that is socially typical, Parliament is not a representative body. Members of both Houses of Parliament are predominantly white, male and middle-class. There is no formal requirement that the membership of either House should be socially typical, and it would be almost impossible to achieve a precise cross section of the population. This is partly because of constraints on who can sit in Parliament (only those aged 21 and over) and the nature of the job.

Being an MP is essentially a middle-class job and its time demands mean that most do not wish to sit for too long beyond retirement age. Indeed, the introduction of a pension has ensured that MPs are more likely now to choose to retire in their sixties, resulting in a more middle-aged House. There are – by virtue of appointment for life – more elderly members in the Lords than in the Commons. Also, as people tend to be elevated to the peerage in middle age, after achieving prominent positions, there are few peers under the age of 40. The removal of most hereditary peers in 1999 took away one mechanism for bringing in young members, since some peers succeeded to their titles while in their twenties and thirties. Lord Freyberg (b. 1970), for example (who remains in the Lords as one of the ninety-two hereditary peers chosen to stay on), entered the House at the age of 23. In 2004, the median age of MPs was just under 50, and the average age of members of the Lords was 67.

The House of Lords is predominantly middle- and upper-class in economic terms. In terms of occupational background, it is notably professional, with a preponderance of lawyers, former civil servants, and teachers of one form or another (Baldwin, 1985, p. 105). As we have seen (in Chapter 2), the House of Commons is now a notably middle-class body. However, the biggest disparity, relative to the population as a whole, is in terms of ethnicity and gender.

In the 1970s and 1980s, it was the unelected House that provided a platform for members drawn from non-white backgrounds. In 1975, Dr David Pitt, a West Indian, was elevated to the peerage. Two years later he was joined by Pratap Chitnis, an Indian, and they have since been joined by other non-white members. The House also boasted more female members – both in absolute terms and expressed as a proportion of the membership – than the Commons. In 1970, there were forty-two women in the Lords. Twenty years later, there were eighty, constituting just under 7 per cent of the membership. Only in 1992 did the elected House pass the unelected House in the proportion of its none-white and female membership. In the general election of 2005, the number of women MPs – and those drawn from ethic backgrounds – reached an all-time high.

The first woman elected to the House of Commons was Countess Markiewicz in 1918. However, she was a Sinn Fein candidate and refused to take her seat. Nancy (Lady) Astor became the first woman to sit in the House after she was elected as Conservative MP for Plymouth in 1919 (in succession to her husband, who had been raised to the peerage); she sat until 1945. The number of women MPs increased only gradually. In the 1983 general election, only twenty-three were elected, by 1987 the number had increased to forty-one – just over 6 per cent of the total – and in 1997 it had reached 120, still less than 20 per cent of the membership, even though women comprise just over half of the population. The number fell to 118 in 2001 but reached 127 in 2005.

Gradually, women have come to occupy leadership positions. Margaret Thatcher was the first female prime minister (1979–90) and Betty Boothroyd the first woman Speaker of the House of Commons (1992–2000). In September 2004, there were five women in the cabinet. Eight of the twenty-one government ministers in the House of Lords were female, including the Leader of the House, Baroness Amos, the third woman to occupy the post.

The first non-white MP was elected in 1892: Dadabhai Naoroji, an Indian, was returned as Liberal member for Finsbury Central with a majority of five. (As some electors found it difficult to pronounce his name, he was dubbed 'Mr Narrow Majority'; Gifford, 1992, p. 33.) Mancherjee Bhownagree became the second Indian to sit in Parliament when he was elected as Conservative MP for Bethnal Green in 1895; he was knighted two years later. A third – Shapurji Saklatvala – was elected as member for Battersea North in 1922, sitting initially as a Labour member; after the 1924 election, he sat as a Communist (Gifford, 1992, p. 40). He lost his seat in 1929.

There was then a gap of fifty-eight years before the return of another non-white member. In 1987, four MPs were elected (Diane Abbott, Paul Boateng, Bernie Grant, and Keith Vaz), all representing Labour. Though the number was small – less than 1 per cent of the House – it constituted the largest number of non-white MPs ever to sit in the House of Commons. The number increased in later elections (including in two by-elections in 2000), and in the general election of 2001, twelve MPs from ethnic backgrounds were elected (Criddle, 2002, p. 197), two of whom were Muslims. The 2005 election saw a further increase, with fifteen MPs elected from ethic backgrounds. Of these, thirteen were Labour (for of them Muslims) and two Conservative. Again, the figure is small, but a historical high. Proportionately, it constitutes 2.3 per cent of MPs, compared with a general population that has well over 5 per cent drawn from ethnic minorities. Paul Boateng became the first black MP to enter the cabinet, in 2002 as chief secretary to the Treasury. Two others, Keith Vaz and David Lammy, have held ministerial office. Two peers from ethnic backgrounds, both women, serve as ministers in the House of Lords.

Other members from different groups have also been returned. The House has had MPs with various disabilities. Of current MPs, one is wheelchair-bound (the Lords has several such members) and another, cabinet minister David Blunkett, is blind. Both Houses have members drawn from a variety of religions. More than twenty MPs are Jewish, including Conservative Party leader, Michael Howard, the first practising Jew to be elected party leader. (Nineteenth-century leader Benjamin Disraeli was of Jewish descent but converted to the Anglican faith.) Chris Smith, the Labour MP for Islington South and Finsbury, was the first MP to declare publicly in the 1980s that he was gay. By the end of 2004, there were eleven openly gay MPs, mainly on the Labour benches but including one Conservative (Alan Duncan) and one Plaid Cymru MP (Adam Price). At one point in the 1997–2001 Parliament, there were three gay members serving in cabinet. In 2005, it was reported that Alan Duncun was interested in running for the leadership of the Conservative Party.

The calls for MPs to be socially typical reflect a particular, but not an uncontested, view of representation. In many respects, it can be seen to hark back to the early view of MPs as representing particular interests. By being drawn from a certain section of society, an MP can speak for that section. S/he, it is argued, will have an understanding of the needs and expectations of that section in a way that someone who is outside it cannot have. Such representation, it is argued, is also important for maintaining the legitimacy of the institution. If particular sections of society do not see some of their own number in Parliament, they feel that their interests are not represented. It was a view with which Burke would have had some sympathy. He argued the case for some sections of society (such as Irish Catholics) that had no MPs to express their interests, to at least have the franchise extended to some of their number (Pitkin, 1967, pp. 177–80). However, as we have seen, he did not see the need for popular election in order to achieve such representation.

This somewhat functional view is in conflict with the liberal view. An MP is elected to represent the individuals who reside in the constituency. An MP does not necessarily have to be drawn from a particular background in order to grasp the needs and interests of constituents. An MP does not have to be tied to particular interests any more than s/he should be a delegate rather than a trustee, and is freely elected. Electors have freedom of choice in voting for whichever candidate they wish: however desirable it may be for MPs to be drawn from particular backgrounds, electors cannot necessarily be relied upon to elect candidates from those backgrounds to Parliament. In some seats, the main party candidates have been women, and in some they have been drawn from ethnic backgrounds, but such cases are in the minority. The maintenance of single-member constituencies, with some degree of local autonomy in candidate selection, makes it difficult to ensure that MPs are socially typical. In the 1990s, the Labour Party introduced provision for all-women short lists in certain constituencies; the result was the increase in the number of female Labour MPs in 1997. The use of such short lists fell foul of sex discrimination legislation in an employment tribunal, and an Act of Parliament had to be passed to enable parties that wished to utilize such short lists to be able to do so. During passage of the bill in the Lords, the House debated the issue of the freedom of choice of the electors as against that of parties to limit local choice in the selection of candidates.

The conflict between the liberal view of representation and that favouring a socially typical House can be argued to be a false dichotomy. If the typically white, male, middle-class MP can act on behalf of all the diverse 70,000 constituents in the constituency, then so can MPs drawn from other backgrounds. As one leading female MP argued, it is a myth 'that women are in Parliament to represent women. Every MP is elected represent all of their constituents, male and female, young and old, and of all political affiliations' (May, 2004, p. 845). They may have a particular affinity with the concerns of a particular section of society, and on rare occasions that might cause the sort of conflict we have already identified between party and conscience, but it is going to be exceptional rather than the norm.

Though such members will normally seek to avoid being single-issue members – not confining themselves to women's issues, black issues and so on – their presence provides the basis for some resonance with members of society with similar characteristics. By being seen to be in Parliament, and in a position to serve some safety-valve function, they can work to enhance the legitimacy of Parliament among groups that otherwise may feel alienated from it.

Symbolic

Parliament fulfils a symbolic role. As with many other parliaments, it has a clear physical presence that is instantly recognizable, in the same way that the Capitol in Washington DC is also instantly recognizable. Some parliaments, such as the European Parliament (lacking a clear single site), have no such presence.

In this respect, the institution of Parliament is important in a physical sense. There is one part of the Palace of Westminster – Westminster Hall – that dates back several centuries, originating in the Norman period, though remodelled at various times since (Field, 2002). However, Westminster Hall aside, the Palace of Westminster is a relatively new building. The old Palace – something of a melange of buildings, set back a little from the Thames – was destroyed by fire in 1834. A grand, mock-Gothic building replaced it; the Lords occupied their new chamber in 1847 and the Commons in 1850. (The chamber of the House of Commons was destroyed by enemy bombing on 10 May 1941. It was rebuilt along the lines of the old chamber.) Despite the addition of various outlying buildings, such as Portcullis House (see Chapter 2), Parliament is still seen solely in terms of the Palace of Westminster, running alongside the Thames, with the Clock Tower (housing the Big Ben bell) at one end and Victoria Tower at the other. The building is iconic. It symbolizes the nation's law-effecting body and, with its mock-Gothic façade, is suggestive of Parliament's long history.

The interior echoes the grandeur of the exterior, with long corridors and high ceilings, and with rooms – particularly in the House of Lords – that are crammed with elaborate fittings and pictures. The chamber of the House of Commons is itself iconic, captured in numerous paintings and now accessible to the public through the medium of television. It has a claim to be the best known debating chamber in the world.

However, there is a potential tension between what it does and what it appears to be. The building exudes grandeur. It conveys a sense of the nation's history. This tends to be reinforced when people visit the Palace, especially on guided tours. Westminster Hall has a plaque to commemorate the fact that Charles I was tried there; other plaques commemorate other historical events. There is the danger of seeing the Palace principally in terms of its history rather than as a working institution, and there is a particular danger of people seeing an incongruence if they perceive a great building housing a politically insignificant Parliament. For Parliament, achieving a balance between the two – conveying that it is entrenched in the nation's history, yet remains relevant through fulfilling important representative functions – arguably constitutes the ideal state for maintaining popular legitimacy.

The challenge to legitimacy

Parliament has had to adapt to the changing political environment. Before the nineteenth century, Parliament's principal relationship was with the executive. There was little direct contact with the people. Since then, it has developed a direct relationship with the expanding electorate, and that relationship has affected, but has also had to accommodate, the pre-existing relationship with the executive. How well, then, has Parliament adapted?

From a pluralist perspective, the expansion of the franchise has weakened Parliament but made the people powerful. The growth of party has enabled the cabinet to dominate Parliament. The cabinet is powerful because it can claim an electoral mandate. The people now exercise a coercive capacity through parliamentary elections: they can decide who sits in the House of Commons and, through those elections, will normally determine which party forms the government. If they do not like the performance of a party in government, they can turn it out at the next election. Election day is, in the words of the late philosopher, Sir Karl Popper, 'judgement day'. The people also exercise a persuasive capacity, through making their views known, through contacting MPs, being polled in surveys, through mass lobbies and marches, by submitting petitions, and through the mass media. As we shall see, they are contacting MPs (and peers) on an ever-increasing and unprecedented scale. MPs – and the government – are driven by the need to be re-elected, and so are responsive to shifts in popular opinion.

However, the coercive power exercised by the people is essentially a blunt weapon. The electorate is not so much a positive driving force as an endorsing body. The electorate assents (or withholds it assent) to the party in government. The relationship between Parliament and government continues to be shaped by the constitutional norms that pre-dated the growth of the franchise. As we have seen, through popular election, the people are endorsing executive dominance and do so through Parliament.

The institutional perspective helps us to identify a problem of legitimacy. If the parliamentary process is to be accepted as legitimate, and the exclusive process for determining issues of public policy, then people have to accept that the House of Commons is a representative body. However, as we have seen, there are inherent tensions within the representative system.

On the one hand, by meeting regularly, by debating, by requiring ministers to justify their actions, by allowing members to express conflicting views, by allowing members to make representations to ministers on behalf of constituents and different groups in society, and by operating generally in a public session – observable by visitors and, now via television cameras – Parliament provides an outlet for tensions, grievances and demands that otherwise might find no outlet. By providing such an outlet – and by being seen to do so – Parliament enhances its own legitimacy in the eyes of the citizenry as well as the legitimacy of the body drawn from it: the government. By engaging in such activity, it is not making policy. It is, however, serving to bolster support for the political system of which it is a core institution. Arguably, it is more active as a representative body than ever before.

On the other hand, the tensions we have identified convey that Parliament's claims to be a representative body are contested. As we have seen, the pre-eminence of the House of Commons derives from the fact that it is the elected chamber. This underpins its legitimacy as the principal assent-giving body. However, perceptions of its legitimacy are affected by the *method* by which it is elected, *who* is elected, and *how* it behaves in defending and pursuing the interests of those who elected it. Since people cannot usually make their views known, regularly and in a structured manner, to government, they rely on Parliament, primarily the House of Commons, to do it for them. Parliament is thus fundamental to making the views of the people known to government. The method of election and who serves in Parliament can be seen to figure in producing a Parliament able to speak for the people. There are, as we have seen, perceived problems with respect to both. This limits the acceptance by some of Parliament as a representative body.

Can it, then, still fulfil a representative role in the first sense of the term? How well have the links between Parliament and people developed, facilitating the capacity of MPs to speak for the people? That is the question we explore in Chapter 9.

9

The Voice of the Constituents

Members of Parliament have a dual but not necessarily incompatible existence. They are in most cases elected under a party label. As we saw in Chapter 8, parties fulfil the role of general representation, aggregating the views of large sections of the population. As such, this form of representation transcends individual constituencies. MPs, as party members, are part of a body that links them with like-minded members, and they generally operate as a collective entity. However, each MP is also elected to represent a particular constituency. Members thus fulfil the role of specific representation, defending and pursuing the interests of individuals and groups within their constituencies. (They may, and do, promote the interests of groups unconnected with, or not confined to, their constituencies, and we shall address this in the next chapter.) Our concern in this chapter is the representation of constituents, which is generally an individual rather than a collective exercise, though MPs from constituencies with a shared interest may work together to defend and promote that interest. Over the years, demands made of members by constituents have changed in nature and increased in volume. Members have sought to meet those demands and have done so in various ways.

The changing nature of constituency demands

There is no formal or definitive job description for a Member of Parliament: it depends in large measure on what the MP makes of it, and it also depends to a large extent on what constituents expect of the MP. Constituents have generally called on 'their' MP to fulfil a range of tasks, or functions. It is possible to identify seven constituency roles fulfilled by MPs (Norton, 1994b, pp. 705–8):

(i)   *safety valve*, allowing constituents to express their views, usually through writing or sometimes having a meeting with the MP;

(ii) *information provider*, giving information, or advice, to those constituents who seek it;

(iii) *local dignitary*, being seen in the constituency and attending civic and other events;

(iv) *advocate*, giving support to a particular cause, either through lending the MP's name to the cause or being active in its support;

(v) *benefactor*, providing benefits to particular constituents who seek them, usually those who are needy or greedy;

(vi) *powerful friend*, intervening with government or other bodies to achieve a redress of grievance for a constituent or constituents; and

(vii) *promoter of constituency interests*, advancing the case for collective interests (such as employment) in the constituency.

The first three are primarily, though not exclusively, internal to the constituency. The rest normally involve action beyond the borders of the constituency, with the MP pursuing some action in relation to other bodies, frequently public bodies, on behalf of constituents. Most are usually pursued as a consequence of approaches made to the MP, though the MP may act as an information provider to constituents collectively (through newsletters, newspaper articles and, nowadays, internet sites), and may also act in pursuit of constituency interests without specific prompting. MPs may also solicit invitations to local events in order to raise their public profile. However, the demands made of MPs at the time of writing are such, both in quantity and quality, that members have little time to adopt a proactive approach in handling constituency matters.

There are two generalizations that can be drawn about the nature of constituency service since the start of the twentieth century. The first is the shift in emphasis from certain roles to others (Rush, 2001, pp. 199–211); and the second is the quantity of demands made of MPs by constituents in fulfilling those roles.

In the nineteenth century and the early decades of the twentieth, the benefactor role was an important one. The MP was frequently invited to support local interests, often financially, and to act to acquire jobs and benefits for constituents. Rush (2001, p. 203) quotes a Liberal MP, Richard Cobden, complaining in 1846, 'I am teased to death by place-hunters of every degree.' Civil service reform helped to reduce the potential for patronage, but other demands continued to be made. The new MP for Ashton-under-Lyne in 1910 – the millionaire Canadian, Max Aitken – faced a daunting array of pleadings from constituents.

These included requests to join societies, or to support local bodies in their activities. According to his biographers:

> Nearly always a donation or subscription was involved ... There was also a stream of begging letters from individuals. All were looked in to; Aitken was prepared to be generous, but hated being taken for granted ... Often he would ask his agents to give a needy family food or clothes rather than cash. (Chisholm and Davie, 1993, p. 85)

The benefactor role remained important for some years but declined as the twentieth century progressed. In part, this reflected the rise of the Labour Party, with MPs who did not have independent financial means. After 1945, it reflected the demise of wealthy members on the Conservative benches (the result of internal party reforms) and, more pervasively, the growth of the welfare state. Citizens could now in certain circumstances obtain, as of right, support from the state, and no longer needed to turn to local benefactors, at least not to the same extent as before.

However, just as the benefactor role declined, many of the others increased in significance, including those of powerful friend and information provider. Public bodies grew in the twentieth century and became a central feature of the state after 1945. The greater the number, and the greater the scope, of public bodies, the greater was the potential for citizens to feel aggrieved by the actions of public officials. When individuals felt they had not received some benefit due to them, or been discriminated against by a public body, they would contact the local MP to intercede on their behalf. Similarly, if they were not sure why they had been treated in a particular way, or needed help in pursing an issue, they would contact the MP. The MP was 'their' MP, and was in a position to act on their behalf in a way that no other body was. There was a limited number of grievance-chasing agencies to approach and none, other than the MP, had direct access to government departments.

The latter half of the twentieth century also saw a growing significance of the MP acting as safety valve and advocate. Post-war years saw an expansion of secondary education and the growth of the mass media. People became more aware of particular issues and were increasingly willing to express themselves (see Inglehart, 1977). They were more likely to join pressure groups; the number of groups increased dramatically in the last four decades of the century. An outlet for their views was the local MP. A British Social Attitudes survey in 1984 found that, in response to an unjust or harmful law being considered by Parliament, most respondents (55 per cent) would contact an MP (Jowell and Witherspoon, 1985, p. 12). This was the most popular course of personal action. The MP was also often sought in order to add his or her name to the campaign, or even to be actively involved in promoting the cause.

The role of local dignitary has remained a prominent one. Some MPs in the nineteenth and early twentieth centuries were drawn from the locality they represented (Rush, 2001, p. 204) and were already local figures of some standing. Others had no connection with the constituency but were accorded status by virtue of their position and this may have been enhanced by infrequent, rather than regular, visits to the constituency. Visits by the local MP were often something of an occasion. When Duff Cooper was elected Conservative MP for Oldham in 1924, he rarely visited the town: 'Although Duff may not have spent long in Oldham, when he was there there was scarcely a Chamber of Commerce dinner or a mothers' meeting which was not graced by a speech from the senior burgess' (Charmley, 1997, p. 48). The role remains important, though now imposing different demands. For reasons we shall explore, MPs spend more time in their constituencies and are keen to be seen locally; they have moved from being Olympian figures, descending occasionally from London, to become local worthies. Their contribution to the constituency has shifted from one of beneficence to one of time.

The other development has been the increase in the demands made of the local MP. There has been a marked increased in the sheer volume of representations made to MPs, especially by constituents. At the beginning of the twentieth century, it was not unknown for members to raise personal constituency cases with ministers (see Chester and Bowring, 1962, pp. 104–5). Requests for action by constituents with problems – war disabilities, unemployment and tax problems, for example – increased as the century progressed. This was reflected in a notable increase in the number of letters that flowed between MPs and ministers. In 1938, for example, the Financial Secretary to the Treasury wrote 610 letters to members. In 1954, the number was 3,349 (Couzens, 1956). There was also a marked increase in the number concerning the Post Office (Phillips, 1949).

However, pursuing cases with departments and other public bodies on behalf of constituents was not extensive. Relatively few problems were brought to an MP's attention. Peter Richards (1959) estimated that a typical MP received between twelve and twenty letters a week; in other words, about two or three a day, though other studies suggest the number may have been higher. By the last quarter of the twentieth

century, the burden of constituency correspondence had increased substantially. In 1967 most MPs estimated that they received between
twenty-five and seventy-five letters a week from constituency sources
(Barker and Rush, 1970, p. 174), but a survey in 1986 found that a
typical MP received between twenty and fifty letters *a day,* with more
than half coming from constituents (Griffith and Ryle, 1989, p. 72). The
quantitative increase is indicated by the number of letters that flow into
the Palace of Westminster. In 2003, no fewer than 12.5 million items of
mail were delivered (*Lords Hansard,* 19 January 2004, *WA117*). It was
estimated that there had been an annual increase of 2.5 per cent in the
number of items of post received since 2001. Of the 12.5 million items,
80 per cent – that is, ten million – were received by the Commons. This
averages more than 15,000 items of mail for each MP. What in 1986
was the highest figure in the range of mail received by MPs was, by
2003, the average amount.

Not all these letters were from constituents. The growth is a product of
increased lobbying by pressure groups (see Chapter 10) as well as representations from constituents. None the less, it does indicate the change in
the volume of letters facing MPs in the twenty-first century compared
with those a century before. The volume varies from one MP to another.
The 1986 survey found that MPs from seats in the South-West of
England received the largest number of letters. It is also generally accepted by MPs that those representing inner-city seats tend to receive more
letters than those representing seats in suburban areas. The former face
particularly problems of housing (though not a responsibility of central
government), urban deprivation and social problems. In some, immigration is also a significant problem that generates substantial casework.

Nor are letters the only means by which constituents make contact
with their MPs. The traditional method of contact has not only been by
letter but also through attendance at an MP's constituency 'surgery',
where the MP makes him herself available at a particular time in the
constituency to see constituents wishing to discuss problems or issues.
One study of just over 1,000 cases dealt with by seven MPs in the 1980s
found that 556 had originated from letters and 366 from surgeries. Just
over 100 had derived from telephone calls (Rawlings, 1990, p. 29).
More recent years have also seen a change in the nature of communication: the letter has been supplemented by the use of e-mail (and voice
mail). Most MPs now use e-mail (see Chapter 12) and, for constituents
and pressure groups, it constitutes an easy and cheap way of making
contact with MPs. In 2002, the Information Committee of the Commons
noted that, typically, '10 to 20 per cent of a Member's correspondence

might be received electronically', adding: 'but this figure seems set to climb' (Information Committee, 2002, p. 9).

MPs' responsiveness

MPs have responded to the demands made of them in two principal ways: one is pursuing constituency casework in the Commons and through contact with ministers, and the other is by spending more time in the constituency.

Some of the mail received by MPs falls into the 'safety valve' category, where the important thing for the writer is simply to have written. As one MP put it, 'The main satisfaction is to the constituent who feels he has gone as far as he can in getting his grievance aired' (Norton, 1982b, p. 65). More frequently, the constituent is contacting the MP as a powerful friend, information provider or advocate. In these roles – especially as powerful friend or information provider – the MP will normally pursue the matter on behalf of the constituents. This may be with a body in the constituency (most often the local authority) or, if concerned with central government, with the relevant government minister. Writing to a minister on behalf of a constituent is a well-established and, as may be inferred from the demands made of MPs by constituents, a growing part of MPs' parliamentary work.

MPs themselves have a fairly standard procedure for dealing with constituents' letters. Those that express an opinion normally receive a standard response, usually acknowledging receipt and thanking the correspondent for passing on their views, and some may provide a substantive answer. Where constituents ask the MP to intercede, as a powerful friend, in a dispute with a government department (or, usually, some agency of the department, such as a local social security office), the constituent's letter is forwarded to the relevant minister for a response. This practice is so standard, and extensive, that printed cards exist for MPs to attach to the letter, absolving them of the need to dictate a covering letter. The ministers' replies are normally then forwarded to constituents. In many cases, MPs thus act essentially as transmission belts for constituents' letters. Only if the minister's response is unsatisfactory, or if the constituent complains further about the response, is the MP likely to pursue the matter. This is done either by writing again to the minister or (especially if correspondence fails to resolve the issue) by a meeting with the minister or by raising the matter on the floor of the House.

MPs will sometimes seek meetings with ministers, on a formal or an informal basis. A formal meeting is one that is scheduled and may take place in the department. This is especially likely to be held where MPs are pursuing their role as protectors of constituency interests, taking up issues such as the closure of a naval dockyard or a hazard affecting the health of local inhabitants. Informal meetings frequently take place in the Palace of Westminster. MPs, as we have noted previously, often make use of the opportunity to speak to ministers when votes are taking place.

Raising a constituent's case or, more generally, a constituency interest, on the floor of the House is something undertaken only if earlier attempts by correspondence or private meetings have failed to resolve the matter satisfactorily. A member may table a parliamentary question for written or oral answer or, if requiring a more detailed response, raise it during the daily half-hour adjournment debate (see Chapter 6). Such debates provide an opportunity for back bench MPs to raise non-partisan issues, either of a general nature or one affecting their constituencies, or, sometimes, particular constituents. A study of adjournment debates in the 1995/6 session found that 43 per cent (61 out of 142) were on constituency issues; and a further 15 per cent were on regional issues (Russell, 1998, p. 29). Debates in Westminster Hall have extended the opportunity to raise constituency issues. The advantage of such debates, whether in the chamber or Westminster Hall, is that the minister's response is on the public record and is more detailed than an answer to a parliamentary question.

Using the floor of the House to pursue constituency issues is something usually kept in reserve. Corresponding with a minister is usually sufficient, and this is the most extensive form of contact between MPs and those of their number who are ministers. Data from the 1980s shows that about 12,000 letters a month were written by MPs to ministers, and that by the end of the decade the figure had reached about 15,000. This would suggest something approaching 200,000 letters a year written to ministers, and this is consistent with data we have for the 1990s. A study of ministerial correspondence revealed that, in 1990, ministers signed about 250,000 a letters a year, most but not all to MPs (Elms and Terry, 1990). In 1997, ministers received 'overall about 200,000 letters' from members of both Houses (*Lords Hansard*, 17 February 1999, col. 746). The number sent varied from department to department. Some departments, such as the Foreign Office, received relatively little parliamentary correspondence, but others had a heavy mailbag. In 1997, the Department of Environment, Transport and the

Regions received just under 32,000 letters, the Department of Social Security received 17,500, and the Home Office 16,831. 'That', as the minister giving the figures put it, 'is the sort of scale we are dealing with as regards correspondence with Members of Parliament' (Lord Falconer, *Lords Hansard,* 17 February 1999, col. 746).

MPs are thus busy dealing with constituency casework, especially through correspondence with ministers. They have also responded to the changing nature of constituency demands by spending more time in their constituencies, a tendency reinforced by greater electoral volatility (and hence instability for incumbents), local party pressure, and by the change in the nature of the work of MPs. The growth of the career politician (see Chapter 2) has increased the dependence on re-election as a necessary condition for career fulfilment.

Responding to pressure from their local parties, new MPs from the 1960s onwards increasingly took up residence in their constituencies. In the 1980s, newly-elected MPs were far more likely than longer-serving MPs to record addresses in or near their constituencies (Norton and Wood, 1993, p. 35). They also spent more time there. Donald Searing (1994, p. 136), in his survey of MPs in the early 1970s, found that recently elected backbenchers were more likely to claim to spend more time in their constituencies than did their longer-serving colleagues. Surveys by the Review Body of Top Salaries revealed that the amount of time MPs claimed to spend on constituency work increased from eleven hours a week in 1971 to sixteen hours a week in 1984 (Norton and Wood, 1990, p. 199), and time spent in the constituency appeared to be even more time consuming. In the early 1970s, most MPs claimed to spend up to fourteen hours a week on 'constituency and party work' in their constituencies; just over 23 per cent claimed to spend between fifteen and forty-eight hours on such work (Searing, 1994, p. 134). In 1984, a survey of members found that, of those who responded, more than 70 per cent spent eight or more days a month in the constituency (Reform Group, 1984). Only 7 per cent spent only two to four days a month in the constituency.

Effects

What, then, are the effects of the changing nature and demands of constituency work? We can see important effects for government, MPs, and for constituents.

Government

Letters from MPs are given priority within departments. By convention, a letter from an MP must receive a reply from a minister. As one former minister recalled, 'I became acutely aware that, whoever had drafted the reply, the responsibility for it lay with me' (Lord Glenarthur, *Lords Hansard,* 17 February. 1999, col. 740). The Cabinet Office gives guidance on best practice, but it is up to ministers as to how they in fact handle the correspondence.

For government, there are benefits as well as costs. The principal benefit is that correspondence from members helps to raise awareness of particular problems, which otherwise might not emerge publicly until much later. By writing, an MP can ensure that a matter, which otherwise might not reach a minister, is brought to that a minister's attention. On occasion, this can be helpful to ministers in identifying issues, not least those that civil servants may prefer not to see raised. Correspondence also serves as something of a barometer of parliamentary opinion, though this is most likely to be the case in respect of policy issues (Norton, 1982b, p. 65). In short, the effect of letter-writing by MPs is to ensure that ministers are better-informed about issues affecting their departments.

There are also costs to government. One is the financial cost of replying. Many letters will require some research or the calling in of files in order to draft a reply. There may be various exchanges between civil servants in a department, including with regional or local offices, before a draft is agreed, and if the minister is not satisfied with the draft, further work may be necessary. Given the scale of the correspondence, there is a burden on departmental budgets, not least on those being forced to handle the greatest volume of correspondence. There is also a cost in terms of time. Checking, sometimes dictating, and signing letters takes up ministers' time. There is an opportunity cost: the ministers could be engaged in more strategic work, or be devoting themselves to more pressing parliamentary and departmental concerns, such as working on bills before Parliament.

There is also a more personal cost to ministers in terms of sheer workload. Those elevated to ministerial office remain MPs and, as such, have constituency responsibilities (see Chapter 3). The fact that they have been, and remain, MPs, is of benefit to members engaging in correspondence with ministers. As parliamentarians themselves, ministers appreciate the importance of constituency correspondence. They can therefore empathize with the MPs writing to them. As constituency members, they may also write to fellow ministers in pursuit of a constituency case. Some find constituency work a relief from departmental pressures, and it may also serve a useful political purpose: 'To work in the constituency obliged one to keep up to date with all the issues being dealt with by ministerial colleagues and served as a useful discipline' (Shephard, 2000, p. 154). However, it adds to their burden of work: 'Ministers who have constituencies to look after don't stop and can't hand over the work to someone else: it just has to be fitted in somehow' (Currie, 1989, p. 233). They have to deal with constituency issues as well as attend to ministerial, parliamentary and party duties. Backbenchers also have parliamentary and party duties, but the pressure on ministers to address party gatherings is normally far greater. The constituency work is ever-present. Seeing Foreign Secretary Douglas Hurd signing constituency letters at an international meeting, a German minister exclaimed that 'Mrs Smith's plumbing problems' could not be the proper responsibility of a minister (Hurd, 2003, p. 312). Hurd took a different view, but the effect of constituency work is demanding. Cabinet ministers not only have to find time to reply to constituency correspondence; they also frequently maintain constituency surgeries. The effect can be exhausting as well as distracting. One cabinet minister (Nott, 2002, p. 123) recalled: 'When I became a Cabinet Minister, these surgeries became something of a burden because I returned to London with a voluminous correspondence about a host of personal problems – sorting them out had to take priority over such insignificant issues as modernisation of the nuclear deterrent!' One minister, in his memoirs (Fowler, 1991, p. 322), outlined a fairly typical week when his 'weekend' did not begin until four o'clock on Sunday. The process, he thought, 'had become dangerously all-devouring. It pushed out everything else'.

MPs

For MPs, whether ministers or backbenchers, there are also benefits as well as costs. It provides them with some self-esteem. The individual backbencher is not likely to have much success in changing public policy. Getting hold of some information for constituents is much easier and can carry with it a significant element of delivering a service. Generally, what constituents want is not so much a changed decision as for the MP to act as a safety valve or information provider. Of the responses to MPs' enquiries in just over 700 cases studied by Rawlings (1990, p. 42), 44 per cent involved the provision of further information and 18 per cent confirmation that the matter was in hand. On other occasions, the MP is able to act as a powerful friend. Some decisions may be – and are – changed as a result of an MP's intervention, especially in such areas as welfare payments and immigration where ministers or officials have some discretion to vary decisions (Rawlings, 1990, p. 168). MPs appear to gain some job satisfaction from their work (see Norris, 1997). It is not uncommon for MPs about to retire to express regret at giving up constituency work. It serves also to bolster their esteem as a local dignitary. In the House of Commons, one is a single member in a 646-member body. In the constituency, one is *the* Member of Parliament.

Constituency work may also have a more political reward. MPs may work hard in order to bolster their electoral base, with the need to do so being seen as more significant in recent decades as a consequence of greater electoral volatility. Even supposedly safe seats can be lost in an electoral landslide, as many Tory MPs discovered in 1997. Constituency work is not thought to persuade many voters to switch their votes, but may serve to retain support that might otherwise drift away. If both the MP's party and the MP are unpopular, this provides little incentive for former supporters, disillusioned with the party, to continue supporting the MP. If the MP's party is unpopular but the MP is popular because of the work done in the constituency, supporters may think twice before switching their vote to another party. There is some evidence that first-time incumbents in some recent elections have managed to achieve a better performance in maintaining their share of the vote than longer-serving members or challengers. The explanation offered for this has been the greater level of constituency activity undertaken by the new MP compared with that undertaken by the MP's predecessor (Norton and Wood, 1993, ch. 7; see also Norris, 1997). Data are not available that would allow us to know whether this is an intergenerational or a life-cycle phenomenon, and it may be a combination of both: new MPs may generally work harder than their predecessors in their first Parliament but nowadays, because of external pressures, may work even harder than previous first-termers.

Constituency work might not only help MPs at election time; it might also serve to fulfil an educative role in between elections. As one put it, it sensitizes MPs 'to the concerns that are pressing on at least a portion of our fellow citizens' (Brandreth, 1992, p. 24). It can help to keep MPs informed about specific local issues or about issues affecting a wide body of citizens. It is a valuable way of connecting with citizens and stops MPs from feeling detached from the rest of the populace. There is

Table 9.1   Influences on MPs' roles as representatives: MPs' evaluations

Q. MPs are expected to represent a number of different interests in Parliament. How important are the following interests in determining your role as a representative?

Answering very important/quite important

	%
My political party	71.5
My geographical constituency	92.7
Individual constituents	91.0
Constituency party	33.0
The nation as a whole	89.4
Sectional interests	33.0
A particular cause	48.0

N = 179

Source: Derived from Hansard Society Commission on Parliamentary Scrutiny (2001, pp. 138–9).

a general perception, not least on the part of MPs, that it keeps them in touch with 'real people'.

However, there are also costs. MPs see constituency work as being to the fore in determining their role as representatives (see Table 9.1). However, while MPs tend to extol the value of constituency service, the public stance is not always consistent with the private one. Though MPs recognize that constituents take priority when it comes to serving as representatives in Parliament, they do not necessarily consider protecting constituency interests to be their most important role in Westminster. They have a collective Westminster role as well as an individual constituency role and, as Table 9.2 reveals, the collective role of holding the government to account is regarded as the most important role by almost twice as many MPs as regard protecting constituency interests as most important.

MPs thus face cross-pressures between their constituency and their Westminster roles (Norton and Wood, 1993). The time-consuming aspect of constituency work has been a concern for many MPs in recent years. Resources available to members have increased (see Chapter 2), enabling them to cope more efficiently with constituency correspondence, but the sheer volume of letters and e-mails, and demands to

Table 9.2   The most important role of MPs: MPs' evaluations

Q. Which of these is the most important role (for an MP)?

	%
Holding the government to account	33.0
Examining legislation	12.8
Speaking in chamber	0.6
Dealing with constituents' grievances	15.1
Voting with political party	2.2
Informing constituents about government activity	0.6
Protecting interests of constituency	18.4
Writing/giving speeches	0.6
Working on departmental select committees	2.2
Appearing on TV	0.6
No reply	14
N = 179	

Source: Hansard Society Commission on Parliamentary Scrutiny (2001, p. 142). By permission of Dod's Parliamentary Communications.

attend constituency functions, means that the overall burden has increased. By 1996, it was estimated that MPs devoted almost 40 per cent of their time to constituency business (Power, 1996, p. 14). Much of this time was devoted to dealing with constituency casework that could be dealt with by other bodies or grievance-chasing agencies. It limits the time available to spend on those collective tasks that MPs alone can fulfil. Recent years have seen a decline in attendance at meetings of select committees and back-bench party committees. One possible explanation (but not necessarily the only one) is the amount of time MPs have to devote to the growing volume of constituency work. Indeed, the House has changed its own procedures in order to accommodate this burgeoning constituency activity. Ten Fridays in each session are designated as non-sitting Fridays, to enable MPs to devote more time to their constituencies, and, as part of the change in sitting hours, the House now normally rises at 7.00 pm on a Thursday evening to allow MPs to return to their constituencies that evening. The House has moved from a five-day week to what amounts, in effect, to a three-day week (late Monday to late Thursday), if that. Most important business is now concentrated on Tuesdays and Wednesdays.

MPs devote, then, considerable time to constituency work, but much of that time is occupied by the concerns of a limited number of constituents who may not be typical of constituents as a whole. An MP may draw generalizations on the basis of a few letters or e-mails from constituents. In some cases, this may suit the MP's purpose, but it may also distort the input the MP has in the political process. Letters tend to be from more literate constituents. In some cases, MPs are well aware that certain constituents who contact them are not representative of others but are simply using the MP to pursue a burning and sometimes irrational grievance. MPs have to cope with what are generally deemed 'crank' cases. These can be time-consuming and, on rare occasions, dangerous. (In 2000, one MP was seriously injured, and his assistant killed, by a mentally disturbed sword-wielding constituent at his constituency surgery.) MPs can find themselves fulfilling a social welfare role that could, and probably should, be fulfilled by professional agencies.

Constituents

Constituents accord priority to the MP's constituency role. Survey data drawn on by Cain *et al.* (1987, p. 38) show that a plurality of respondents identified the protection of the district, or constituency, as the most important representative role. ('Keeping in touch' came second.) Dealing with policy and engaging in oversight came bottom of the list. The attachment to protecting the constituency was even more highly rated by people in Britain than in the USA: 'The constituency service roles, protecting the district and helping people, were ranked highest by one-quarter of the American respondents and by nearly half of the British. Indeed, protecting the district was the highest-ranking role in Britain' (Cain *et al.* 1987, p. 39). This finding was reinforced by a later survey, undertaken for a study for a House of Commons committee, which found that two-thirds of respondents thought that MPs ought to be 'working on behalf of individual constituents' (Select Committee on Televising the Proceedings of the House, 1990, p. 85).

MPs generally appear to achieve what constituents expect of them. In many cases, this is an authoritative explanation of why some action has been taken. A letter from a minister, or an agency chief executive, forwarded by the MP, demonstrates not only action by the MP on the constituent's behalf but also usually provides a substantive response to the constituent's concerns.

Constituents not only expect their MP to be active on behalf of the constituency but they also appear to have some knowledge of the MP and, in the case of a substantial minority, call on the services of the MP. One survey found that almost two-thirds of respondents could name their MP; this compares with just over 30 per cent of Americans who could name their member of Congress (Cain *et al.*, 1987, p. 28; though see Modernisation Committee, 2004, p. 9). In the 1985 Social Attitudes Survey, 11 per cent of respondents claimed to have contacted their MP, a figure that is 1 per cent to 3 per cent higher than earlier estimates. According to Cain *et al.*, 25 per cent of citizens have received mail from their MP.

The work that is undertaken by MPs appears to attract a positive evaluation, and that response appears to be most positive in the event of contact. One survey in the 1970s found that, the closer the contact, the greater the belief that the MP was doing a good job. As Ivor Crewe (1975, p. 322) memorably put it, on reviewing the data: 'familiarity appears to breed content'. Members' responsiveness may also have encouraged more constituents to make contact. The responsiveness of members also appears to elicit a favourable reaction. One survey found that, of those who contacted their MP, 75 per cent reported a 'good' or 'very good' response (Cain *et al.*, 1979, pp. 6–7). More generally, constituents believe that the local MP is doing a good job. The State of the Nation surveys undertaken for the Joseph Rowntree Trust show that roughly twice as many people think the local MP is doing a good job as those believing the s/he is doing a bad job. Table 9.3 shows that the relative position has remained largely unchanged in recent years. As the Commons Modernisation Committee reported in 2004, the evidence it had received showed that individual MPs 'remain fairly credible in the public eye' (Modernisation Committee, 2004, p. 9).

Table 9.3   Evaluations of local MPs

Q. On balance, are you satisfied or dissatisfied with the job the local MP is doing for this constituency?

	1991	*1995*	*2001**
Satisfied	43	43	42
Dissatisfied	23	23	19
Don't know/no opinion	34	34	39

Note: * Satisfied combines 'very/fairly satisfied', dissatisfied combines 'fairly/very dissatisfied', don't know/no opinion combines 'neither satisfied nor dissatisfied' and 'don't know'.
Source: MORI, *State of the Nation, 1995* (London: MORI, 1995) for 1991 and 1995, MORI, 'Polls and survey archive 2001' accessed at www.mori.com for 2001.

On the face of it, constituents thus seem to be well served (and appear to regard themselves as being well served) by their local MP. However, there are problems. As we have seen, only a minority of constituents make contact with their MP. This could reflect contentment (or a lack of discontent) on the part of those who do not make contact. As we have seen, more think the local MP is doing a good job than those who think the s/he is doing a bad job. The proportion expressing satisfaction, however, is a minority. More than a third of constituents do not have an opinion on the work of their MP (see Table 9.3). Levels of satisfaction also appear to vary, depending on the nature of the constituency. By parliamentary tradition, constituency cases are dealt with by the local MP. If a constituent writes to another MP, that MP will pass the letter on to the constituency MP. The constituent is thus dependent on the quality of the local MP in pursuing casework. Some are more competent, persistent and interested than others. Though MPs generally accord significance to casework, not all treat it in the same way. There is anecdotal (and some hard) evidence that some MPs are fairly disdainful of constituency work (see Searing, 1994, pp. 137–8): Labour MP Tony Banks, for example, when announcing in 2004 his decision to retire from the Commons, declared that he had found constituency work 'tedious in the extreme' (BBC News Online, 27 November 2004). Also, MPs are not trained in grievance-chasing roles; they are essentially amateurs in the task. In the words of one MP, they are 'unspecialised, ill-equipped, amateurish and over-worked' (Alan Beith, cited in Norton, 1982b, p. 66). They are expected to pursue grievances in a wide range of areas, many of which will not fall within their field of specialization or interest. They are also expected to pursue grievances with bodies, most notably local authorities, for which they have no responsibility. The number of such bodies is, if anything, growing: 'The number of government functions and services privatised, contracted-out or deregulated has further reduced the scope for the MP to exert direct influence. They may apply pressure by dint of their position, but only to get access to the people who do make the decisions' (Power, 1996, p. 15).

There is also a problem in terms of pursuing the grievances of constituents where that grievance is expressed in a collective form. A letter written personally by a constituent will normally elicit a response by the MP. The local MP may also decide to take action if s/he perceives a threat to a local interest, such as the mooted closure of a factory. However, when constituents petition an MP in favour of some particular action, the exercise is largely a wasted one. This is not necessarily the fault of the MP, but rather of the process for dealing with petitions.

Citizens may spend hours, even days, soliciting signatures for a petition to be presented to Parliament. Some of these have a few signatures and some have several thousand. A petition is sent to an MP – the local MP where it affects a local interest (as, for example, with the closure of a local hospital) – who then presents it, either formally on the floor of the House, or informally, by placing it in a bag behind the Speaker's chair. The formal presentation is very short, with no substantive speech being allowed. Petitions are not debated and, though now sent to the relevant select commitee, are largely ignored by government. The Procedure Committee of the House noted in 1992 that the process 'may lead to some false expectations on the part of the public' (Select Committee on Procedure, 1992). One MP, in writing to the Procedure Committee, noted that petitioning was one of the few ways in which the public could feel in some way 'connected' to what went on inside Parliament. Under existing arrangements, that connection is largely broken. As the Hansard Society Commission on Parliamentary Scrutiny (2001, p. 86) recorded, 'there is little sense that petitions to Parliament result in any concrete action on the part of MPs'. So much so that citizens are now more likely to submit a petition to the prime minister than to Parliament. As the Hansard Society Commission reported, the number of petitions presented each year to the Commons is now fewer than a hundred. In the two-year period from January 1999 to January 2001, 492 petitions with over 200 signatures in each were presented to Downing Street: citizens are by-passing Parliament in favour of the head of government.

Conclusion

The link between Parliament and citizen, in terms of direct contact, is through the individual Member of Parliament. That link historically is well established and is reinforced by the nature of the electoral system. Research by Bowler and Farrell (1993) shows election by geographic constituencies is more likely to encourage constituency service than election by list systems of proportional representation. Constituents expect 'their' Member of Parliament to take action on their behalf, independent of the MP's collective and party roles. MPs, as we have seen, have fulfilled a number of roles as constituency MPs, and those roles have changed as the nature of MPs has changed, and as constituents' expectations have grown. Constituents contact their local MP in increasing numbers to take action on their behalf, typically by requesting information or confirmation that a matter is being investigated.

A growing number also write to express opinions on issues of public policy. MPs have sought to meet constituents' expectations and have devoted more time to constituency service.

Constituency activity is an intrinsic part, then, of the work of the MP. However, as we have seen, it is not problem-free. From a pluralist perspective, it is possible to identify what may be considered as the principal concern. The emphasis on constituency work reinforces the realization that MPs are not able to utilize their coercive capacity, or, for that matter, much persuasion, in affecting outcomes of public policy. Members therefore absorb themselves in constituency work, which may engender a degree of satisfaction and occasionally result in a changed decision, but which none the less constitutes a distraction from the collective task of members. This view is best encapsulated by the observation of Greg Power that

> there are many MPs who work assiduously on behalf of their constituents and achieve much success in doing so. But such work largely fails to call on the expertise or skills of the MP, and almost totally fails to utilise their role in Parliament. At a time when Parliament is failing to act as a check on the power of the Executive, there is a serious question as to whether this role is the best use of an MP's time and resources. (Power, 1996, p. 15)

The institutional approach enables us to look at constituency work from a different perspective: it stresses the extent and institutionalization of the process by which MPs pursue constituents' concerns. There is a well-established process by which MPs take up issues on behalf of constituents. It is highly institutionalized, encompassing an acceptance by ministers as well as backbenchers that it is legitimate and should therefore be undertaken. As we have seen, despite the time-consuming nature of the work, MPs accept it is as a necessary part of their work, and equally important, so too do ministers. As we have seen, they abide by the convention that letters from parliamentarians to ministers must receive a reply from a minister, and not from a civil servant. Much of this activity does not result in changed decisions; it absorbs a great deal of time of ministers and officials and it potentially detracts MPs from other, collective, activities. None the less, it delivers a service to citizens, one that they expect and appear to appreciate. Citizens attach importance to the constituency role and rate it above the collective, or Westminster, role of MPs.

The evaluation of the work undertaken by the MP as a constituency member exists independently of citizens' evaluation of the collective role undertaken by MPs. As we have seen from Table 9.3, evaluations of the work done by the local MP remained stable, as well as positive, over the decade from 1991 to 2001. The same MORI State of the Nation poll shows considerable variation in the popular view of the job done by Parliament, however. In 1991, for example, 59 per cent of respondents thought that Parliament did a good job; in 1995, this had dropped to 43 per cent. Though MPs collectively are deemed to do a good job, voters appear to be able to distinguish the service provided by the local MP from the institution of the House of Commons.

The institutional approach also alerts us to the complexity of addressing the demands imposed nowadays by constituency work. To expect MPs to devote more time to work in Westminster requires either reducing the demands of constituency work, ignoring it or providing more resources to cope with it. There is little obvious scope for reducing the demand, other than through a widespread educative process. Ignoring it has the potential to build up tension within the political system. Expanding resources may enable MPs to keep pace with the demands made of them. Some MPs have been able to deploy their staff and office resources in such a way as a enable them to concentrate on their role in Westminster. However, increasing the resources available to each MP does not address the structural problem that has developed. The institutional limitations in dealing with petitions are apparent, not least in comparative perspective. Petitions committees are common features of West European Parliaments (see Norton, 2002a), a category that encompasses the Scottish Parliament. Though the process of dealing with correspondence from constituents is well developed, and may serve to encourage constituents to make more contact, that for dealing with petitions is not, and may be deflecting citizens in the direction of other outlets for the expression of their collective views.

10

The Voice of Organized Interests

Members of Parliament are elected for defined constituencies. As we saw in Chapter 9, constituents expect them to give priority to local interests and an increasing amount of time is devoted by members to constituency casework. However, members also devote considerable time to listening to, and expressing the demands of, different groups in society. Some groups may be composed of a member's constituents: a local charity or the local chamber of commerce, for example. Others may have no direct constituency connection but believe they have a case that will engage the MP's attention.

Like constituency casework, the task of pursuing the demands of different groups is a growing one. However, unlike constituency work, it is not confined to the House of Commons. Peers are also important targets for groups seeking to have some influence on the content of public policy. By expressing the views of different groups in society, members of both Houses fulfil a number of functions, not unlike to those carried out by the MP as a constituency member. They act as safety valves, advocates and powerful friends.

The role of party

For more than a century, the most important organized interest has been that of party (see Chapter 2). MPs are elected on the basis of their party label; parties serve to aggregate interests, and candidates stand on the basis of their party's manifesto and are expected, if elected, to support the party in implementing the promises made to the electorate. The result of this, as we have seen, has been party cohesion in Parliament. Within Parliament, and especially the House of Commons, parties dominate not only voting but also most other aspects of parliamentary behaviour. Debate is frequently, though not always, partisan, and members are called to speak on the presumption that it *is* (hence they are called from alternate sides of the chamber). Question Time is seen increasingly as representing a partisan tussle between government and opposition front benches (see Franklin and Norton, 1993), especially on Wednesdays when there is a gladiatorial contest between the prime minister and the leader of the opposition. Standing committees, as we have seen, are essentially the chamber in miniature, with proceedings dominated by the party clash and the operation of the whips.

This domination by party has advantages for the political system. It ensures some degree of coherence, and electors know what they are voting for. The names of individual candidates may not mean much to them, but they understand the party label. Parties compete essentially for the all-or-nothing gains of electoral victory. Once returned with a majority of seats, a party can implement a particular programme of public policy and is then answerable to the electorate at the next general election. Electors are offered a choice, and they can turn a government out.

A number of problems have been identified in this system. Some critics have queried whether there is much to choose between the parties. The more they resemble 'catch-all' parties (Kirchheimer, 1966), the less differentiated a choice they offer. Other critics have contended that at various points the choice has been far too stark, with little point of contact between the main parties – as, for example, in the 1983 general election. As we have seen in Chapter 8, some critics of the political system have also challenged the basic legitimacy of an electoral system that can produce an absolute majority of seats on the basis of less than 50 per cent of the votes cast. There is also an important question of legitimacy stemming from popular perceptions of party domination.

The stance of electors towards Parliament and its members presents a conundrum. On the one hand, voters elect MPs on the basis of the party label, but on the other, they expect the MP to do far more than merely support the party in Parliament, and greater emphasis is given to a local than to a national role. For MPs, there is thus an important balance to be maintained, loyally supporting the party on whose label they were elected, while at the same time carving out a role independent of party, not least in order to pursue constituency demands. At times, the roles may conflict, as when local interests are threatened by government policy and the local MP is a member of the governing party.

In post-war decades, the balance has been tipped predominantly, if not overwhelmingly, in favour of party. Party cohesiveness reached its peak in the 1950s. Independent activity by members was extremely limited and the stranglehold of party rendered Parliament essentially a closed institution, with no means of independent access (Norton, 1991a). Though party was essential for ensuring a coherent system, its hegemony conveyed the appearance of MPs as 'lobby fodder' and the institution as a body for little more than rubber-stamping decisions taken elsewhere. The consequence was frustration for MPs wanting to have some effect on the political system, and a tendency for organized groups to ignore Parliament and to concentrate their efforts on government. Government neglected Parliament in favour of pressure groups, generating what Richardson and Jordan (1979) dubbed 'a post-parliamentary democracy'. There were few opportunities for members of the public to follow what was going on, and little point in making the effort (Norton, 1991a, pp. 223–4).

However, the situation was to change in the last quarter of the twentieth century. As discussed in Chapter 2, the stranglehold of party was relaxed. The change was relative, but significant. The demands made of MPs by constituents increased, and so too did the demands made by organized interests. Increasingly, MPs – and peers – found themselves the targets of representations, better known as lobbying (a phrase deriving from those who used to hover in the lobby of the New York state capitol to seek special favours; Congressional Quarterly, 1987, p. 2), from a vast range of organized interests. The most important organized interest, still largely determining their parliamentary behaviour, was that of party. But it was no longer the exclusive interest determining their actions. Parliament became a more open institution.

The impact of groups

Since the 1960s there has been a massive increase in the lobbying of members of both Houses by organized interests, such interests including large companies, professional bodies, charities, unions, consumer groups and a vast array of pressure groups seeking a change in public policy.

Lobbying by such interests is not new. As early as 1910, for example, the National Farmers' Union appointed a 'Parliamentary Lobbyist' (Wootton, 1975, p. 216). The presence of lobbyists was noted in the 1950s and 1960s (Finer, 1958, p. 23; Walkland, 1968). What has changed is the extent and the visibility of such lobbying. Organized interests now impinge massively on the time and consciousness of members of both Houses. One survey in 1986 of more than 250 organizations – encompassing the range just noted (companies, charities,

Table 10.1   Group contact with Members of Parliament – a survey of 253 organized interests conducted in 1986

Q. Do you or does your organization have regular or frequent contact with one or more Members of Parliament?

	N	%
Yes	189	74.7
No	64	25.3
Total	253	100.0

Source: Rush (1990; p. 280). By permission of Oxford University Press.

consumer groups and the like) – found that three-quarters maintained 'regular or frequent contact with one or more Members of Parliament' (see Table 10.1).

That contact is sometimes in person, not least during the committee stage of bills. The representatives of groups with a particular interest in a bill will normally be present during sittings, and committee members will sometimes be seen leaving the room for a quick discussion in the corridor with a lobbyist for a group on whose behalf the member is speaking. Such lobbyists are frequently in evidence in the public gallery during the report stage of bills and on occasion fill the public seating during select committee hearings.

More frequently, the contact is by correspondence. The increase in constituency mail has been supplemented by mail from pressure groups of one type or another. The 1986 survey of organizations found that 34 per cent of them sent information or briefings regularly or often to MPs, and almost 60 per cent did so occasionally. Only 6 per cent of them did not send such material (Rush, 1990, p. 280).

The burden is not just in the number of letters written to members: there has been a qualitative change as well. Correspondence has become more complex and more technically demanding. Groups interested in a particular clause of a bill will write to explain why it needs amending. Finance bills and those that impose regulatory regimes can be highly detailed, requiring knowledge of the subject in order to grasp the arguments being advanced by those seeking changes to the measures.

For members, then, the burden lies in more than simply being the recipients of straightforward information. The material is often intricate and involves the member being invited to take some action. Of the 189 organizations found in the 1986 survey to maintain contact with

MPs, 83 per cent had asked an MP to table a parliamentary question. Most had also asked an MP to arrange a meeting at the Commons (78 per cent), to table an amendment to a bill (62 per cent) and to table a motion (51 per cent). Approximately half of the groups had also asked MPs to arrange meetings with ministers. More than a third had asked a member to sponsor a private member's bill (Rush, 1990, p. 281).

During the passage of a bill, members will draw on material supplied by groups in order to question provisions and to propose amendments. The extent of group activity is frequently apparent from explicit references to their briefing material. Thus, for example, during second reading of the Children Bill in the Commons in September 2004, there were various references to briefings received by members from bodies such as the Children's Society, the National Children's Bureau, the National Society for the Prevention of Cruelty to Children, the Refugee Children's Consortium, Save the Children, Shelter, and Women's Aid. The most frequent references were made by those speaking for the main opposition parties. However, the most intensive lobbying tends to take place at committee stage. The names of members of the standing committee are published, and organizations seeking changes direct their efforts to wards those members. Committee members will often be swamped with letters and briefings. Such lobbying is not confined to government bills. Private members' bills can be the subject of even more intense pressures. Bills on abortion, mercy killing and animal welfare, for example, elicit extensive lobbying by pressure groups and their supporters.

Nor is such lobbying confined to MPs:

> the House of Lords offers fruitful ground for inserting relatively technical amendments which may be important to a pressure group's members. Even if the amendment is not pressed to a vote, it may be used to extract further assurances from the government. (Grant, 2000, p. 158)

Of the groups surveyed in 1986, 70 per cent had used the Lords to try to influence public policy. Of the groups that had attempted to influence legislation, almost 80 per cent had contacted one or more members of the House of Lords; indeed, this was the most popular form of action (Rush, 1990, pp. 289, 284). A later survey by Baggott found that half of the groups surveyed were in touch with peers at least once a month, and almost one in five were in contact on a weekly basis (see Baggott, 1995, pp. 93, 164). Groups utilizing regular contact with the House, and understanding the legislative process, will not only identify particular problems with a bill but also offer the text of amendments. The House is valuable also for raising issues through debates and questions, thus ensuring that the issues are on the public record and elicit a ministerial response. One survey of active peers found that almost all of them had asked written questions on behalf of pressure groups. More than 60 per cent had tabled starred questions, and a similar proportion had raised a point in debate (Baldwin, 1990, pp. 162–3).

The extent of lobbying of the House of Lords is indicated by the data reported in Chapter 9 regarding the volume of mail received in the Palace of Westminster. In 2003, 2.5 million items of post flowed into the House of Lords: an average of more than 3,500 items per peer. This total does not include e-mails, a form of communication that various lobbying groups have begun to use. Although some individuals will write on what are essentially constituency matters (and hence matters for MPs), the bulk of correspondence comes from organizations or individuals dealing with current issues – especially bills before the House – or keeping the target member informed of activities; it is common to receive newsletters and magazines.

Members of both Houses are thus subject to extensive lobbying by organized groups, and not simply through occasional letter writing or the submission of briefing material. Many organizations will have a degree of contact that is semi-institutionalized, not least through the burgeoning all-party groups (see Chapter 6) and through having staff permanently employed to deal with parliamentary affairs. A good illustration is provided by Wyn Grant:

> the Chemical Industries Association employs a Parliamentary Adviser, and administers the All Party Parliamentary Group for the Chemical Industry with a membership of some seventy MPs together with members of the House of Lords. The group meets to hear about developments in the industry and to discuss relevant legislation, and its members are also individually briefed on a large number of subjects. A piece of legislation which is particularly important to the CIA may involve the Parliamentary Adviser attending every debate and committee session in the Commons and Lords; briefing individual committee members, civil servants and ministers; and commenting on large numbers of amendments put down by MPs. (Grant, 2000, p. 150)

The result is extensive contact between organized groups and parliamentarians. Despite the realization that policy originates with government – and that measures brought forward by government will pass – groups none the less perceive some utility in lobbying Parliament and engage in such lobbying on an ever-increasing scale.

Explanations of change

As with the growth of constituency demands, there is no single explanation for the increase in parliamentary lobbying by organized interests.
There are several independent developments that appear to have coin-
cided, producing this phenomenon (Norton, 1991b, pp. 65–9). Changes
in the nature of groups, of government and of Parliament have contributed to the change.

Pressure groups

The most significant change in organized groups in recent years has
been the increase in their numbers. As we saw in Chapter 2, interests
began to organize during the nineteenth century more extensively than
before. That trend continued into the twentieth century and has been
pronounced in the period since 1960. With increased education and
political awareness – what Inglehart (1977) has termed cognitive mobilization – more and more people have been willing to join together to
seek some change in public policy. There has been a marked increase
in the number of pressure groups, not least those created to promote a
particular cause – for example, environmental or lifestyle – rather than
to defend a specific sectional interest (Smith, 1995, p. 2): 'To some
extent, the 1980s and 1990s have been a period of increased pluralism.
More groups are involved in politics and more people are involved in
pressure groups' (Smith, 1995, p. 110). Groups are now notable both for
their number, their different forms, and the support that they enjoy. The
National Trust and the Royal Society for the Protection of Birds (RSPB)
have memberships that far exceed the membership of any political
party.

Growth in the number of groups has led to an increase in demands
made of members of both Houses of Parliament. However, there has
also been a change in the resources available to groups to engage in parliamentary lobbying. One has taken the form of improved technology,
providing the facility for more rapid communication. Much of the material received by MPs and peers is now the product of personal computers and desktop publishing facilities. E-mail is an efficient and cheap
way of making contact, enabling all parliamentarians with e-mail
addresses to be contacted at the press of a button. The other change has
been in the professional bodies available to undertake such lobbying
activities. Some organizations have in-house lobbyists. Others now
employ lobbying firms, known formally as political consultancies. The
1980s and 1990s were growth periods for such bodies (see Grantham,

1989; Grantham and Seymour-Ure, 1990). Such firms, often composed of former civil servants, parliamentary officials, party officials and MPs offer a range of services, including the monitoring of activities in Westminster – and Whitehall – for clients, advising on how to lobby effectively, and lobbying politicians and civil servants on behalf of clients. The range of bodies using their services grew and their use soon became widespread among organizations seeking to influence public policy (see Grantham and Seymour-Ure, 1990, pp. 50–6). Not only do such consultancy firms facilitate lobbying, it is also in their commercial interest to encourage it. The more they engage in such activity, especially if it appears to have some effect, the more it encourages other organizations to use their services. However, as we shall see, their activities have proved to be controversial.

Government

In the years from 1945 to 1979, government drew on organized interests in developing public policy. There was co-operation between government, labour and business; in essence, the post-parliamentary democracy identified by Richardson and Jordan (1979). That co-operation came under pressure as economic conditions worsened and government had to move from distributive to redistributive policies. Groups were forced to compete for a share of resources that were not expanding. The relationship then changed substantially during the era of Conservative government from 1979 to 1997: 'The election of Mrs Thatcher heralded a new approach to pressure group relationships' (Grant, 2000, p. 3). The government sought greater autonomy in policy-making (Gamble, 1994), resulting in more distant relationships with organized interests, especially at the level of high policy (such as economic policy). Bodies such as the Trades Union Congress were virtually frozen out of policy discussions. The more groups perceived that they lacked the access they previously enjoyed to government, the more they turned to Parliament as a means of achieving some input into the deliberations on public policy. Though the perception that government distanced itself from organized interests was greater than the reality (extensive contact was maintained between departments and outside bodies), this perception affected behaviour, and the lobbying of Parliament has continued under a Labour government that has also exhibited some autonomy in policy-making. Despite developing relationships with various organizations, 'there was no reversion to the old style corporatism of the 1970s' (Grant, 2000, p. 4).

Parliament

Groups thus turned to Parliament in various ways. At the same time, there were developments internal to the institution that increased its attractiveness. The greater behavioural independence of MPs (see Chapter 2) meant that changes to public policy, in particular to the detail of bills, might be achievable as a result of back-bench pressure. Following the removal of most hereditary peers from the House of Lords in 1999, the House has appeared to be more self-confident in challenging government.

The introduction of the departmental select committees in the Commons has also provided groups with a very clear focus for their activities. Select committees determine their own agendas, the evidence they take is published, and the government responds in writing to a committee's recommendations. For groups, select committees are a valuable conduit for getting their views on the public record and before government. As one Labour member of the Trade and Industry Committee once observed, 'trade unions are delighted with the committee ... the main benefit is to put into the "public domain" information that otherwise might not be available' (Judge, 1990, p. 192). They may also serve to influence the recommendations. The degree of committee attractiveness to groups is reflected not so much in the oral evidence provided by the representatives of groups – they attend by invitation of the committee – but in the volume of written evidence submitted. Many pressure groups ensure that they are on committees' mailing lists, and once an enquiry in their area of interest is announced they prepare and submit written evidence. Committees are often inundated with memoranda.

The same consideration applies to committees in the Lords. When the Constitution Committee in the Lords embarked on an inquiry into the role of regulators in 2003, it received extensive submissions from a wide range of bodies, not least those subject to regulation (Constitution Committee, Home of Lords, 2004a). There was a notable flurry of memoranda from disgruntled independent financial advisers writing about the role of the Financial Services Authority. The evidence taken by the committee was published in two volumes.

In terms of the legislative process, the growth of pre-legislative scrutiny since 1997 also offers a particular opportunity to pressure groups. As we have seen in Chapter 4, input at the formulation stage of legislation enhances the opportunity to influence the content of bills. Consultation on bills has enabled the views of interested organizations

to be given to the sponsoring department, but scrutiny of draft bills by
a parliamentary committee provides a particular focus for group lobbying in order to influence the committee's recommendations. With the
growth in pre-legislative scrutiny, parliamentary lobbying by pressure
groups is likely to become even more pronounced.

Parliament may also have increased its attractiveness to organized
groups as a result of the televising of proceedings. Since cameras were
introduced in the Commons, it has achieved more public prominence. A
particular feature of the twenty-first century is the use of cameras to
interview members within the Palace of Westminster. This, and the
growth of 24-hour news coverage, has meant that back-bench MPs are
now more likely than before to be interviewed by the media. They are
therefore more attractive to groups seeking a public outlet for their
views.

These various developments have coalesced to produce the increase
in parliamentary lobbying. The volume of such lobbying shows no sign
of receding; quite the reverse, in fact. But what effect has it had?

Consequences

As with the increase in constituency casework, the burgeoning of lobbying by pressure groups has had several consequences for the political
system. Such lobbying has served to strengthen members of both
Houses in carrying out a number of tasks; and it has served to enhance
the legitimacy of Parliament among organized groups. In addition, it
appears to have contributed towards some changes in public policy.
Against this must be set the fact that there are problems of popular legitimacy as a result of perceived inequities in group influence and, as with
constituency casework, problems for parliamentarians in trying to cope
with all the demands made of them.

Benefits

Much of the material that is sent to MPs and peers is of little use to most
of the recipients. Some is outside the members' areas of interest, and
some is so badly prepared and argued, and sometimes too late, to have
any effect. Much, if not most, of the material is discarded, often unread.
As one MP wrote: 'Throughout the year the brown tide of letters pours
in. The basic weapons for mail warfare are a paper knife and a large
waste paper basket – known in the trade as "the circular file"' (Flynn,
1997, p. 61). His advice to new members: 'Be ruthless.'

However, what is more important is the fact that not all the material sent is discarded. The material supplied by organizations outside Parliament ensures that members, and committees, of both Houses have a source of information independent of government and party. This material adds to the members' store of knowledge and provides the basis for questioning the detail of provisions laid before them. Such is the value of the material supplied by interested organizations that members will sometimes actively solicit it (Norton, 1990b, p. 197). Within the context of their particular enquiries, departmental select committees do so on a regular basis.

Given their own limited resources, MPs and – especially – peers use outside groups almost as substitutes for research assistants, their own areas of interest and political predispositions serving as a filter for the material they are sent. Information likely to be of use is read and retained; the rest is discarded. For members who may be critical of a particular measure, or may have been unaware of inherent problems with it, the information supplied by groups can be invaluable. As a result, it adds to their critical capacity and ensures that Parliament is a more effective body of scrutiny than it otherwise would be.

Well-briefed members are in a stronger position to press amendments and to challenge government than would be the case if they were reliant on government for information. Pressure from members, especially government backbenchers, and the quality of argument may be sufficient to persuade ministers to accept changes to their bills. The House of Lords offers particular scope to pursue amendments. Government is less in control of proceedings – and the outcome of votes – in the Lords than in the Commons, and peers with a particular knowledge of a subject can pursue it in order to elicit a response from government. The capacity of members to have a significant impact on the legislative process remains limited (see Chapter 5), but the link with outside groups ensures that it is not quite so limited as it once was.

Similarly, well-informed select committees have had some impact on public policy, or rather, as was noted in Chapter 6, the *detail* of policy. Outside organizations have ensured that the committees have material that supplements or challenges that provided by ministers and officials. Knowing that committees may obtain information from other sources can have an effect on departmental thinking and intentions. Again, the impact of departmental select committees may be limited, but their existence – and their extensive use of evidence from organizations independent of government – has provided a new dimension to parliamentary scrutiny. That dimension has increased as a result of the greater number of bills published in draft and subject to pre-legislative

Table 10.2   Group influence on legislation

	N	%
Q. Speaking generally, how would you rate your efforts in seeking to influence legislation before Parliament?		
Very successful	15	7.2
Quite successful	100	48.3
Not very successful	80	38.6
Unsuccessful	12	5.8
Total	207	99.9

Note: There were four non-respondents.
Source: Rush (1990, p. 285). By permission of Oxford University Press.

scrutiny. As we have seen (in Chapter 4), most bills subject to pre-legislative scrutiny have been scrutinized by departmental select committees.

The pursuit of group demands by members of both Houses (and the effect it sometimes has) has also helped to enhance the legitimacy of Parliament among such groups. The perception of groups is generally a positive one. The 1986 survey found that, of those groups that had sought to have some influence on legislation, more than half claimed to have been successful (see Table 10.2). Lobbying is often inefficient (see Norton, 1990b, pp. 193–6) but none the less, the perception of groups involved in the exercise is that it has some effect. As can be seen from Table 10.2, less than 6 per cent of the groups questioned deemed their efforts to have been unsuccessful.

The value of Parliament extends to agenda setting. By giving evidence to committees, groups can place their views on the public record and influence the committee's recommendations. Even if the recommendations are not accepted, the fact of their publication can help to place the issue on the public agenda: 'Coupled with pressure through other channels, this raises the possibility of a more positive outcome in the longer term' (Baggott, 1995, p. 148). For many groups, getting their views on the record in an authoritative forum is an end in itself; they have had an opportunity to express themselves. Parliament thus serves as an important safety valve for groups as well as for individuals. The possibility of actually influencing some change in public policy is an added attraction, enhancing the legitimacy of the institution.

And the legitimacy of the institution, in the eyes of pressure groups, is also enhanced by the fact that it serves as an important transmission belt between groups and government. As we have seen, this role has acquired greater significance since 1979. Parliament offers not only an opportunity to give a public airing to group demands, but it can also help to channel those demands to government, both publicly and privately. As we have seen, half the groups questioned in the 1986 survey had asked MPs to arrange meetings with a minister (Rush, 1990, p. 281). Through arranging such meetings, through tabling questions, and through tabling amendments to bills, members in both Houses can ensure that group demands are considered by government.

The significance of these activities should not be exaggerated. Public policy is determined by government (see Chapter 4). For the purposes of groups, ministers and senior civil servants remain the principal targets of their lobbying activities. Despite the arm's-length relationship of government to many economic groups since 1979, the contact between departmental ministers and organized interests remains extensive and continuous (Norton, 1999c, pp. 19–21). Parliament remains a supplementary rather than a primary point of contact. While half the groups questioned in 1986 may have asked MPs to arrange meetings with ministers, the other side of the coin is that the other half did not. Equally remarkable is the number of groups who fail to recognize and exploit the value of the House of Lords in influencing legislation.

None the less, Parliament occupies the time and attention of organized interests on a more extensive basis than before. While persuading government remains the essential and normally sufficient task for most groups seeking some change in policy, Parliament fulfils an important role in providing groups with a safety valve and another opportunity to fight a battle that may have been lost in Whitehall. Their activity also adds to the store of members' knowledge, thus providing them with the means to adopt a more critical stance and, in so doing, reinforce the legitimacy of the institution in the eyes of citizens.

Limitations

Though the increased activity of groups may have helped to bolster perceptions of Parliament's legitimacy among such groups, there are problems of popular legitimacy arising from the access that such groups enjoy. There are perceived inequalities of access between groups, and between groups and the individual citizen.

Larger and more powerful organizations can afford the services of professional lobbyists, and there is a perception on the part of less powerful groups that they are squeezed out. As the representative of one voluntary organization put it, 'those like us with little money, staff and resources can't mount such a good show and tend to be overlooked' (Grantham and Seymour-Ure, 1990, p. 76). Wealthy groups are believed to be able to buy influence. This perception was compounded in the 1980s and 1990s by the fact that a significant proportion of parliamentarians were themselves consultants or retained by consultancy firms. Influence-buying had been alleged in earlier decades (Norton, 1999a, p. 34) but claims of MPs being in the pay of outside groups reached new heights during this period. In 1989, 180 MPs – 137 of them Conservatives – were retained by outside groups as parliamentary consultants or advisers (Grantham and Seymour-Ure, 1990, p. 67).

Stories about links between MPs and organized interests attracted critical press stories and a number of books appeared, their titles reflecting the critical content: for example, *Corruption and Misconduct in Contemporary British Politics* (Doig, 1984), *Westminster Babylon* (Doig, 1990) and *MPs for Hire* (Hollingsworth, 1991). The links also attracted a growing body of academic literature (see Rush, 1990; Jordan, 1991). Investigation of lobbying by the Select Committee on Members' Interests in the Commons tapped unease about the activities of lobbyists among some MPs, some of whom gave voice to perceived misuse of Commons facilities by lobbyists (Select Committee on Members' Interests, 1990). Allegations of abuse were common, though rarely substantiated. Stories about links between MPs and lobbying organizations affected the public perception of members. A MORI poll in 1985 found that 46 per cent of respondents agreed with the statement that 'most MPs make a lot of money by using public office improperly', against only 31 per cent who disagreed. Just over two-thirds of those questioned (67 per cent) agreed with the statement that 'most MPs care more about special interests than they care about people like you'. Less than one in five (19 per cent) disagreed with the statement.

The issue of MPs' links with outside bodies attracted particular media attention in 1994 as a result of allegations that MPs were being paid in return for tabling parliamentary questions. The 'cash for questions' scandal led to the than prime minister, John Major, setting up a Committee on Standards in Public Life (the Nolan Committee) to make recommendations. Against a background of growing public disapproval, and a marked increase in the number of people (64 per cent in 1995) believing that most MPs make a lot of money by using public office improperly, the Commons agreed to a number of recommendations emanating from the Nolan Committee. Despite some opposition, the House voted to ban paid advocacy by MPs (members could still advise outside interests for payment, but could not raise an issue on their behalf in Parliament); to require disclosure of income derived from activities relating to their work as an MP (in effect, tightening up the rules on its existing register of members' interests); to establish a code of conduct; to create a parliamentary commissioner for standards (to maintain the register of interests, to advise MPs, and to investigate complaints of breaches of the rules); and to create a Select Committee on Standards (the new committee succeeded the Select Committee on Members' Interests and was then merged with the long-standing Select Committee on Privileges) (Rush, 1998, pp. 106–10; Norton, 1999a, pp. 35–6; Riddell, 2000, pp. 144–8). The House of Lords subsequently tightened its rules of disclosure, making them even more rigorous than those of the Commons.

Allegations of misconduct – subsumed under the term 'sleaze' – continued to be made, including under the Blair Government (Riddell, 2000, pp. 149–51). There remain problems in that Parliament continues to regulate itself and there are no means of appeal (Rush, 1998, pp. 117–18; Riddell, 2000, pp. 153–9). Though the issue has subsided in terms of popular consciousness, the perception of sleaze has attached itself to the House and, as Peter Riddell has noted, 'the two Houses have to demonstrate to the public that high standards are being maintained' (Riddell, 2000, p. 159).

The other negative consequence is the impact on members' workloads. The more they are lobbied, the less time they have to devote to other activities, sifting the unsolicited material received into useful and useless material is itself a time-consuming exercise. Office staff can carry some, but not all, of the burden, and the qualitative as well as the quantitative change adds to the burden. The fact that members have limited research resources means that they often rely on the material they are sent by outside groups. However, those limited resources also mean that the members have difficulty in evaluating its significance.

Lobbying by groups extends beyond corresponding with members. Meetings will be sought. A good portion of material from groups is in the form of invitations, usually to presentations or receptions. MPs often accept such invitations in order to demonstrate support or to find out more. Attending such events eats into the members' time. Meeting rooms, and especially dining rooms, are booked well in advance. Most lunchtimes and evenings, the private dining rooms in the Palace of Westminster are full, with members hosting events for outside groups or constituency bodies.

Lobbying by outside groups adds considerably to the burden of parliamentarians, forcing them to establish priorities in terms of their parliamentary activities and the demands made of them. As a consequence, some activities may be abandoned. Lobbying contributes significantly to the potential of parliamentary overload.

Conclusion

Members of both Houses of Parliament are lobbied heavily by organized interests and on an ever-increasing scale. From a pluralist perspective, the activity appears to be somewhat perplexing. Parliament is essentially a body for approving legislation, not making it. Anyone seeking to change public policy should address their attention to ministers and civil servants, and not to Parliament. Parliament may use its coercive capacity to change a measure, but it is extremely rare that it does so. The House of Commons in 1986 defeated the Shops Bill (see Chapter 5) but that was an exceptional event. Members may more often use their persuasive capacity to affect outcomes. Ministers may be influenced by the arguments put before them or may feel it unwise to antagonize their backbenchers on a particular issue. Such occasions, though, are not easily quantifiable, and do not appear to be extensive. On the face of it, the impact of Parliament on legislation appears to be sporadic and minor. Furthermore, from a pluralist perspective, what influence that groups have through Parliament is not only limited but also distorted. In pure pluralist theory, groups should enjoy equality of access to the policy-making process, including to Parliament, but in practice, some groups are seen to have better access than others.

The pluralist conundrum is well summarized by Baggott (1995, p. 142):

> Although MPs can in certain circumstances have a direct impact on government policy and legislation, the scope for achieving even a modification of the government's position is fairly limited on the vast majority of issues. As long as the government has a majority its view will generally prevail on the key issues. Indeed, if the direct impact of Parliament upon legislation were the sole reason why groups lobbied MPs, it is doubtful that the scale of parliamentary lobbying would be at its present level.

It is possible that groups have misunderstood the role of Parliament, assuming it to be more powerful than it is, and being overawed by the very institution of Parliament itself, nestling in the iconic Palace of Westminster. However, there is arguably more to it than that. Here, the other approaches to power provide some useful insights.

Why do a great many groups send their newsletters and other publications to members of both Houses, and why do they hold receptions or exhibitions for the benefit of MPs and peers? Lobbying takes two basic forms. One is what is known as 'fire brigade' lobbying, in essence having to respond quickly to a piece of legislation that affects one's interests adversely. The other is essentially that of building goodwill among parliamentarians. This is long-term and it can benefit groups in two ways. One is in terms of building support among parliamentarians who may one day be ministers (or, indeed, may already be – ministers attend variously parliamentary receptions) and hence in a position to determine public policy. The other is in terms of developing, and demonstrating, such strong support in Parliament that it would be a foolhardy government that decided to legislate against the interests of the group.

The fact that ministers are drawn from, and remain within, Parliament (see Chapter 3) is important in this context. MPs may become ministers. Backbenchers mix with ministers, enjoying a proximity that is not available to most outside organizations. The head of a major company may be invited to meetings with ministers at the Department of Trade and Industry more often than a back-bench MP, but s/he is unlikely to bump into DTI ministers in the division lobby of the Commons or in the tea room and dining rooms in the Palace of Westminster. Junior ministers want to be senior ministers, and support from parliamentary colleagues may help one's reputation. Perhaps more importantly, hostility from one's parliamentary colleagues may destroy prospects of advancement. Ministers therefore have good reason to listen to backbenchers. Nor should it be forgotten that partisanship in the chamber is not necessarily replicated outside. Friendships exist across parties as well as within them; in the Lords, party is often irrelevant in terms of social relationships. Members may thus serve to convey a particular view, but one that is not necessarily on the public record nor one that has an immediate or perceptible impact on public policy.

MPs and peers thus serve to articulate the views of outside groups to government. As such, they have helped to open the process more to groups in society. From an institutional perspective, Parliament is important because of the processes that exist for views to be expressed. It provides not only the mechanisms for those views to be conveyed, but also provides a structured, and public, forum in which competing views can be pitted against one another. Groups involved on the two sides of an argument make representations to MPs and peers. The groups may not talk directly to one another, but they talk indirectly through Parliament. Both Houses provide a forum in which each side can be heard and assessed, including by government and by the media. If one side is going to be expressed, the other is likely to organize and lobby MPs and peers.

Parliament thus has an appeal, a necessary appeal, to organized groups. Its continued relevance, in terms of popular perception, is shown in the number of mass lobbies that occur. It is shown in the fact that demonstrations against particular measures are held, not outside a particular ministry, but outside Parliament. When Parliament was debating lowering the age of consent for homosexuals in 1994, gay rights organizations staged a candlelight vigil outside the Palace. In 2004, when the House of Commons was debating the Hunting Bill, the Countryside Alliance held a mass demonstration in Parliament Square. Even if MPs and peers do not act in the way the demonstrators want, Parliament is still the focus for activity and, through that attention, is the means of sending out a message to government and the wider public.

Parliament thus constitutes an important body for organized interests. It can serve to articulate their interests to government; and MPs and peers can serve as advocates, sometimes even powerful friends (or at least friends) in seeking a change to a bill going through Parliament. Groups consider it legitimate to lobby Parliament to achieve change, not necessarily seeing Parliament as the target but rather as a channel for reaching their ultimate target – the government. Their activities, and the failure of some MPs to distinguish their public duty from private gain, have undermined the standing of MPs in popular perception. Both Houses have sought to address the problem, and have necessarily done so through regulating the conduct of members rather than seeking to prevent groups making representations to members. Party may limit the capacity of MPs to determine outcomes, but it also serves as a protective shield against undue influence by special interests. By getting the processes right, Parliament can serve as the basic – and legitimate – link between organized interests (which, in many cases, are organized groups of citizens) and government.

11

Other Voices, Other Interests

We have already identified (in Chapter 8) the tasks of general and specific representation. The former is largely fulfilled by party and the latter by MPs acting individually or forming groups on particular issues to defend or promote the interests of constituents or particular elements (see Chapters 9 and 10). Specific representation is predominantly the product of the demands made of MPs by individual constituents and groups who seek action. However, only a minority of constituents ever make contact with their MP. Those groups that do make contact with parliamentarians have some degree of coherence and organization. What about those who are not organized or are unaware of the means by which to contact, or utilize the services of, Members of Parliament?

Many people in society lack an organized voice. On some issues, it may be a majority of people. An issue may suddenly arise on which the parties have no opinion, or no united opinion, and for which no other groups exist to express citizens' views. There is at least one major group – women – that lacks any clear, unified organization to speak for it.

More frequently, the unorganized voice will be that of a minority. The form and size that each minority takes will vary enormously. It may be a particular body of citizens that is definable by location, ethnic background, physical condition, or simply a shared ideology or instincts: for example, local residents may be aggrieved about a decision to site a remand hostel in the locality; citizens of Afro-Caribbean descent may feel they are being unfairly singled out for attention by the police; people who suffer from particular phobias may feel that not enough is being done to meet their needs; or pacifists may feel that government is pursuing policies at odds with their fundamental beliefs.

Taking cognizance of the views and needs of unorganized sections of society is a significant task for Parliament. We have already seen that people in the UK put particular emphasis on an MP's local role (see Chapter 9), attaching greater importance to MPs protecting the constituency, 'keeping in touch' and 'helping people' than they do to the collective roles of oversight and policy-making (Cain *et al.*, 1987, p. 38). Yet the task of pursuing the views and needs of particular unorganized sections of society is in many respects a hidden task, rarely featuring in surveys of MPs and citizens.

Recognizing and considering the views of unorganized minorities that are not just within but also extend beyond constituency boundaries have important implications for the maintenance of parliamentary legitimacy. It is possible to hypothesize that being seen to consider the interests of such groupings is likely to enhance Parliament's standing in the eyes of those comprising such groupings, and hence to build up diffuse support – what Packenham (1970) identified as latent legitimization – for the political system. A failure on the part of Parliament may undermine it, especially if it fails to express the generalized demands of the majority, but also if it ignores the particular needs of minorities.

How, then, are the views of the unorganized in society heard and acted upon by Parliament? Given that they are, by definition, not organized, how can they compete with the interests that *are* organized?

The twentieth century and into the twenty-first

For much of the twentieth century and into the twenty-first, Parliament has been a relatively closed institution to those lacking an organized voice. Indeed, unorganized opinion has suffered from similar difficulties to opinion that has been marshalled through established organized groups. Party has provided a cocoon (see Chapter 10), and party has acted as a means of aggregating and channelling opinions, but what of those interests and opinions not catered for by party programmes? For most of the twentieth century, the party stranglehold resulted largely in such views finding little or no outlet through parliamentary means.

The dominance of party has ensured that there has been little time for consideration of issues outside the context of partisan debate. It has also ensured, for most of the period up to the time of writing, members' commitment to Westminster. As was noted in Chapter 9, the first half of the twentieth century witnessed relatively little direct contact between MPs and their constituents. Members were motivated by partisan considerations and their time was occupied by activities at Westminster and by outside business and more leisurely pursuits.

There were thus few points of contact between parliamentarians and unorganized interests. By definition, the interests lacked organization, and hence a clear means of channelling their views to Parliament. Parliamentarians were essentially reactive rather than proactive in dealing with problems affecting citizens; they did not go out and solicit the views of constituents.

There were exceptions, however. Some members did voice the concerns of particular and not well-organized interests, and did so independent of party. But if the problems of particular sections of society were recognized and voiced, it was usually through the medium of party. Party could thus be useful, indeed – if it was the governing party – invaluable. But it could also be, and was, a major obstacle to allowing an outlet for other groups in society.

A good illustration is to be found in the case of disabled people, of whom there are nearly 10 million in Britain. Despite post-war decades seeing some organizations being formed to make demands on behalf of disabled people, this group was still an under-represented and ill-organized sector of society, and the problems suffered were only dimly perceived by the public and by politicians:

> Before ... 1964 disablement had simply not figured on the parliamentary agenda at all. There had been no mention of the problems of the disabled in either of the major party manifestos, and there had been no debate on disablement in the whole of the parliamentary term from 1959 to 1964. (Topliss and Gould, 1981, p. 4)

Another example is that of homosexuals. Though there were organizations such as the Homosexual Law Reform Society, founded in 1958 (see Grey, 1992), the voice of those who were gay was hardly heard in the corridors of Whitehall or Westminster. There were other groups, formed in the 1970s, campaigning for homosexual equality, and some support from bodies such as the National Council for Civil Liberties, but, as Read and Marsh (1998, p. 26) noted, 'this growth in institutional support for homosexual equality was not universal, with conservative views remaining prevalent both in society and (especially) at Westminster'. Others not well organized included – to take just a few examples – students, the homeless, retired people, the unemployed, travellers, and prisoners. For such people in society, there was a danger of seeing Parliament as having little to offer them. MPs represented parties and could use party as a cloak to protect them from having to deal with issues that did not engage the support of their party or constituents.

A growing voice

Recent years have witnessed a number of changes that have affected Parliament's capacity to heed the views and needs of those who have traditionally lacked an organized voice. The changes are disparate and have largely been chronicled in preceding chapters. They can be grouped under four headings; greater organization; greater knowledge – on the part of Parliamentarians; greater willingness, and greater opportunities.

Greater organization

Possibly the most important development in recent years affecting those who are unorganized is the fact – already chronicled in Chapter 10 – that many have ceased to be unorganized. As we have seen, there has been a remarkable growth in the number of organized groups formed in recent years, especially since 1960. In the field of disablement, for example, the 1960s and 1970s witnessed a burgeoning of groups such as the Disablement Income Group, the Central Council for the Disabled, the National Campaign for the Young Chronic Sick, the Disabled Living Foundation, and a range of other voluntary organizations geared to particular needs (see Topliss and Gould, 1981, pp. 4–5). The poverty lobby gained a powerful voice through the Child Poverty Action Group (Field, 1982, pp. 42–4). The range as well as the volume was extensive, and by the beginning of twenty-first century, the interests of the disabled were well represented. Indeed, in 2000, Parliament created a Disability Rights Commission to stop discrimination and promote equality of opportunity for disabled people.

Similarly, the period since the late 1980s has seen a remarkable growth in bodies promoting gay rights. The most prominent has been the campaign group Stonewall, formed in 1989 in reaction to the enactment of Section 28 of the Local Government Act 1988, which prohibited the 'promotion' of homosexuality by local authorities. Stonewall soon developed as a highly organized political lobbying organization, with professional staff, and was to the fore in lobbying MPs and peers in order to achieve a reduction in the age of consent for homosexual sex and the repeal of Section 28, both of which were eventually achieved. It has campaigned for gay couples to adopt children, and for civil partnerships. By 2004, it had a staff of twenty, engaged in research and education as well as lobbying, and had charitable status (www.stonewall.org.uk). Other gay rights organizations also came into being or established a greater prominence, including within each of the main political parties.

The reasons for this change have been touched on in Chapter 10. A more educated and politically confident population has become more organized in order to make demands of the political system. As groups have been formed, others with opposing interests and views have found it expedient also to organize in order to counteract their influence. They have been aided in recent years by the development of the internet, which provides a relatively cheap and effective way of communicating, not least by those who are isolated and have difficulty in meeting others face to face. There are websites, for example, for disabled people (see www.disabled-world.com). As we shall see in Chapter 12, the internet is valuable not only for communicating information about shared concerns but also for keeping abreast of developments within government and for obtaining information about Parliament and the means of making contact with MPs and peers. Consequently, the extent of the unorganized groupings in society has diminished as the organized sector has increased.

Greater knowledge

The growth of mass communications and investigative journalism has extended public and parliamentary awareness of previously neglected groups in society. The growth of 24-hour news reporting and the internet has encouraged a much greater awareness of issues that were previously little reported or not reported at all. The growth of regional television and local media has also served to extend awareness of more localized problems. Local opposition to a new airport, concern over drug use in an estate, or demands for road safety measures are all newsworthy items. If people group together to protest, this is both immediate and visual. The use of the internet has facilitated such protests. Protest marches, as with anti-war marches in 2003, can be arranged more quickly and efficiently than was the case before the introduction of the Internet. Coverage by the media of such issues, especially where the reaction of MPs may be sought, ensure that members know about them.

Greater willingness

There is a greater willingness on the part of MPs to act on behalf of constituents (see Chapter 9), and the same applies to more general constituency views and those of wider interests, for he reasons we have previously identified. MPs are more career-orientated; they want to stay in Parliament, and are less willing to call it a day and go off and pursue other interests. At the same time, there is a greater sense of insecurity on the part of MPs (see Norton, 1994c, pp. 103–21). The old class-based support cannot be taken for granted in the way it once was; to maintain support, parties have to work harder. And to maintain support locally, MPs see a need to work harder. Hence an increased responsiveness to local demands, not just those coming from individuals but also those channelled through the local media.

The problems of constituents will not necessarily be constituency-specific. The different unorganized groups mentioned in the opening paragraph are not confined to a particular town or city. They may group more extensively in some areas, in which case their potential impact may be even greater; they form a more substantial part of the local electorate than would be the case if they were spread evenly throughout the country. In some marginal constituencies they may have the potential to affect the outcome.

This greater willingness, though, is not confined to the elected House. The changes in the House of Lords that have taken place in recent decades (see Chapter 2) have resulted in a different and more active House. Peers come from a range of backgrounds, in some cases professional ones – such as the medical and caring professions – that provide them with knowledge and experience of the problems faced by certain sectors of society. The extent of this knowledge should not be exaggerated – the numbers are often small in each sector – but the willingness to contribute of those with current expertise in particular sectors has been a significant feature of the House in recent decades. Various peers in the medical profession – such as Baroness Finlay of Llandaff, a specialist in cancer and palliative care – have been especially active, for example, in raising the problems faced by those suffering from particular medical conditions.

Whereas electoral pressures may increase MPs' willingness to acknowledge the existence and needs of particular groups, the absence of electoral pressures may have the effect of allowing peers to consider the interests of minorities that might be unpopular and about which, consequently, MPs are reluctant to speak. For example, the late Lord Longford, who died in 2001, did not necessarily endear himself to the public in speaking on the issue of prisoners' rights, including those of child murderer Myra Hindley. Given the relative lack of partisanship on the part of peers, there is arguably a greater willingness on their part – compared with their counterparts in the Commons – to take up controversial social issues outside the context of party.

Greater opportunities

Even if parliamentarians are more willing to pursue such wider interests, do the opportunities to do so exist? To a limited extent, they do, and on a slightly greater scale than before. The traditional opportunities we discussed in Part I; questions, debates, and private members' legislation are the most prominent. They are used in various ways to raise the needs and concerns of unorganized groups in society. Private members' bills introduced in 2002–3, for example, covered such topics as female genital mutilation, a commissioner for older people's rights, patients' protection, sex discrimination in private clubs, and traveller law reform. In the Lords, the opportunity exists not only through questions but also through unstarred questions and the monthly balloted motions, allowing back bench peers to raise what has proved to be a large and wide range of issues. On the remaining debate days, when topics are selected by party or the cross-benchers, the opportunity may also be used to raise such issues. In March 2004, for example, on the day allocated to cross-bench debates, Lord Sutherland of Houndwood (president of Alzheimer's Scotland – Action on Dementia) initiated a debate on the needs of those suffering from Alzheimer's disease and other forms of dementia. Relevant to our foregoing discussion, he noted that it was the twenty-fifth anniversary of the foundation of the Alzheimer's Society. General debates and unstarred questions occupy between 20 per cent and 30 per cent of the time of the House (House of Lords, 2003, p. 68).

The opportunities in the Commons have been extended through the creation of the departmental select committees and, more recently, the introduction of debates in Westminster Hall. Select Committees on occasion investigate topics affecting unorganized or largely ill-organized groups. In 2002–3, for example, the Environment, Food and Rural Affairs Committee examined the role of gangmasters (people who ran gangs of people engaged in work such as cockle-picking) – the concern was not the gangmasters themselves but those who worked under them; the Trade and Industry Committee looked at the impact of direct payment on post offices and their customers; and the Transport Committee looked at overcrowding on public transport. In undertaking such enquiries, committees have not only called evidence from officials and bodies with particular responsibilities for providing the services under consideration but have on occasion in fact gone out and held hearings in the area where the problem exists.

Westminster Hall debates have added considerably to the opportunity to raise issues affecting those who are not organized. To take examples from September and October 2004, in one debate on 15 September, Julia Drown, MP for Swindon South, raised the issue of the international trafficking of women; and on 12 October 2004, the first debate covered the effect of the closure of many public telephones on those

living in rural areas, and the second was on helping those with osteo-
porosis, which affects about three million people in the UK.

The opportunities thus exist for members of both Houses to raise and
discuss the views and needs of people who are not organized, or not particularly well organized, and, as we have seen, the willingness to do so
is greater than before.

Limitations

Despite these developments, there are a number of variables that continue to militate against the interests of those who are unorganized being
heard and pursued in Parliament. Though many previously disorganized
interests have now come together and achieved a structured means of
expressing themselves, many still remain disorganized. Others – such as
the elderly, the unemployed and the young – have seen some attempt at
organization but still remain largely unorganized or poorly organized.

Unorganized groups still often go unnoticed or the full extent of their
problems goes unrecognized. There are various explanations for this,
many not particular to the United Kingdom. Some groupings may have
a culture that militates against seeking to express themselves politically
(such as Jehovah's Witnesses). Some may not feel that their needs are
such as to require a remedy through the political process (left-handers,
for example). Some may be formed of individuals with little knowledge
of the existence or location of others with the same characteristics (individuals with extraordinarily rare medical conditions, for example).
Some may not know how to get organized and may not feel that there
is much point in organizing for political purposes. Gangs of inner-
city youngsters may have some form of organization, but not one geared
to making demands of elected representatives. When the then
Environment Secretary, Michael Heseltine, visited Liverpool in the
wake of the riots there in 1981, he asked some disaffected youngsters
whether they had contacted their local councillors. The response was:
'What's a councillor?' (Norton, 1982a, p. 27).

There also remains the problem of competition. Even if parliamentarians are aware of the views of such groupings – be it a particular
minority body or more widespread public opinion – there is still the
dominant influence of party; party still dominates in terms of the political agenda. If a party takes up an issue on behalf of an unorganized sector of society, then that sector will find its concerns on the agenda.
Without that, it has to rely on one or more parliamentarians exploit-

ing the still limited opportunities. Furthermore, the competition now is arguably greater than ever before, with organized interests competing energetically for attention. We have already noted the disparity of resources between organized interests. Even if MPs and peers are keen to ensure a fair hearing for all interests, organized or not, there is still the danger of smaller or unorganized groups believing that they can never achieve the same attention as that achieved by the better-resourced groups. The observation of the representative of one small group cited in the preceding chapter – 'those like us with little money, staff and resources can't mount such a good show and tend to be overlooked' – illustrates a perception that is likely to be even stronger among those who lack any organization, and hence staff and resources, to express their interests.

This disparity may be reinforced by economic considerations. At times of economic decline or when government is keen to reduce the burden on the public purse, there is less to go round. Those who lose out as a consequence of this may find their plight is given voice by a political party but they none the less feel alienated from the political system. Those who lose out, such as the unemployed, are often the unorganized.

Conclusion

Many previously unorganized groups in society have become organized. Members of both Houses of Parliament have proved more willing and able in recent years to elicit and express the grievances and needs of unorganized sectors of society. But does this make much of a difference? From a pluralist perspective, there are grounds for scepticism. In his study of the Brazilian congress, Packenham (1970) found that the congress had little decision-making power, so it made 'little sense for interest-group representatives to present their demands to congressmen and to try to have political conflicts resolved in congress'. Parliament, as with the Brazilian congress, is not a decision-making body. In order to affect outcomes, the focus of group activity should be, and is (principally if not exclusively) ministers and officials. From this perspective, devoting resources to lobbying Parliament is inefficient and likely to be ineffective.

Parliament none the less does have a utility. On occasion, it can serve to resolve particular conflicts in society. There are some issues that government is reluctant to address, and it hands over the decision to Parliament. There is thus a relevance for those affected by the issue to organize themselves and to lobby Parliament. The issue of the age of consent has been one such issue; and others in recent years have included stem cell research and euthanasia. The House of Lords has proved to be a particular forum for debating the merits and demerits of allowing terminally ill people who wish to do so to receive medical help to die. (Lord Joffe in 2003 introduced the Patient (Assisted Dying) Bill and returned to the issue in 2004 with the Assisted Dying for the Terminally Ill Bill.) Even if Parliament is not making the decision, it can ensure that ministers hear the case for those who have previously not been heard. MPs and peers, as we have seen, have the facility to seek to influence the policy-makers. Parliament is a way of reaching government. Through Parliament, different parts of society can be heard by government.

The institutional view of power offers a further perspective on the utility of Parliament. By raising the needs and concerns of those in society who are not organized, or not well organized, parliamentarians serve as an important safety valve, interest articulators and legitimizers. Those previously ignored have acquired, to some degree, an authoritative outlet for their views. Parliament can ensure that the interests of different 'publics' are articulated and heard by decision-makers. The more parliamentarians engage in such activities, the more they legitimize Parliament in the eyes of those who may previously have felt alienated from the political system.

Furthermore, by listening to the different groups, Parliament may enhance its own legitimacy as an arbiter between them. Ian Marsh's study of pressure groups involved in giving evidence to select committees in the 1981–2 session found that 70 per cent regarded the select committee process as fairer than departmental procedures, and more than 40 per cent regarded MPs as more legitimate arbitrators of an issue than departmental officers (Marsh, 1986, pp. 173–4). This study was of organized interests but it is suggestive of what Parliament may be able to achieve beyond those groups. The more that previously excluded sectors of society are brought into this process, the greater the capacity for Parliament to help lessen and possibly even resolve conflict.

Perhaps the most noteworthy aspect, from an institutional perspective, is the extent to which Parliament still serves as a focus for group activity. Previously ill-organized or unorganized sections of society get organized and direct their activity towards the Palace of Westminster. Mass lobbies are arranged, letters are written and briefing material sent. Stonewall, for example, has devoted considerable resources to lobbying Parliament, meeting sympathetic MPs and peers, and providing briefings for parliamentarians when issues such as gay adoption and civil partnerships are before the House. Though it seeks to influence government, it none the less recognizes the need to ensure that parliamentarians are supportive of what it seeks to achieve. Parliament remains an important forum in which different views are pitted against one another; when issues affecting gay rights are before Parliament, MPs and peers will receive briefing material from the Christian right, in the form of the Christian Institute, and from gay rights groups such as Stonewall. When Lord Joffe's bill on assisted dying was introduced in 2003, many people affected by the bill – on both sides of the argument – wrote to peers arguing their case. When demonstrations are held, the focus is usually on Parliament. Demonstrators may march down Whitehall but they also march past the Palace of Westminster and often congregate in Parliament Square.

Parliament has gone further than before in being able to identify and raise the views and needs of unorganized groups. By voicing their concerns and demands, members of both Houses can ensure some government response. None the less, major problems remain. In terms of the linkage between Parliament and citizen so far considered, this remains the weakest. Party remains a conduit for expressing the demands of different sectors, but unorganized interests that are not accommodated by party remain at a disadvantage in seeking to have some input in the political process. There are also structural problems. If people come together to organize a petition, then – as we have seen in Chapter 9 – that petition goes into a parliamentary black hole. Not all groups that have come into being in recent decades necessarily recognize the utility of Parliament. Some, such as a number of environmental protest groups, or the radical gay rights group, Outrage, prefer direct action. Environmental protestors have tied themselves to trees to block development; members of Outrage, led by gay rights campaigner, Peter Tatchell, have disrupted religious ceremonies. Many groups in society remain unorganized and largely unheard. For example, many people in Britain suffer from acrophobia – an extreme fear of heights – and can be affected by such things as the design of public buildings (if, for example, they have open walkways, exposed stairs and escalators). However, government has no figures on how many people are affected by acrophobia, and the issue has hardly ever been raised in Parliament. Unorganized or previously unorganized groups also remain at a disadvantage compared with those who are organized and able to express their demands directly, frequently and extensively in both Houses.

Disparities thus remain. However, they are less pronounced than before. Parliament has, if anything, increased in relevance, enabling previously unheard voices to be heard within the political process. MPs and peers sometimes complain when there are mass lobbies, or when demonstrators gather outside Parliament, displaying banners and chanting. Though their activities may upset members, the institution of Parliament would be in a parlous state if they neglected the institution altogether.

12

Reaching the Public

Individual citizens, and a vast array of groups in society, both organized and unorganized, make demands of Members of Parliament. MPs raise the concerns of constituents, groups and different sections of the public in Parliament, and can ensure that the government takes note. The flow of communication in this relationship is essentially from those outside Parliament to those inside; but what about the communication from Parliament to those outside?

One of the functions ascribed to Parliament by Walter Bagehot (1867) was that of 'teaching' – 'to teach the nation what it does not know' (see Chapter 1). A century later, Samuel Beer identified the potential of legislators to mobilize popular support for policies. He had in mind policies approved by Parliament that imposed often complex requirements on citizens. Such policies, he contended, were numerous and a consequence of having a welfare state and a managed economy:

> A great deal is expected of the citizen in the form of new necessities that oblige him to conform his behaviour to the complex requirements of economic and social policy ... To win both the mind and the heart of the citizen to an acceptance of these coercions is a major necessity, but a severe problem. (Beer, 1966)

If the policies were explained to citizens, then support would more be likely to be forthcoming, thus facilitating the desired effect. However, Beer argued, the potential was not one that had been fulfilled by the British Parliament.

To what extent, then, does Parliament in the twenty-first century educate and raise support for measures to which it has given its approval? Are citizens better-informed and more supportive of policies as a result of the activities of parliamentarians?

Lack of contact

The developments of the nineteenth century have resulted in party domination of Parliament and an increase in both the volume and complexity of legislation. As was shown in Chapter 2, Parliament failed to keep
pace with these developments. Successive governments were prepared
to use their party majorities to prevent detailed and critical scrutiny by
Parliament. They were prepared to rely on the mandate of a general
election victory and the resulting party majority as sufficient to legitimize their measures.

The consequence was a Parliament that was able and prepared to
debate policy on a partisan basis but denied the resources (and largely
lacking the political will) to subject that policy to informed and detailed
scrutiny. Lacking information about the detail and the case for particular provisions of the bills they were approving, Members of Parliament
were in no position to mobilize popular support for those provisions.

The position was exacerbated in post-war decades, with the realization of the 'closed' institution outlined in Chapter 10. Legislation
became more specific and reached more than ever before into the economic and social lives of the citizenry. Far from being in a position to
inform and mobilize support among citizens, parliamentarians appeared
increasingly to have little scope for action independent of assenting to
what government placed before them. MPs and peers were generalists
struggling to cope with a mass of highly detailed legislation. They had
no mechanism for specialized enquiry. Their inability to engage in
independent action appeared to lessen interest in their activities and
hence their capacity to influence those affected by the measures they
were approving.

During the 1950s and 1960s, there was little opportunity for individuals to find out what Parliament was doing. Continuous daily
reporting of Parliament was confined to the serious press. Television
and radio coverage was limited, and the BBC had a self-imposed rule
prohibiting the broadcasting of any statement or discussion on matters
to be debated in Parliament within a period of fourteen days. The 'four-
teen-day rule' was not removed until 1957. For those interested in
knowing what was being said throughout an entire debate, it was a case
either of sitting in the public gallery or consulting *Hansard,* the official
report of proceedings. Sales of *Hansard* of both Commons and Lords
were small.

For individuals, there was little incentive to find out what was being
said in debate. For pressure groups and all bodies affected by legisla-

tion, there was some reason to follow what was going on, but attempts to do so do not appear to have been extensive. Occasions when either House debated matters of interest to a particular group would, in any event, be few and far between.

Individuals and groups were thus faced with an institution that was essentially enveloped by party and which appeared to offer little of relevance to them (see Chapters 10 and 11). Parliamentarians had limited contact with constituents (see Chapter 9) and what they said in the chamber had a very small audience. The communication from members of the two Houses to the outside world could thus be described as extremely muted, making little contribution to understanding on the part of individuals and organizations.

This was the position recognized and sketched by Samuel Beer in 1966, but it was to change soon after his words were published.

Developing links

In his analysis of Parliament, Beer contended that there were two obstacles that clearly stood in the way of Parliament being able to mobilize support in the period between general elections. One was secrecy, both in government and in Parliament itself. The other was the lack of specialized committees for investigating what government was doing: 'If the public is to be given a greater sense of participation, not only must secrecy be reduced, but MPs must be given better instruments for understanding, explaining, and – inevitably – criticizing what the government is doing' (Beer, 1966). Both obstacles have been tackled. If they have not been removed totally, they have at least been substantially eroded. They have been supplemented by another fundamental change that has constituted a further instrument for communicating with citizens: the growth of the internet.

More openness

Parliament itself has moved towards greater openness in its proceedings. There is long-standing openness in terms of voting behaviour, and division lists are published the day following the vote. Both Houses retain absolute power to determine whether proceedings should be open or closed to the public. The public are granted access to watch the proceedings in each chamber unless the House votes to go into secret session, as occasionally happened during the Second World War. In the

Commons, select committees often sat in public in the nineteenth and early twentieth centuries. However, private sittings became the norm after the Second World War. This only changed in the latter half of the 1960s. Today, public sessions for evidence-taking are the norm among the departmental select committees.

Exceptionally, a departmental select committee will go into closed session, the most obvious example being the Defence Committee when hearing sensitive details affecting national security. (The published proceedings appear with the sensitive information 'sidelined' – that is, omitted.) Some of the domestic committees, such as the Privileges Committee, used to hold closed meetings, but generally no longer do so. Meetings of standing committees are open to the public unless the committee votes otherwise. Consequently, the position now is one where closed committee hearings are rare.

However, meeting in public session is necessary but not sufficient to ensure that parliamentary activities are widely known about. Media coverage was limited, but this changed dramatically in the 1980s, with the admission of television cameras to the chamber and the committee rooms of both Houses.

An early attempt by the BBC in the 1920s to be allowed to broadcast special occasions in Parliament came to nothing (Griffith and Ryle, 1989, p. 81). Little then happened until 1966, when a select committee in the Commons recommended a closed-circuit experiment, on the basis of which the House could decide whether limited public broadcasting should be permitted. The recommendation was defeated by 131 votes to 130. The House of Lords was less reticent and passed a motion declaring that it 'would welcome the televising of some of its proceedings for an experimental period as an additional means of demonstrating its usefulness in giving a lead to public opinion'. The reason given reveals sensitivity to Bagehot's teaching function. The experiment duly took place, in 1968, but was not pursued, partly for technical reasons, partly because of the expense, and partly because the Lords did not wish to be out of line with the practice of the Commons (Wheeler-Booth, 1989, pp. 511–12).

In 1975, the Commons approved an experiment in sound broadcasting and, following the experiment, both Houses approved the principle of proceedings being broadcast on radio. The decision was taken in principle in 1976, and sound broadcasting began in both Houses in April 1978.

Pressure for proceedings to be televised continued. In 1983, the Lords voted to endorse its earlier decision of 1966 and take steps to implement it. An experiment began in 1985 and it was agreed in 1986 that broadcasting be made permanent. The Commons, as in 1966, was more reticent. In 1985, the House voted by 275 to 263 against the idea. Three years later, by 318 votes to 264, it reached a different conclusion, approving in principle the conducting of an experiment in television broadcasting. After some delay, the cameras eventually started transmitting proceedings on 21 November 1989. The following year, the House agreed that broadcasting was to be made a permanent feature.

During the period of broadcasting solely from the Lords, coverage of the Upper House was more extensive – and more popular – than had generally been expected by either broadcasters or parliamentarians. The same proved true initially of Commons coverage from November 1989 onwards, though the extent of coverage declined after the first decade or so of broadcasting. At the time of writing, parliamentary proceedings are broadcast on the Parliament Channel, enabling viewers to follow proceedings live in the Commons and to see the recorded broadcasts of proceedings in the Lords. But as we shall see, broadcasting is not confined to the chambers.

Both Houses have also proved more willing to give access to the media in order to report proceedings and to provide interviews with both MPs and peers. Broadcasting companies have their Westminster headquarters at 4 Millbank, just across the road from the Palace of Westminster. In 2000, the Commission to Strengthen Parliament, established by Conservative leader William Hague and chaired by this author, advocated that instead of parliamentarians having to troop over to 4 Millbank, greater efforts should be made to get 4 Millbank into the Palace of Westminster. To some degree, this has happened, with a relaxation of the restrictions on where the media can broadcast from within the Palace. Permission was given for filming in an alcove off the Central Lobby. Now, reporters can broadcast from Central Lobby – an attractive venue because of its convenience for parliamentarians and because of the backdrop for the cameras. The extent to which Parliament is relevant to the broadcast media is reflected in the number of parliamentary passes held by representatives of the broadcasting companies. In October 2004, 111 security passes were held by people employed by or contracted to the BBC, and 78 passes were held by representatives of other broadcasting organizations (Lords *Hansard,* 14 October 2004, *WA 65*). Parliament now attracts the media in a way that it did not do, and could not do, a quarter of a century before.

Specialization

By the end of the twentieth century, Parliament was a far more open institution than at any time in its history. It was also a far more specialized institution. The most significant change occurred, as we have seen already, in 1979, with the creation of the departmental select committees. This specialization has had two consequences. One has been to render government more open, and the other has been to provide a more precise and extensive link between Parliament and outside groups.

By taking evidence from ministers and civil servants, the departmental select committees have elicited information that otherwise would not be on the public record. The committees (see Chapter 6), have proved to be prolific in taking evidence and producing reports. During the lifetime of a Parliament, the committees will usually interview at least 200 ministers and more than 1,000 civil servants (see Norton, 1991b, p. 73). The committees have become more experienced at questioning witnesses and teasing details from them.

Obtaining such information benefits the committees: they are better informed than they would otherwise be. By virtue of each committee's concentration on a particular sector, and by each acquiring information and issuing reports, usually with recommendations for particular action, committee activity has also attracted the attention of a wide array of interested organizations. The creation of the committees has provided groups with a clear parliamentary target for lobbying activities (see Chapter 10). Groups lobby committees to investigate a particular topic. They submit evidence when enquiries are undertaken. Of more than 250 groups surveyed in 1986, two-thirds had presented written evidence to a Common's select committee or a joint committee of both Houses (Rush, 1990, p. 283).

Select committees, then, have acted as magnets for such groups. However, groups are not simply providers of inputs to committees. They are also consumers of the outputs. Representatives of organized interests are frequently present during committee hearings. They will be avid readers of committee reports in order to find out what impact their evidence has had. One survey of more than a hundred groups giving oral evidence to committees in the early 1980s found that virtually all of them had obtained the committee findings (Marsh, 1986, p. 171). Through their reports, committees thus reach an important audience. The televising of proceedings reaches both the general public and, to some extent, outside groups (just over two-thirds of groups questioned in 1986 used television as one means of keeping in touch with what goes on in Parliament), whereas select committee reports reach essentially the outside groups.

The House of Lords, as we have seen, has given a lead in terms of greater openness; it has also now developed its use of specialized committees. As we have seen, the number has expanded notably in recent years (see Chapter 6). As with reports from Commons committees, reports from Lords committees also serve to engage with affected sections of the public; the Constitution Committee's inquiry into economic regulators in 2004, for example – the first major inquiry into the subject – engaged with a wide range of regulatory bodies (Constitution Committee, 2004a). Some of the *ad hoc* committees established by the House, such as that discussing the 1994 Chinook helicopter crash on the Mull of Kintyre that killed leading security experts, have also attracted media attention; the committee was appointed in 2001 and reported the following year. The importance of the output side of committee work has also been recognized by both Houses, with the appointment of staff responsible for arranging the publication date of reports and press releases. Press conferences are arranged to launch the publication of the more significant reports.

Use of the internet

The development of the internet has also facilitated communication between Parliament and the public. This has been at both collective and the individual levels.

At the collective level, Parliament has introduced its own website (www.parliament.uk). It has been expanded and redesigned since its inception, a new design being introduced in 2002. It embodies a mass of data and provides access to *Hansard* as well as to committee reports and proceedings. The Commons site alone hosts over 9,000 pages and over a million pages of linked publications (Modernisation Committee, 2004, p. 17). The transcripts of committee hearings are now put on the website shortly after the hearings take place. Bills before Parliament, as well as explanatory notes to them, are available on the site. There is also a large volume of information about Parliament and its work, and data on members and details of how to contact them. Anyone with internet access can now examine material immediately in a way that previously was either impossible or very time-consuming – and expensive. Committee reports, which in paper form may cost £20 or £30 each, and sometimes considerably more – the three volumes of the Lords Constitution Committee's report on the regulatory state in 2004, for example, cost £70.50 – can be accessed at no charge on the website. The same applies to copies of *Hansard;* the weekly edition of the Commons *Hansard* in 2004 cost £12 and the daily edition £5. The internet has thus enabled Parliament to put a great deal of information in the public domain in a more accessible manner than ever before. The Modernisation Committee noted in May 2004 that, since the redesign of the website, there had been over 2.5 million page requests on the main server, and over 5 million hits from 300,000 users on the publications server in the month of January 2004 (Modernisation Committee, 2004, p. 17).

The internet has also made possible greater access to committee proceedings. Meetings are televised on a selective basis – only a limited number of committee rooms are equipped for television coverage – but all chamber and committee proceedings are now webcast, so anyone wanting to listen to proceedings can do so via the internet. The webcasting began on an experimental basis in January 2002 and was made permanent in October 2003 (Parry, 2004, p. 2). The website www.parliamentlive.uk carries audio-visual coverage of both chambers, and of sittings in Westminster Hall and of some committees. All committee proceedings are available in audio format. During the first year of the experimental period of webcasting, more than 200,000 visits to the site were recorded and, in the run-up to the war in Iraq, up to 600 users were logged on at any one time (House of Commons Commission, 2003, p. 38).

Some committees also use the internet not only for dissemination of their evidence and reports but also for consultation. The use of online forums has been developed especially in respect of pre-legislative scrutiny. The Joint Committee on the Draft Communications Bill in the 2001–2 session, for example, employed an online forum and reported:

> Of the 80 online forum participants who returned the evaluation survey, over a quarter had watched the webcasts of our evidence session and 13 had watched on BBC Parliament (about the same proportion as had attended a hearing in person). Taken as a whole, we feel the innovative features of our inquiry such as the online forum have enhanced the openness of our deliberations. We are particularly pleased that nearly 400 people registered for the forum. (Joint Committee on the Draft Communications Bill, 2002; annex 5)

There have also been online consultations on family tax credit, electronic democracy, the Constitutional Reform Bill, and hate crimes in Northern Ireland. The Modernisation Committee also commissioned an online consultation for its inquiry into connecting Parliament and the public. Online consultations have also been employed by the Parliamentary Office of Science and Technology, on flood management, and by the all-party group on domestic violence, the latter encouraging input from people who otherwise might not have been able or willing to contribute to a parliamentary inquiry. Professor Stephen Coleman of the Oxford Internet Institute told the Modernisation Committee:

> On-line consultations are something that you [Parliament] have in fact pioneered, and have done better than any other parliament in the world. There is quite a lot of data suggesting that these consultations have had an effect on the fairly small minority of people who have engaged in them – because they have been deliberative, because they have been expansive over a period of a month, and because you have taken people seriously. (Modernisation Committee, 2004, pp. 20–1)

The internet has thus opened Parliament to a much wider audience than previously existed. Professor Coleman pointed out to the Modernisation Committee that more people now visit Parliament virtually than physically. The Committee also received evidence that more people access *Hansard* online than receive the printed edition. Peter Riddell of *The Times* told the MPs that the internet was now the principal means by which Parliament as an institution communicates with voters, significantly reducing the importance of press reporting of Parliament (Modernisation Committee, 2004, p. 16).

At the individual level, MPs are also making great use of the internet to communicate with citizens: in 2004, 560 MPs had e-mail addresses listed on the Parliament website, and 430 MPs had their own websites, though at the time of the research nineteen of them were not working. Research undertaken at the University of Hull revealed that, of the MPs with working websites, 97 per cent provided the means by which they could be contacted; 28 per cent provided the opportunity for constituents to receive electronic bulletins – most of these (18 per cent) being party bulletins or a mix of the party's and the MP's bulletins; and 10 per cent offered their own individual bulletins. Some MPs are also developing their own weblogs (known as 'blogs') – in effect, daily or regular electronic postings (see Ferguson and Howell, 2004). The first to do so was Tom Watson, MP for West Bromwich East, who started weblogging in 2003 (www.tomwatson.co.uk). Weblogs can enable citizens to respond to the MP. As one MP noted, 'They are a platform for an MP's views, and they allow for feedback from readers, of a sort you don't get anywhere else' (Ferguson, and Howell 2004, p. 5).

The internet has thus provided the means for Parliament and for MPs individually to reach citizens in a way that was not previously possible, and for a greater degree of interaction than was possible before. Parliament is now more open to citizens than it has ever been in its long history.

Consequences

Since the time that Beer was writing, in the 1960s, both Houses have thus moved to dismantle the obstacles he identified, to achieve the capacity to mobilize support for measures of public policy. But have greater openness, specialization and the use of new technologies served as teachers and mobilizers of popular support?

The positive impact

The effect of a more open Parliament, particularly through the medium of television and the internet, would appear to be a more informed public. The reaction to televised proceedings has generally been positive (Negrine, 1998, p. 69). Televised proceedings, which mean essentially televised extracts, reach a large audience, especially through news and regional programmes. Once televising began, dedicated programmes attracted audiences of between 200,000 and over 1 million (Select Committee on the Televising of Proceedings of the House, 1990, p. xxix). Not surprisingly, coverage of the chamber increased significantly compared with the period before 1989. Negrine compared coverage in 1996 with that of 1986. The number of items, including audio or audio-visual material from the chamber, increased by 188 per cent, and within these items the total number of seconds recorded in the chamber increased by 127 per cent: 'The percentages indicate a dramatic increase in the time for which politicians are seen in the chamber and illustrate the importance of the introduction of television cameras for news producers' (Negrine, 1998, p. 79). The use of the internet has also facilitated Parliament reaching a wide audience and, unlike television coverage, has provided the means for more direct contact between MPs and citizens; it has also provided the means for some interaction between committees and citizens, and between individual MPs and citizens.

Contact between members and constituents is growing rapidly (see Chapter 9). MPs are more likely than before to exploit the local media, not least because there are more local media than before. The internet now provides the means for more direct, in effect unmediated, contact between MP and constituents. E-bulletins can be sent at regular intervals to those requesting them. Weblogging provides a means for constituents to provide feedback to MPs' comments.

As we saw in Chapter 10, contact between individual backbenchers – in both Houses – and organized groups is also more extensive than before. The contact is two way. Of the groups surveyed by the Study of Parliament Group in 1986, over half (56 per cent) relied on direct contact with back bench MPs as one means of keeping in touch with what is going on in Parliament. Almost 45 per cent used contact with back bench peers (Rush, 1990, p. 292). Groups now have the means of utilizing the internet to access reports and proceedings and, indeed, to keep track of proceedings and forthcoming business. The internet has been a boon for those responsible for monitoring parliamentary proceedings, providing not only immediate access but also the capacity to track down specific material through search engines.

The effect of greater specialization also appears to have produced more attentive groups, learning from the process and the substance of committee work. The most extensive data on such effects were gathered by Ian Marsh from groups that gave oral evidence to committees in the 1981–2 session. Of the groups, just over half reported positive 'learning' of some kind and/or forming new links to other groups (Marsh, 1986, p. 169). Forty-one per cent received extra information about the issue, or government or department attitudes. Virtually all, as we have already noted, got copies of the committees' findings; most then reported to their members on their participation in the enquiry (Marsh, 1986, p. 171). In terms of the impact of the enquiry process on the attitudes and judgements of the groups, 55 per cent reported 'important' or 'very important' alterations of attitude (Marsh, 1986, p. 173). Most were also stimulated to undertake fresh research.

Similarly, among the unorganized public, members are playing a greater – though not such an extensive – role. By utilizing local media and the internet, MPs inform as well as learn. The greater the number of MPs – and, indeed, select committees – utilising the internet to connect with the public, the more they may benefit in terms of information and in building links between citizens and Parliament. The internet has facilitated contact that might otherwise have proved impossible. We have already referred to the online consultation on domestic violence in 2000. Nearly 1,000 messages of evidence were received from women survivors of domestic violence, some of whom were 'voices largely unheard by hon. Members, including Irish women travellers and Bangladeshi women' (Commons *Hansard,* 6 November 2001, col. 108). The potential value to MPs of such contact was emphasized by Graham Allen, MP:

> The more voices that are allowed to be heard, the more likely we are to get the ideas to make good legislation even better. Many of the legislative disasters that Governments have imposed on Parliament ... could probably have been avoided. To refer to my own experience, I led for my party in opposition on the Child Support Act 1991, which had to be re-written about five times. I have no doubt that had we had a sensible process of pre-legislative scrutiny – either online or offline – and had we listened to the practitioners and to those whom it affected, we would have been able to make that law far better, far earlier. (Commons *Hansard,* 6 January 2004, col. 3WH)

Allen's comments bring together two recent developments – pre-legislative scrutiny and online consultation – in a manner that demonstrates the capacity of Parliament to have a greater influence on legislation. The forum in which he was speaking – Westminster Hall – also emphasizes the utility of another recent innovation.

The greater the capacity Parliament has to reach people, then the greater the capacity it has to inform and educate. The capacity of Parliament to hear the views of those outside may also help in the legislative process and in bringing issues on to the political agenda. The more groups and individuals are involved, the greater the likelihood of them being supportive of the resulting legislation and of the parliamentary process. In combination, then, this increase in contact between parliamentarians and those outside Westminster provides a greater capacity for teaching and for mobilizing the support of the public for particular measures of public policy. What evidence we have suggests that, to a small extent, that capacity is being realized.

Limitations

The capacity of parliamentarians to teach and to mobilize is none the less limited. Coverage of proceedings in news broadcasts and other programmes is in the form of extracts rather than an extended coverage or continuous feed. Coverage of a large part of a debate is exceptionally rare. There is a particular concentration on Prime Minister's Question Time, which may generate heat but very little light. Hence opportunities for increasing knowledge on the substance of issues are limited. Viewers may gain some understanding of Parliament, but increased knowledge of particular issues will tend to be confined to major issues that are already the focus of public discussion.

Negrine has also drawn attention to the focus on the chamber. Televising proceedings has resulted in coverage of the chamber to the detriment of other locations:

> This greater attention to the institutional political arena provides the audience with a visual taste of the world inhabited by the politician, but it could also be argued that it offers a restricted register of workplaces. Other institutional locations are neglected – committees, departments, overseas, and so on. It is arguable, therefore, whether this concentration on the chamber is a positive thing. (Negrine, 1998, p. 82)

The Modernisation Committee has also reported 'widespread dissatisfaction' with the website. Professor Coleman told the Committee that the website worked for those who knew exactly what they were looking for, but not for the majority of people. He did not think the website could be said to be performing a democratic function unless it was able to reach people 'who cannot find what they might need but they do not even know is there' (Modernisation Committee, 2004, p. 18). The Commons Information Committee also noted problems with e-mails. It noted that MPs considered e-mails both an opportunity and a threat, fearing that such communication might generate demands they could not meet, and e-mail could add to paper mail rather than be a substitute for it. There was particular concern that interest groups would utilize e-mail addresses for mass campaigns. As the committee noted, some members therefore declined to publish their e-mail address. The committee cautioned against this approach:

> Our view is that the demand for Members to adapt to e-mail and other communication technologies is great that a more pro-active strategy is required. The reputation of Members – and of the House – could be damaged by a refusal to embrace such technologies at a time when they are becoming standard in most other organisations. (Information Committee, 2002, p. 9)

The Hansard Society used a citizen jury to monitor some political blogs. Though jurors tended to like the presentation, they were not impressed with the content. Although they were optimistic about the capacity of blogs to enhance political participation, the vast majority said they would not return to the blog they were monitoring. 'More worryingly still, not a single juror felt that his or her political participation and awareness had been enhanced by the blogs' (Ferguson and Howell, 2004, p. 2).

The capacity to educate and mobilize support among particular groups is also limited. The bi-partisanship of select committees is a strength but also a weakness, as it discourages committees from addressing some central issues that are the subject of party conflict. Of the impact that committee reports have on group attitudes, most of those identified by Marsh took the form of clarifying attitudes. Less than one in five mentioned developing attitudes towards other issues as an important or very important outcome (Marsh, 1986, p. 172). Marsh noted that his findings 'suggest substantive bases for mobilizing consent' (Marsh, 1986, p. 178). However, he then immediately conceded that 'the process is clearly in an elemental stage. It can be observed in embryo, so to speak ... Further deliberate leadership from committees – further effort deliberately aimed at interest groups – is required for a forthright judgement about committee potential' (Marsh, 1986, pp. 178, 179).

Though contact between committees and groups, and between individual members and constituents, has increased, and members have displayed a relatively greater willingness to act independently of their party leaders, party none the less continues to act as the principal barrier to mobilizing support behind a particular policy. Where there is cross-party agreement, the potential is considerable. Where the parties take opposing stances, the opportunity to inform and mobilize support behind particular provisions is limited. As we saw in Chapter 5, the partisan conflict in standing committees results in much of the detail being neglected in favour of argument over the contentious clauses. Individual members often find it difficult to avoid giving their communications with constituents – particularly speeches and press articles – a partisan slant, but once this practice has been recognized, constituents tend to discount it accordingly.

The capacity for parliamentarians to educate and, more particularly, to mobilize support for particular provisions of public policy thus remains restricted. For members of either House to engage in a teaching role, they have first to be informed on the issue and be prepared to communicate with individuals, groups and less organized sections of the public to inform them. Limited time and resources restricts the opportunity to obtain the information. Partisanship also acts as a barrier to both obtaining and disseminating information, and more particularly to offering a united front to the public.

Conclusion

In recent decades, both Houses of Parliament have acquired a greater potential to educate the public, and particular groups, and to mobilize support for specific provisions of public policy. Relative to past practice, both Houses are more open than before and, indeed, more open than some other legislatures. Both Houses have utilized new media of communication to reach the public. There is much greater contact between parliamentarians and those outside Westminster – individuals, organized groups and the unorganized public.

From a pluralist perspective, there are clearly significant limitations. The affect of such communication between Parliament and people on policy outcomes is limited. Party principally dictates what happens. Most people who see parliamentary proceedings on television are essentially passive recipients. They have not actively sought to watch or listen to what is happening in Parliament, and are not likely to be influenced to take any particular action as a result.

However, from an institutional perspective, channels of communication are expanding and being embedded in the political system. The number of people seeking information from and about Parliament has increased significantly. Educating citizens is sometimes achieved by Parliament, and on occasion – primarily where there is cross-party agreement – members are able to assist in mobilizing popular support behind a particular policy. The development of such channels has the capacity to strengthen the linkage between Parliament and people. Partisanship, though, continues to limit what the institution can achieve and the means for informing people are not as fully exploited as they could be. The opportunity exists to engage in a more extensive dialogue with the public; it is an opportunity that both Houses, as well as individual members, have started to exploit, but it is an opportunity not yet fully realized.

13

Conclusion: Parliament – The Power and the Future

Writing in the 1970s, Peter Self concluded an article on whether Britain was worse governed than before, with the words: 'This article hardly mentions Parliament. I suggest the reader asks himself why' (Self, 1977). The (male) reader was clearly expected to come up with one particular answer. However, there were two answers that the discerning reader might supply.

Perceptions of decline

One – the expected one – is that Parliament is not a central actor in the determination of public policy. That perception has persisted. If anything, Parliament is seen in the twenty-first century as being more marginal than ever before. Parties have, in many respects, tightened their grip. Central control of candidate nomination has been extended (Commission to Strengthen Parliament, 2000, p. 12). As we have seen (in Chapter 7), the core function of Parliament – that of giving assent to measures of public policy – has in some areas been transferred to other bodies (the institutions of the EU and the Scottish Parliament). The courts have acquired the capacity to strike down provisions of Acts of Parliament as being contrary to EU law. Under the Human Rights Act 1998, the courts can certify that legislative enactments are incompatible with the European Convention on Human Rights. The policy-making power that remains with British government has been concentrated in Downing Street, under a prime minister who has distanced himself more from Westminster than any of his predecessors. The neglect of Parliament by Tony Blair is in many respects a continuation of a trend, discernible since the period of the 1867 Reform Act:

> Prime ministerial activity in the Commons has decreased overall and narrowed down to a few forms of participation, especially the now highly for-

malised and very brief prime minister's question time … These results establish unequivocally that the direct parliamentary accountability of the prime minister has fallen sharply over the whole period since 1868, and that this change has accelerated in the last decade and a half. (Dunleavy and Jones, 1995, pp. 295–6)

The neglect has been pronounced under Blair, who has the worst record of attendance of any modern prime ministers (Rose, 2001, pp. 134–5; Tyrie, 2000). Blair, according to Richard Rose, 'appears to be heading for a new record in distancing Downing Street from the Palace of Westminster only a few hundred feet away. Ministers appear to have followed suit' (Rose, 2001, p. 139). Blair displays no great interest in Parliament or strengthening Parliament in fulfilling its tasks. When the House of Commons debated the report of the Commission to Strengthen Parliament in 2000, the prime minister claimed that the issues it covered were 'good issues for academics and constitutional experts' but were not the 'big issues' that Parliament should be debating (Commons *Hansard*, 13 July 2000, col. 1098). He has shown a remarkable degree of detachment both from Parliament and from his own government, exacerbating perceptions of a presidential form of government (Norton, 2003b, pp. 547–52).

The consequences of these developments have been summarized by Labour MP Graham Allen:

Traditionally, electors have voted on the party label but they now increasingly vote on the personality of the leading Prime Ministerial candidates. Legislators evolved into rubber stamps for Executive laws and now have become mere appendages at their own elections, being grateful for the pre-election photo opportunity with the Presidential candidate every four years. What further humiliation is needed to sting MPs into action? (Allen, 2001, pp. 12).

The patronage available to the prime minister, according to Allen, has confirmed the House of Commons as 'the House of Government' – 'hardly conducive to producing a Parliament with an alternative view which can serve as a serious basis for negotiation and exchange with the Executive' (Allen, 2001, p. 13) – and the unelected nature of the second chamber maintains electoral legitimacy for the Commons and, hence, for the executive. He produces what amounts to the pluralist conclusion to Self's question:

These developments over many centuries, the product not of conspiracy but of events, [have] led to where we are today – 'The Lost World' of Western democratic evolution. Viewed in economic terms the British political system can be characterised as a political monopoly – all power controlled by one player, the UK Executive. (Allen, 2001, p. 14)

To the pluralist, Parliament makes little or no difference to the outcome of issues once on the political agenda. Measures placed before Parliament emerge largely or wholly in the form that the government wants. Parliament engages in the 'daily theatre of Parliamentary politics' (Allen, 2001, p. 1). MPs sit in Parliament because of ambition: they want power, which in this case means ministerial office (Paxman, 2002, pp. 43–4). For those denied office, it is a case of going through the motions. The view of Richardson and Jordan, that the significance of Parliament is its very insignificance appears, if anything, to be confirmed.

The wider picture

There is, however, a second response to Self's question, namely that, even within a pluralist framework, this view of Parliament is partial and that, by adopting a pluralist perspective, it is unduly narrow.

Philip Cowley notes that there is a perception of Parliament having been marginalized under the Labour government under Blair, adding: 'Yet it was ever thus':

> The first problem with most of the criticisms made of Parliament under Labour is not that they are wrong – because they are not – but that they pretend to be describing something that is new. Lamenting the decline of parliament was a popular sport throughout the twentieth century. (Cowley, 2002b, p. 123)

The criticisms follow those of Lowell (1896) and Bryce (1924) (see Chapter 1). Examples are scattered throughout the twentieth century (see Norton, 1981, pp. 201–4). As Cowley notes, government defeats in Parliament may have been rare, but they basically always have been; defeats were not that frequent in the nineteenth century – the number of government defeats in the seven-year period from 1972 to 1979 was comparable with the number from 1863 to 1869 (Norton, 1980, p. 42). Both periods were exceptional. Prime ministers have neglected Parliament before. Governments have normally been able to get their way. It is not clear, therefore, what Parliament has 'declined' *from*. Some of the problems may have been exacerbated in recent years, but –

apart from the consequences of constitutional changes of recent years – they are hardly novel. Even the constitutional changes may not have had the dramatic effect that critics claim. The transfer of decision-making power has, in reality, been the transfer of executive power.

Even within a pluralist perspective, the contention that Parliament is marginalized is based on a narrow perspective. It derives historically from the view that Parliament is a 'law-making' body and it is not using its coercive capacity to constrain government or to ensure the outcomes that it wants. What this neglects is the persuasive capacity of Parliament (see Chapter 1). It can be contended that this is the most vital aspect of Parliament's capacity to affect outcomes.

Given that the executive has normally been able to ensure the outcome it wants in parliamentary votes, MPs have had to rely on persuasion to get ministers to act in a way that otherwise they would not. The problem for pluralist analysis is that influence is not always observable or measurable. The fact that MPs troop loyally into the lobby at the request of the whips does not mean that members have not been affecting outcomes. 'Concord and peace,' as Sir Ian Gilmour once observed, 'may signify back bench influence, not dull obedience' (Gilmour, 1971, p. 269). Under the Labour government returned in 1997, many Labour MPs who have voted with the government have done so because they support what the government is doing: 'it is the cohesion of those who are perfectly happy to be cohesive' (Cowley, 2002b, p. 123). Those who have disagreed have, as we have seen (see Chapter 2), been willing to vote against the government.

However, it is what is happening away from the chamber that is just as important, if not more so, than what is happening in the chamber. Ministers have been prepared to listen to backbenchers and to act on their demands. As Cowley notes, 'Where the government has adopted a more consultative approach, being prepared to sugar the legislative pill – as with the treatment of asylum seekers in June 1999 – rebellions have been muted, if not non-existent' (Cowley, 2002b, p. 124). Furthermore, there are other means of persuasion than the threat to embarrass the government publicly by voting against it. Pre-legislative scrutiny has added a new dimension to parliamentary influence at a formative stage (see Chapter 5). Select committees have become a central part of the parliamentary landscape (see Chapter 6), in effect engaging in a dialogue with ministers and other political actors. Members also have at their disposal other formal as well as informal means of putting a particular point to ministers in order to induce action. The correspondence that flows between members and those of their number who are ministers is now a voluminous one, requiring ministers to respond to a wide range of concerns affecting individuals and groups in society.

Indeed, what is apparent from our foregoing chapters is the extent to which Parliament has, to some degree, adapted to its external environment. Given that government has normally achieved the measures it wants – a feature of most of Parliament's history – measuring the extent to which Parliament actually employs its coercive capacity is not particularly salient. What is arguably more pertinent is assessing the extent to which it has been able to utilize its persuasive capacity to affect outcomes.

The institutional impact

The pluralist focus on the coercive capacity of Parliament is thus misleading; it exaggerates the perception of Parliament as a powerless body. Furthermore, as one view of power, it is unduly narrow. Other views help us to see Parliament in a different light. As we have seen, the elite view of power has some utility inasmuch as it draws our attention to the importance of anticipated reaction. In effect, it takes us beyond the pluralist view of persuasion as observable activity and into the realm of unseen persuasion. Ministers cannot ignore Parliament. They can and do anticipate reaction. Some proposals that ministers may instinctively wish to pursue may never reach the stage of being articulated within government because of the negative response expected from MPs and peers. The problem with this is, as we have noted, that of measuring it. However, the plausibility of the claim that ministers have to anticipate Parliament in a way that affects their actions is reinforced when we consider the institutional view of power.

As we have seen throughout this work, the institutional view of power provides a different way of assessing the significance of Parliament within the British polity. As we noted in Chapter 1, institutions are not neutral in their effect. Parliament is a powerful institution inasmuch as the route to ministerial office flows through the House of Commons. This, as we have seen (in Chapter 3), has a number of consequences. Especially important in this context is that ministers are socialized into the parliamentary process. They learn the norms of parliamentary behaviour and are sensitized to the needs and expectations of members. Even though, by definition, ministers are not back bench members, they remain constituency members and have normally spent time as backbenchers. Serving an apprenticeship for office has important effects. As Rose observed, 'In his fourteen years in the Commons [prior to becoming prime minister], Tony Blair had never been a minister answering questions from the government benches. Less experience of life in the Commons goes along with a Prime Minister being less inclined to treat the House as his or her political home' (Rose, 2001, p. 133). Membership of the House helps to shape ministers in their perceptions and their acceptance of the institutional processes of Parliament. Remaining as members also keeps them in the proximity of other members of the House. They have offices in their departments, but they also have offices in the Palace of Westminster.

The House of Commons thus acts as a magnet for those intent on ministerial office. Of even greater significance is the fact that the measures that government want enacted have to go through a highly institutionalized procedure within Parliament. There is, crucially, no alternative. If ministers wish to limit the right to trial by jury, or to impose a new tax, they have to bring a bill before Parliament. We have detailed the stages (see Chapter 5) in both Houses. Within the legislative process, there is scope for MPs and peers to affect the details of a bill. Procedures may be exploited, especially in the House of Lords, where the government does not enjoy a majority. Though government may seek to constrain debate, especially through programme motions in the Commons, it is only so far that constraints can be imposed:

> the parliamentary process is historically well established and complex. Governments entering office find themselves facing a body of rules and procedures that are highly institutionalised. Attempting to change those procedures has an immediate political cost. Changing rules takes time. Governments have to work within the rules in order to change the rules. It may have to invest time to persuade other actors – and there are several – to support the changes. It also has to invest in intellectual resources – you have to know the rules in order to change the rules. (Norton, 2001b, pp. 25–6)

The twenty-third edition of *Erskine May*, the bible of parliamentary procedure, was published in 2004 and runs to over 1,000 pages (McKay, 2004). Those familiar with its contents tend to be the clerks, not ministers, and clerks answer to the Speaker, not to the government. Furthermore, Parliament proceeds on the basis of consensus. The opposition recognizes that the government has a right to pursue its business, and the government recognizes that the opposition has a right to be heard. The opposition could withdraw its co-operation and disrupt or hold up proceedings, and government could use its majority, at least in the Commons, to restrict the rights of the opposition. Both sides recognize that is in their interests to abide by the rules, and do so. Similar considerations apply to the relationship between government and backbenchers as a whole, and between government and its own supporters. There is thus what has been termed an equilibrium of legitimacy: 'Each accepts the legitimacy of the other in what it seeks to do. If either side upsets the equilibrium, it delegitimises their role and therefore threatens to destabilise the parliamentary process and what they gain from it' (Norton, 2001b, p. 28). There is also a potential political cost if the government is seen to be skewing the rules excessively in its favour. Government needs the legislative process to be accepted as legitimate as a precondition for passage of its own measures to be accepted as valid.

Bills have to go through a detailed process. As we have seen, the extent and nature of this process is constricting. That is, only so many bills can be processed in any one session of Parliament. As we have noted, more bills are put before cabinet than there is parliamentary time available to consider them. As a result, the Legislative Programme Committee of the cabinet has to make choices. It will take into account whether bills are likely to encounter problems in their passage, but the most important constraint is not anticipated reaction but rather the limited time available. Institutional constraints force the cabinet, or rather the Legislative Programme Committee, to make choices which, in an ideal state for government, it would not have to make.

The institutional view of power also sensitizes us to the other consequences of Parliament identified by Robert Packenham (1970) (see Chapter 1). This moves us beyond the narrow focus of executive–legislative relations and enables us to bring in the voters. Parliament serves as a representative assembly. There are, as we have discussed (see Chapter 8), problems with how Parliament is seen as a representative body, deriving from the different definitions of representation. As an elected body, it legitimizes executive power, but serves also to link citizens with the political process. It fulfils consequences as a safety valve and articulates the interests of different bodies in society to government. As we have discussed (see Chapter 8), Parliament fulfils the task of both general and specific representation. MPs serve to ensure that the requests and grievances of constituents are pursued with government. In the UK, the task of 'errand running' for constituents ranks much higher in its significance than the place accorded it by Packenham and, indeed, should be rendered as a specific consequence.

Indeed, if we take the functions identified by Packenham, adapt them and render them in terms of their significance within the British

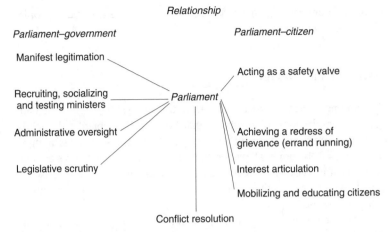

Figure 13.1   The functions of the UK Parliament

political system, we produce a ranking as shown in Figure 13.1. The list encapsulates the principal consequences discussed in the preceding chapters. The ordering is a rough and necessarily subjective one, designed to give some sense of the relative position of the consequences that have so far been discussed in compartmentalized form. It deals with Parliament as a whole. If the two chambers were to be considered separately, then legislative scrutiny would rank as the principal function of the House of Lords. For reasons discussed in Chapter 1, we have not included 'latent legitimation', as this flows from the fulfilment of the functions rather than standing as one of them.

Two generalizations can be drawn from Figure 13.1. The first is that it puts in perspective the pluralist emphasis on observable decision-making. In short, there is more – far more – to Parliament than affecting the content of law through engaging in legislative scrutiny, or saying 'no' to government. The second is the emphasis on functions that relate to the relationship between Parliament and citizens as much as those that relate to the relationship between Parliament and government. The functions, though, are not mutually exclusive and reinforce one another, emphasizing Parliament's pivotal role in the British polity.

The significance of Parliament to the public is reflected in the extent to which it remains a magnet for the expression of opinion and dissent. As we have already recorded, millions of letters flow into the Palace of Westminster each year. Organizations arrange mass lobbies of MPs. Protestors stand with banners and megaphones outside the Palace.

Huge demonstrations are sometimes held. For a great many people, Parliament remains relevant.

Whither Parliament?

What conclusions are we to draw from this analysis? There is the danger of complacency, of assuming that because Parliament still clearly remains significant in fulfilling a range of functions, there is nothing that needs to be done. However, there is a far more persuasive conclusion. That is, far from making a case for no change, it makes a case for much wider change than that advanced by those adopting a narrow pluralist focus.

Parliament has to be seen in the round. As we have seen, representative democracy was superimposed on an existing structure of executive dominance. Parliament has served as the body through which the executive is chosen, legitimized and constrained. Between elections, party serves as a body for aggregating opinion but limits Parliament inasmuch as it claims a monopoly as the expression of popular opinion. Given that party cannot encapsulate the opinions of all sectors of society, nor of all individuals, Parliament serves to compensate for the limitations of party.

Given this analysis, the basic questions to be asked about Parliament are: how effective is it in listening to the people; how effective is it in making sure that government hears, and acts, on what it says; and how effective is it in speaking to the people?

Listening to the people

Parliament is arguably better able now than ever before to listen to electors. As we have seen, it has become more adept at fulfilling the task of specific representation. MPs are more active in their constituencies than before, devoting considerable time to being in the constituency and to dealing with issues raised through letters, e-mails and constituency surgeries (see Chapter 9). They are also active in seeking to influence public policy on behalf of a range of organizations and bodies (see Chapter 10). Bodies seeking a change in the law have increasingly recognized the value of lobbying MPs and peers. As we recorded in Chapter 10, 12.5 million items of post flowed into the Palace of Westminster in 2003. MPs have responded to demands made of them, utilizing the now more extensive formal and informal means available to achieve a response from government.

There are, none the less, problems. Not all groups enjoy the same access to the corridors of Westminster, and perceptions of undue influence undermine Parliament's credibility. While mechanisms have been put in place to address the problem, the perception lingers. Though MPs deal with a large volume of cases raised by constituents, the cases are exceptional; only a minority of constituents get in touch and most MPs have no means of assessing the views of the majority of people living in the constituency. Even if some members are proactive in soliciting constituents to get in touch, they are still not able to assess 'constituency' opinion on issues of public policy on a regular basis. Earlier research in the USA has pointed to the fact that elected representatives' views of constituency opinion do not always correlate particularly well with what constituents' in fact think (Miller and Stokes, 1963; Hedlund and Friesema, 1972). For most of the time, members do not see this as a particular problem, falling back on the party line, but on some issues it becomes important. When opposition grows to policies being pursued by government, with the opposition transcending party lines – as, for example, on issues such as gambling and the licensing laws – what can MPs on the government benches do? Fall back on unthinking party loyalty, follow their own views, or try to discern opinions in the constituency? There is also the problem of finding out the views of different groups in society, who may not be organized (see Chapter 11), and who may not have a particular champion in the Commons or Lords. As we have seen, MPs and peers hear the views of citizens on a much wider scale than before, but on an imperfect basis.

So how can the problem be addressed? There has been relatively little attention given to the issue. The limited pluralist analysis has focused more on constraining the executive than on enabling the voice of citizens to be heard. There is none the less a growing awareness of the problem. The most recent manifestation of this is the report of Modernisation Committee of the House of Commons, *Connecting Parliament with the Public,* published in June 2004 (Modernisation Committee, 2004), followed by the report of the Constitution Committee of the House of Lords, *Parliament and the Legislative Process,* published in October 2004 (Constitution Committee, 2004b). Both recognized the need for citizens to be heard in the parliamentary process. The Modernisation Committee ranged over how people could learn about Parliament as well as feed in their views; the Constitution Committee focused on how opinions could be expressed while legislation was being considered. What emerged from the two reports was how people could have a greater input into parliamentary deliberations. Principal among the recommendations of one or both reports were:

- giving a greater role to public petitions through referring petitions to the appropriate departmental select committee;
- providing that bills should normally be published in draft and available for consultation, thus allowing interested bodies the opportunity to comment;
- ensuring that each bill at some stage during its passage was considered by a committee empowered to take evidence from witnesses;
- putting more bills out to online consultation;
- empowering committees considering bills to meet outside Westminster and take evidence; and
- enabling committees to commission opinion polls to discover public attitudes on a particular measure.

The proposals – the first of which has already been accepted – might not necessarily address all the problems we have identified. MPs will probably continue to have imperfect awareness of constituents' views. Constituents who have no awareness of the local MP and no access to the internet may encounter problems of which the MP is, and will remain, unaware. As we have seen, MPs have had difficulty keeping pace with existing demands made of them. Resources have expanded, enabling them to cope with demands but not to the extent that they can be unduly proactive in addressing concerns not already brought to their attention.

None the less, there is greater scope for involvement by the public, or more frequently particular groups, in parliamentary deliberations, especially in considering legislation. The proposals advanced by both committees offer significant scope for greater involvement. The experience of online consultation on domestic violence (see Chapter 12) suggests that it may be possible to generate involvement by people who previously would not have been involved and who may be able to speak from experience in a way that informs parliamentarians. As the Modernisation Committee recorded, the experiments with online consultation 'have generally been successful and have proved effective as a way of engaging members of the public in the work that we do and of giving a voice to those who would otherwise be excluded' (Modernisation Committee, 2004, p. 21).

Each proposal may have a beneficial effect in enabling Parliament to hear more from citizens but, in combination, they have the potential to enhance considerably the links between citizen and Parliament. Hearing what people have to say is facilitated if they have an awareness of what Parliament is doing and an understanding of its procedures. Parliament has to be accessible and ensure that people know what it is doing. We shall return to this in looking at how Parliament reaches the public.

Making the government hear

The task of ensuring that the government listens to Parliament is one that has engaged parliamentary reformers for as long as there has been awareness that party has facilitated the dominance of the executive. This is more familiar territory from a pluralist perspective. Reform proposals have littered the parliamentary landscape. Some reform, as we have seen, has taken place – such as the introduction of the departmental select committees and the use of pre-legislative scrutiny – but Parliament still remains limited in its capacity to influence government. As we saw in Chapter 5, there has been no fundamental change to the legislative process within Parliament; the weakest part of the process is to be found at the committee stage in the House of Commons. MPs go through the motions of considering some amendments (though not all of those that have been tabled) and do so often within specified time constraints. Similarly, in Chapter 6, we have seen that – despite the development of means available to MPs and peers – the capacity of Parliament to scrutinize government remains limited.

The need to strengthen Parliament in ensuring that government listens to it has resulted in a range of proposals from a number of bodies. Among the most prominent reform proposals in recent years from bodies outside Parliament have been the Hansard Society Commission Report on the Legislative Process, *Making the Law,* in 1992; the report of the Conservative Party's Commission to Strengthen Parliament, *Strengthening Parliament,* in 2000; and the report of the Hansard Society's Commission on Parliamentary Scrutiny, *The Challenge for Parliament: Making Parliament Accountable,* in 2001. A number of parliamentary committees have also come forward with proposals for change. These have included the Modernisation Committee, especially its reports on *The Legislative Process,* in 1997, and *Modernisation of the House of Commons: A Reform Programme,* in 2002; the Liaison Committee in its report, *Shifting the Balance,* in 2000 – dealing with select committees; and the Lords Constitution Committee in *Parliament and the Legislative Process* in 2004. They have tended to advance proposals that are complementary to rather than in conflict with one another. A number of their proposals have been implemented. However, most of their recommendations remain precisely that. Among the more prominent proposals are those designed to achieve:

- greater parliamentary control of proceedings;
- strengthened select committees; and
- enhanced legislative scrutiny.

The House of Commons is unusual among Western legislatures in the extent to which the parliamentary timetable is determined by the government and not by the House itself. Research has shown that parliamentary control of the timetable does not prevent government from getting its business transacted (Commission to Strengthen Parliament, 2000, p. 28), but what it does permit is for the chamber itself to ensure that adequate time is allocated to scrutinizing bills and the executive. Having ownership of the process would enable the Commons to allocate time more effectively in order to fulfil the functions shown in Figure 13.1. It would enable more time to be given to debating select committee reports, not least those that may arise from petitions presented by members of the public.

Although departmental select committees have significantly enhanced scrutiny of the executive, they labour under the constraints identified in Chapter 6. There is an argument both for further strengthening their links with the chamber and for giving them greater resources. Holding short debates on reports, doing so at prime time and possibly on substantive motions (to approve rather than take note) may generate greater interest in the House and beyond (Commission to Strengthen Parliament 2000, pp. 28, 32). Expanding the resources of the committees will also enable them to fulfil their work more effectively and, potentially, to extend their role. We have described their growing role in undertaking pre-legislative scrutiny (see Chapter 4). In carrying this out, they are able to draw on experts (lawyers, accountants, economists) who serve in a Scrutiny Unit, set up to assist committees in the analysis of draft bills and to examine departmental estimates. Expansion of the Unit would provide committees with the support necessary to examine more draft bills. The Constitution Committee in the Lords also envisaged a role for select committees in post-legislative scrutiny. Recognizing the burden this would impose, it recommended that they be empowered to commission independent research on the effects of an Act (Constitution Committee, 2004b, pp. 45–6). In that way, they would retain ownership of the process, and would have the discretion to conduct an inquiry in the light of the findings, but would not necessarily have to undertake the principal work of investigation. This would enhance Parliament's scrutiny role considerably, through extending it to all stages of the process by which law is formulated, discussed, approved and implemented. As such, it would have the potential to enhance Parliament's relevance to people outside the House as well as have the capacity to improve the quality of legislation.

The legislative process could also be enhanced, as we have suggested above, by utilizing more regularly the power to draw on the views and expertise of those outside Parliament. While select committees can take evidence, standing committees cannot. Bills are rarely committed to select committees or to special standing committees, which are empowered to take evidence (see Chapter 5). The Hansard Commission in 1992 argued that bills should normally be considered by special standing committees. As we have noted already, the Constitution Committee in 2004 argued that a bill should normally be considered by an evidence-taking committee at some stage during its passage. In the course of the Committee's inquiry, former Leader of the House of Commons, Robin Cook, declared:

> I personally think that there is a mistake in having two set categories: a Standing Committee, which proceeds normally, and a Special Standing Committee, which has the unique capacity to call witnesses. Frankly, I would just re-write the procedure book and let every Standing Committee call witnesses if they wish to, and leave that decision to Standing Committees. (Constitution Committee, 2004b, p. 35)

The attraction of extending such evidence-taking capacity is twofold. It allows for greater input from those outside Parliament with an interest in the bill, and at the same time lessens the grip of government on the content of a measure. If expert evidence suggests a particular provision is not workable, it makes it difficult for government to proceed with it. Giving the House of Commons greater ownership of the legislative timetable would also enable it to ensure that bills were not overly rushed. Enabling bills to be carried over from one session to another will also permit the staggered introduction of bills and a more equitable distribution of parliamentary time to deal with them.

Speaking to the people

Enabling Parliament to speak to the people – in other words, to ensure that people have an appreciation of what the institution is doing, and why it is endorsing particular policies – is the most difficult task facing parliamentarians. It can be seen as a cultural problem on two levels. The first is the parliamentary level. Historically, Parliament has been wary of 'strangers' following its proceedings. As we have seen (in Chapter 12), it is only recently that the two Houses have allowed television cameras to record proceedings. It is even more recent that television reporters have been permitted to broadcast from the Central Lobby. Parliament is developing a culture of greater openness, but this has been slow in developing and problems remain. We have already detailed in Chapter 12 the limitations on the way that material is disseminated. The problem, in part, is attitudinal, reflected in some MPs remaining wary of the use of e-mails. It is also presentational; problems remain with the Parliament website. Partisanship also gets in the way. MPs are good at promoting themselves individually but not at banding together to promote the institution of which they are members. There is a wariness about disseminating material that does anything other than explain proceedings.

Perhaps more fundamental, though, is the culture external to the institution. However much Parliament makes information available about itself, it cannot force people to look at it or to take an interest. Parliament increasingly has to compete in a crowded market to attract attention. It cannot take it for granted that people will rush to watch parliamentary proceedings, or to read a detailed report of proceedings. What coverage there is tends to be skewed, focusing on the televisual aspects of partisanship, primarily Prime Minister's Question Time, and however much politicians bemoan the limited coverage, that by itself will not bring any changes.

For Parliament, the challenge is to render what it does relevant to people outside and to engage with them. To some people, there is a problem in the proceedings and language of Parliament. However, that in large part appears to derive from a focus on proceedings in the chamber, especially at Prime Minister's Question Time. The greater problem is in ensuring that people are aware that many of the issues of concern to them are in fact considered by MPs and peers. One only has to look at the topics covered by select committees (listed in Chapter 6) to recognize that issues that impinge on different sections of society are discussed, and in some depth, by Parliament.

There is only so much Parliament can do to compete with alternative attractions. Some of the reforms designed to ensure that Parliament listens to the people, listed above, are also designed to ensure that people are more aware of what Parliament does and can offer. Other proposals designed to enable Parliament to reach members of the public, put forward by the Modernisation Committee (2004), include:

- exploiting the digital broadcasting of Parliament;
- sending a weekly newsletter, by post or e-mail, to all those interested in receiving it;

- carrying out a radical up-grade the Parliament website; and
- sending a new voter's guide to all young people around the time of their eighteenth birthday.

The Committee recognized that the digital broadcasting of proceedings could provide some interactivity with viewers. However, not all committee proceedings are recorded for audio-visual transmission. Only a few of the committee rooms in the Palace (as distinct from those in Portcullis House) can be used for broadcasts. Ensuring that all committee rooms were fitted with cameras would be a starting point. Exploiting digital broadcasting for interactivity, and the internet for more e-consultations, would enhance the engagement with those interested in the subjects under consideration.

As Peter Riddell has emphasized (see Chapter 12), the internet provides a considerable opportunity for Parliament; but it does not represent a panacea. There are dangers in placing too much emphasis on what it can deliver. Equally, there are dangers for Parliament if it does not exploit the internet, as well as digital broadcasting, as a means of ensuring that people are aware of what is going on in Parliament and, through interactivity or a greater awareness of procedures, are able to have some input.

The Modernisation Committee also recognized the importance of the education process. Citizenship is now part of the national curriculum. The committee wanted ministers to re-examine the balance of the citizenship curriculum because, while it recognized that other matters were also crucial aspects of citizenship education, 'an understanding of the country's democratic institutions is also of fundamental importance to today's young people, and to the engaged voters of tomorrow' (Modernisation Committee, 2004, p. 13).

It is thus possible to identify changes that would build on recent developments and enable Parliament to fulfil its pivotal role between government and citizen more effectively.

Achieving change

Identifying the changes that may help Parliament to engage more with the public is the easy part of the task; the difficult part is delivering those changes. If they are to be achieved, there needs to be the political will to implement them.

If reform is to be achieved within Parliament, then MPs and peers have to exercise the will to deliver it. There is the danger of parliamentary reform being seen as the preserve of a select few. Many of the proposals we have detailed above emanate from what are colloquially known as 'the usual suspects'. When Labour MP, Mark Fisher, was asked in 2004 how many members the parliamentary reform movement, Parliament First, had, he replied 'there are about thirty', adding: 'The smallness of our group does not indicate the scale of support, but even if we recruited everybody we could of like mind it would be still a very small proportion of our House' (Fisher, 2004, p. 94). His Conservative colleague, Douglas Hogg, took an even gloomier view:

> I am deeply, deeply, deeply pessimistic. I think that if any change is incremental it can only come through shame. There is no great political will on the floor of the House to change and I think that the parties will keep their nasty little grip on the Members of Parliament for as far ahead as I can see. (Hogg, 2004, p. 94)

This is arguably an extreme view, though one that reflects a truism: that interest in parliamentary reform is not widespread in the House of Commons. The House of Lords has generally been more willing to change and has been somewhat more attuned to the need to ensure that the public is aware of what it does. It was the first House, for example, to appoint an information officer, and still disseminates information material not matched by the Commons. One hypothesis for this is that MPs enjoy the legitimacy of election and therefore take their positions for granted in a way that members of the House of Lords do not; many of the latter take the view that they have to work to prove their legitimacy.

There are some grounds for optimism based on the changes that have occurred in recent years, not least the development of pre-legislative scrutiny and the introduction of debates in Westminster Hall. Reform may thus occur as a result of incremental change but the question then becomes one of whether it is ever likely to be quick enough to enable Parliament to meet popular expectations. Survey data reveal that though respondents generally have a high regard for the local MP, there is a declining level of trust in politicians. According to the Modernisation Committee, 'Politicians have always scored low on levels of trust but even so there is a noticeable downward trend, with fewer and fewer people trusting politicians. Lower levels of trust are translating into a disconnection from the institutions of democracy' (Modernisation Committee, 2004, p. 9). The problem, as the committee noted, was not that people were not interested in politics; they *are* interested, but the challenge for Parliament is how to harness that interest. Parliament for many appears to be part of the problem as much as part of the solution. In terms of trust, survey data presented to the committee showed that, on a scale of 0 to 10, with 10 representing the top end of the scale, more than half of those questioned rated the House of Commons on the bottom half of the scale; the average score for the Commons was below 4 (Modernisation Committee, 2004, p. Ev 48). Respondents showed greater trust in the courts, the civil service, banks, the police, and other people, and only the government, the EU and politicians attracted lower levels of trust than the House of Commons.

Though the data are not necessarily a cause for panic – when questioned, more people say Parliament works well than say it doesn't (Dunleavy *et al.*, 2001, p. 76) – they are a cause for concern, especially when put in a wider context. The Joseph Rowntree Reform Trust's survey in 2004 found a growing support for demonstrations at a time when 90 per cent of those questioned believed that ordinary voters 'should' have 'a great deal' or 'a fair amount' of influence over government policy, but only a third in fact believed that they *did* have such influence (Joseph Rowntree Reform Trust, 2004). Given the perceptions of what people expect of Parliament, this suggests that Parliament is not acting – at least not as much as it could – as the voice of the people to government. The challenge for MPs is to ensure that it does.

Conclusion

What conclusions are to be drawn from this study of Parliament in British politics? There are three basic conclusions.

First, Parliament matters. Parliament is a core institution of the state. No democratic country exists without a legislature. Government needs Parliament to legitimize both its existence and its measures of public policy. Parliament is not a law-making body, but it is the essential law-effecting body of the United Kingdom. Acts of Parliament dictate behaviour. They stipulate what is and, more pervasively, what is not permissible. They are enforced by the agencies of the state, including the courts and the police. There are few aspects of daily life not now affected by Acts of Parliament and regulations made under them. The process by which Acts are made – a process exclusive to Parliament – renders it an indispensable institution. For the purpose of governing the nation, Parliament may not be sufficient, but it is necessary.

Second, Parliament matters more than is popularly realized. Views of Parliament, and of legislatures generally, have been affected by a longstanding pluralist perception of decline. From a pluralist perspective, Parliament is a marginal actor in the making of public policy. However, as we have seen, this is both a skewed and a narrow perspective. A more rounded pluralist approach, and other views of power, helps us to appreciate the significance of Parliament. Parliament fulfils a range of functions and in so doing underpins the health and legitimacy of the parliamentary process. Parliament operates at the interface between government and citizen; it is the authoritative channel through which citizens make themselves heard by government. Government necessarily operates through Parliament in order to maintain effectiveness and consent. In terms of public policy, the effect of Parliament is far from neutral. Parliament's structure and activity shape ministers' behaviour and constrain the government's legislative programme. Its most important effect is not to be found by analysing its influence on bills laid before it, but in the number of proposed bills that never see the light of day.

Third, Parliament could matter more than it does. Parliament has adapted to a changing constitutional and political environment, but it remains limited in the extent to which it is able to inform the people, listen to them and make sure that the government hears and acts upon what they say. As we have seen, Parliament could be strengthened in scrutinizing and influencing government; it could be more effective in making itself heard by the people; and it could be more effective in hearing the concerns and wishes of the people. There have been several developments that have strengthened Parliament, but they are limited relative to the pressures it faces. In terms of institutional change, Parliament is running in order to stand still. Recognizing the importance of the pivotal position of Parliament between government and citizen helps us to appreciate the range of changes that may be necessary. Reform has previously focused too heavily on the Parliament–executive relationship and not enough on the Parliament–citizen relationship. In many respects, the citizen has been left out. The good news is that recent reform agenda cover both aspects of the relationship. The bad news is that identifying what needs to be done is only half the battle. The other, most important, half is doing it.

Further Reading

Facts and figures

The most substantial work available providing extensive facts and figures on parliamentary activity is the second edition of *Griffith and Ryle on Parliament: Functions, Practices and Procedures* (Blackburn and Kennon, 2003). There is also useful material, and a good guide to procedure, in the second edition of Child (2002). Valuable quantitative material for each parliamentary session is to be found in the *Sessional Information Digest* produced each year by the House of Commons Information Office. This contains sections covering sittings of the House and dates of session, legislation, the work of committees, documentations, membership of the House and addresses. The *Digest* draws together material published throughout the session in the *Weekly Information Bulletin*. Both the *Digest* and the *Bulletin* are published in paper form, but may also be accessed on the Parliament website at: www.parliament.uk/directories/hcio.cfm. Useful data on the House of Lords are published each year in the House of Lords *Annual Report*, including statistics on sittings and government defeats. The report is published in paper form, and copies of each of the annual reports can also be found on the Parliament website at www.publications.parliament.uk/pa/ld/ldlordsrep.htm.

The rules, precedents, practices and law of Parliament are detailed in *Erskine May's Treatise on The Law, Privileges, Proceedings and Usage of Parliament* (McKay, 2004). The first edition first appeared in 1844. Though essentially for the parliamentary specialist (and, for reasons of cost, the library), it contains some useful historical material and information on both Houses of Parliament.

Parliament and government

The responsibility of ministers to Parliament is covered in Woodhouse (1994). Other coverage of the relationship of ministers to Parliament is to be found in Part 5 of Brazier (1997). Data and a succinct analysis of Parliament's developing role in pre-legislative scrutiny are provided in the article in *Public Law* by Andrew Kennon (2004). Details of legislative scrutiny are to be found in Norton

(1990b), Blackburn and Kennon (2003), and in the report of the House of Lords Constitution Committee, *Parliament and the Legislative Process* (2004b). For a discussion of the legislative passage of constitutional bills, see the article by Seaton and Winetrobe (1998). On Parliament and conscience issues, see Cowley (1998b). The most recent comprehensive study of Question Time remains Franklin and Norton (1993), though there is up-to-date material in Rogers and Walters (2004). On select committees, there is useful material in Chapter 3 of the report of the Hansard society Commission on Parliamentary Scrutiny (2001) as well as in Maer and Sandford (2004) and Blackburn and Kennon (2003). Much useful data are included in the annual reports of the House of Commons Liaison Committee, comprising select committee chairmen; see, for example, Liaison Committee (2004), available at www.publications.parliament.uk/pa/cm200304/cmselect/cmliaisn/446/446.pdf.

On Parliament and the European Union, see Norton (1996) and Giddings and Drewry (2004). The reports of the European Scrutiny Committee in the House of Commons (2002, 2003) are available at www.publications.parliament.uk/pa/cm200102/cmselect/cmeuleg/152-xxxiii/152.pdf and www.publications.parliament.uk/pa/cm200203/cmselect/cmeuleg/63-xxiv/63-xxiv.pdf and contain valuable material. On Parliament and devolution, see Trench (2004b). The relationship of Parliament to the law, including human rights law, is covered in Oliver and Drewry (1998).

On MPs, see Searing (1994) and Rush (2001). Data on members' backgrounds are to be found in Byron Criddle's chapter in the Nuffield study covering each general election (see Criddle, 2002) and in the annual *Dad's Parliamentary Companion*. On parliamentary behaviour, see especially Cowley (2002a). Up-to-date information on parliamentary rebellions is to be found on www.revolts.co.uk.

On the House of Lords, see especially Carmichael and Dickson (1999) which covers the House in both the legislative and judicial roles. See also Russell (2000) and Part IV of Blackburn and Kennon (2003). There is much useful material to be found in the report of the Royal Commission on the Reform of the House of Lords (2000); the report is available on the internet at www.archive.official-documents.co.uk/document/cm45/4534/4534.htm. More generailly, see the volume edited by Baldwin (2001).

Parliament and citizen

On the concept of representation, the classic work is that of Hanna Pitkin (1967). For recent scholarship in the context of the United Kingdom, see Judge (1999a, 1999b). On the relationship of MP and constituent, see Cain *et al.* (1987), Norton and Wood (1993) and Power (1998). There are also valuable data in the article by Pippa Norris in *The Journal of Legislative Studies* (1997). Flynn (1997) offers an entertaining insight into the work of the MP. The most substantial academic study of the relationship between Parliament and pressure groups remains the volume edited by Rush (1990). On Parliament and the media, see Negrine (1998), and on Parliament and the internet, see Coleman and Van De Donk (1999). See also the report of the Modernisation Committee (2004), available at www.publications.parliament.uk/pa/cm200304/cmselect. cmmodern/368.368.pdf.

Parliament and reform

There are various reform tracts. The most recent include the reports of the Commission the Strengthen Parliament (2000) (printed copies of the report are now difficult to obtain, but it is available at www.conservatives.com/pdf/ norton.pdf), the Hansard Society Commission on Parliamentary Scrutiny (2001), the House of Commons Modernisation Committee (2002) (available on the Parliament website at www.publications.parliament.uk/pa/cm200102/cmselect/ cmmodern/1168/1168.pdf), and the House of Lords Constitution Committee (2004b) (also available online at www.publications.parliament.uk/pa/ld200304/ ldselect/ldconst/173/173.pdf) See also Peter Riddell (2000) for a critique of Parliament by an informed observer.

Parliamentary publications

Parliamentary publications are accessible on the Parliament website (www. parliament.uk). As already mentioned in Chapter 12, the Commons site alone hosts 9,000 pages and over a million pages of linked publications. The website includes *Hansard*, the text of bills before Parliament (as well as the explanatory notes), reports from select committees (as well as the transcripts of hearings held as part of current inquiries), details of business, information on members, and a host of archival and educational material. Paper copies of publications can be ordered from the Stationery Office. For a comparative study, the websites of other parliaments can be reached through the website of the Inter-Parliamentary Union (www.ipu.org).

Journals

Articles on Parliament are variously carried in journals, most notably *The Journal of Legislative Studies* and *Parliamentary Affairs*. Both are published quarterly.

Bibliography

Allen, Graham (2001) *The Last Prime Minister* (London: Graham Allen).

Arter, D. (2004a) 'The Scottish Committees and the Goal of a 'New Politics': A Verdict on the First Four Years of the Devolved Scottish Parliament', *Journal of Contemporary European Studies,* vol. 12, no. 1, pp. 71–91.

Arter, D. (2004b) *The Scottish Parliament: A Scandinavia-Style Assembly?* (London: Frank Cass).

Bachrach, P. and Baratz, M. (1962) 'Two Faces of Power', *American Political Science Review,* vol. 56, pp. 947–52.

Bagehot, Walter (1867) *The English Constitution* (London: Chapman & Hall).

Baggott, Rob (1995) *Pressure Groups Today* (Manchester: Manchester University Press).

Baldwin, Nicholas D. J. (1985), 'The House of Lords: Behavioural Changes', in P. Norton (ed.), *Parliament in the 1980s* (Oxford: Basil Blackwell).

Baldwin, Nicholas D. J. (1995) 'The House of Lords and the Labour Government 1974–79', *The Journal of Legislative Studies,* vol. 1, pp. 218–42.

Baldwin, Nicholas D. J. (ed.) (2001) *Second Chambers* (London: Frank Cass).

Barker, Anthony and Rush, M. (1970) *The Member of Parliament and His Information* (London: George Allen & Unwin).

Beard, Charles A. and Lewis, J. D. (1959), 'Representative Government in Evolution', in J. C. Wahlke and H. Eulau (eds), *Legislative Behavior: A Reader in Theory and Research* (New York: The Free Press of Glencoe).

Beer, Samuel H. (1966) 'The British Legislature and the Problem of Mobilising Consent', in E. Frank (ed.), *Lawmakers in a Changing World* (Englewood Cliffs, NJ: Prentice-Hall).

Beer, Samuel H. (1969) *Modern British Politics,* revd edn (London: Faber).

Beetham, David, Byrne, I., Ngan, P. and Weir, S. (2002) *Democracy Under Blair: A Democratic Audit of the United Kingdom* (London: Politico's).

Berry, Roger (1996) 'A Case Study in Parliamentary Influence: The Civil Rights (Disabled Persons) Bill' *The Journal of Legislative Studies*, vol. 2, pp. 135–44.

Birch, Anthony H. (1964) *Representative and Responsible Government* (London: George Allen & Unwin).

Blackburn, Robert and Kennon, A. (2003) *Griffith and Ryle on Parliament: Functions, Practice and Procedures,* 2nd edn (London: Sweet & Maxwell).

Blondel, Jean, Gillespie, P., Herman, V., Kaati, P. and Leonard, R. (1970) 'Legislative behaviour: Some Steps towards a Cross-national Measurement', *Government and Opposition,* vol. 5, pp. 67–85.

Bowler, Shaun and Farrell, D. (1993), Legislator Shirking and Voter Monitoring: Impacts of European Parliament Electoral Systems upon Legislator-Voter Relationships', *Journal of Common Market Studies*, vol. 31, pp. 45–69.

Bowman, Sir Geoffrey (2004), Evidence, *Parliament and the Legislative Process,* Select Committee on the Constitution, House of Lords, 14th Report, Session 2003–4, HL Paper 173–II; pp. 96–109.

Bown, Francis A. (1990), 'The Shops Bill', in M. Rush (ed.), *Parliament and Pressure Politics* (Oxford: Clarendon Press).

Brandreth, Gyles (1992) 'Post Haste', *The House Magazine,* 5 October.

Brandreth, Gyles (1999) *Breaking the Code* (London: Phoenix).

Brazier, Rodney (1997) *Ministers of the Crown* (Oxford: Clarendon Press).

Bromhead, Peter (1958) *The House of Lords and Contemporary Politics 1911–1957* (London: Routledge & Kegan Paul).

Bruyneel, Gaston (1978) *Interpellations, Questions and Analogous Procedures for the Control of Government Actions and Challenging the Responsibility of Government* (Geneva: Association of Secretaries General of Parliaments).

Bryce, Lord (1921) *Modern Democracies* (London: Macmillan).

Buck, Philip W. (1963) *Amateurs and Professionals in British Politics* (Chicago, Ill.: University of Chicago Press).

Butler, David (1963) *The Electoral System in Britain Since 1918,* 2nd edn (Oxford: Clarendon Press).

Butler, David (2004) 'Electoral Reform', *Parliamentary Affairs,* vol. 57, pp. 734–43.

Butler, David and Butt, S. (2004) 'Seats and Votes: A Comment', *Representation,* vol. 40, pp. 169–72.

Cabinet Office (2004) *The Government's Response to the Report of the Joint Committee on the Draft Civil Contingencies Bill,* Cm 6078 (London: Cabinet Office).

Cain, Bruce E., Ferejohn, J. and Fiorina, M. (1979) 'Popular Evaluations of Representatives in Great Britain and the United States', California Institute of Technology Working Paper No. 288 (Passadena, Calif.: California Institute of Technology).

Cain, Bruce E., Ferejohn, J. and Fiorina, M. (1987) *The Personal Vote* (Cambridge, Mass.: Harvard University Press).

Campion, Lord (1952) 'Parliament and Democracy', in Lord Campion (ed.), *Parliament: A Survey* (London: George Allen & Unwin).

Cannon, John and Griffiths, R. (1988) *The Oxford Illustrated History of the British Monarchy* (Oxford University Press).

Carmichael, Paul and Dickson, B. (1999) *The House of Lords* (Oxford: Hart Publishing).

Cazalet-Keir, Thelma (1967) *From the Wings* (London: Bodley Head).

Charmley, John (1997) *Duff Cooper: The Authorised Biography,* paperback edn (London: Phoenix).

Chester, Norman and Bowring, N. (1962) *Questions in Parliament* (Oxford University Press).

Child, Susan (2002) *Politico's Guide to Parliament,* 2nd edn (London: Politico's).

Chisholm, Anne and Davie, M. (1993) *Beaverbrook: A Life* (London: Pimlico).

Clayton, Richard (2004), 'Judicial Deference and "Democratic Dialogue": The Legitimacy of Judicial Intervention under the Human Rights Act 1998', *Public Law,* Spring, pp. 33–47.

Coleman, Stephen and Van De Donk, W. (1999) *Parliament in the Age of the Internet* (Oxford University Press).

Commission to Strengthen Parliament (2000) *Strengthening Parliament* (London: The Conservative Party).

Committee on Standards in Public Life (2004) *Survey of Public Attitudes Towards Conduct in Public Life* (London: Committee on Standards in Public Life).

Congressional Quarterly (1978) *The Washington Lobby,* 5th edn (Washington DC: Congressional Quarterly Inc).

Conradt, David (1986) *The German Polity,* 3rd edn (New York: Longman).

Constitution Committee, House of Lords (2003) *Devolution: Inter-Institutional Relations in the United Kingdom,* 2nd Report, Session 2002–3, HL Paper 28 (London: The Stationery Office).

Constitution Committee, House of Lords (2004a) *The Regulatory State: Ensuring Its Accountability,* 6th Report, Session 2003–4, HL Paper 68-I, 68-II, 68-III (London: The Stationery Office).

Constitution Committee, House of Lords (2004b) *Parliament and the Legislative Process,* 14th Report, Session 2003–4, HL Paper 173-I (London: The Stationery Office).

Cook, Robin (2003) *The Point of Departure* (London: Simon & Schuster).

Corston, Jean (2004) Written Evidence, *Parliament and the Legislative Process,* Select Committee on the Constitution, House of Lords, 14th Report, Session 2003–4, HL Paper 173-II, pp. 164–7.

Couzens, K. (1956) 'A Minister's Correspondence', *Public Administration,* vol. 34, pp. 237–4.

Cowley, Philip (1998a), 'Unbridled Passions? Free Votes, Issues of Conscience, and the Accountability of Members of Parliament', *The Journal of Legislative Studies,* vol. 4, pp. 70–88.

Cowley, Philip (ed.) (1998b) *Conscience and Parliament* (London: Frank Cass).

Cowley, Philip (2002a) *Revolts and Rebellions* (London: Politico's).

Cowley, Philip (2002b) 'Legislatures and Assemblies', in P. Dunleavy, A. Gamble, R. Heffernan, I. Holliday and G. Peele (eds), *Developments in British Politics 6* (London: Palgrave).

Cowley, Philip and Norton, P. (1999) 'Rebels and Rebellions: Conservative MPs in the 1992 Parliament', *The British Journal of Politics and International Relations,* vol. 1, pp. 84–105.

Cowley, Philip and Stuart, M. (1997) 'Sodomy, Slaughter, Sunday Shopping and Seatbelts', *Party Politics,* vol. 3, pp. 19–30.

Cowley, Philip and Stuart, M. (2004a) 'The Mother of all Rebellions: Iraq and the PLP', Paper presented at the Political Studies Association Annual Conference, University of Lincoln, April (accessible on www.revolts.co.uk).

Cowley, Philip and Stuart, M. (2004b), 'Parliament: More Bleak House than Great Expectations', *Parliamentary Affairs,* vol. 57, pp. 301–14.

Cox, Gary W. and Morgenstern, S. (2002) 'Epilogue: Latin America's Assemblies and Proactive Presidents', in S. Morgenstern and B. Nacif (eds), *Legislative Politics in Latin America* (Cambridge University Press).

Crewe, Ivor (1975) 'Electoral Reform and the Local MP', in S. E. Finer (ed.), *Adversary Politics and Electoral Reform* (London: Anthony Wigram).

Crick, Bernard (1964) *The Reform of Parliament* (London: Weidenfeld & Nicolson).

Criddle, Byron (2002) 'MPs and Candidates', in D. Butler and D. Kavanagh, *The British General Election of 2001* (London: Palgrave).

Crossman, Richard H. S. (1963) 'Introduction' to W. Bagehot, *The English Constitution* (London: Fontana).

Crowe, Edward (1986) 'The Web of Authority: Party Loyalty and Social Control in the British House of Commons', *Legislative Studies Quarterly* vol. 11, pp. 161–85.

Currie, Edwina (1989) *Lifelines* (London: Sidgwick & Jackson).

Cygan, Adam (2003) 'Democracy and Accountability in the European Union – the View from the House of Commons', *The Modern Law Review,* vol. 66, no. 3, pp. 384–401.

Dawes, Derek (1993) *Power on the Back Benches? The Growth of Select Committee Influence* (Bristol: SAUS Publications).

Dicey, A. V. (1959) *An Introduction to the Study of the Law of the Constitution* (first published 1885), 10th edn (London: Macmillan).

Dod's Parliament Companion (annual) (London: Dod's Parliamentary Communications).

Doig, Alan (1984) *Corruption and Misconduct in Contemporary British Politics* (Harmondsworth: Penguin).

Doig, Alan (1990) *Westminster Babylon* (London: Allison & Busby).

Double, Paul (2004) 'The Impact of European Community Law on the British Legislative Process', in A. Brazier (ed.), *Parliament, Politics and Law Making* (London: The Hansard Society).

Drewry, Gavin (1985) 'Public General Acts – Now and a Hundred Years Ago', *Statute Law Review,* Autumn, pp. 152–61.

Drewry, Gavin (ed.) (1989) *The New Select Committees,* revd edn (Oxford: Clarendon Press).

Dunleavy, Patrick and Jones, G. W. (1995) 'Leaders, Politics and Institutional Change: The Decline of Prime Ministerial Accountability to the House of Commons, 1868–1990', in R. A. W. Rhodes and P. Dunleavy (eds), *Prime Ministers, Cabinets and Core Executives* (London: Macmillan).

Dunleavy, Patrick, Margetts, H., Smith, T. and Weir, S. (2001) *Voices of the People* (London: Politico's).

Edwards, Richard A. (2002) 'Judicial Deference under the Human Rights Act', *The Modern Law Review*, vol. 65 no. 6, pp. 859–82.

Electoral Commission (2004), *Delivering Democracy?* (London: The Electoral Commission).

Elms, Tim and Terry, T. (1990) *Scrutiny of Ministerial Correspondence* (London: Cabinet Office Efficiency Unit).

Engle, George (1983) '"Bills are Made to Pass as Razors are Made to Sell": Practical Constraints in the Preparation of Legislation', *Statute Law Review*, Spring, pp. 7–23.

European Scrutiny Committee, House of Commons (2002) *Democracy and Accountability in the EU and the Role of National Parliaments*, 33rd Report, Session 2001–2, HC 152-xxxiii-I (London: The Stationery Office).

European Scrutiny Committee, House of Commons (2003) *The Convention on the Future of Europe and the Role of National Parliaments*, 24th Report, Session 2002–3, HC 63-xxiv (London: The Stationery Office).

European Scrutiny Committee, House of Commons (2004) *The Committee's Work in 2003*, 8th Report, Session 2003–4, HC 42-viii (London: The Stationery Office).

Evans, Paul (2004), 'The Human Rights Act and Westminster's Legislative Process' in A. Brazier (ed.) *Parliament, Politics and Law Making* (London: The Hansard Society).

Ferguson, Ross and Howell, M. (2004) *Political Blogs – Craze or Convention?* (London: The Hansard Society).

Field, Frank (1982), 'Backbenchers, the executive and theories of representation', in Royal Institute of Public Administration, *Parliament and the Executive* (London: RIPA).

Field, John (2002) *The Story of Parliament* (London: Politico's/James & James).

Finer, Samuel E. (1958) *Anonymous Empire* (London: Pall Mall).

Fisher, Mark (2004) *Parliament and the Legislative Process*, Select Committee on the Constitution, House of Lords, 14th Report, Session 2003–4, HL Paper 173–II, pp. 83–95.

Flynn, Paul (1997) *Commons Knowledge: How to Be a Backbencher* (Bridgend: Seren).

Foley, Michael (1993) *The Rise of the British Presidency* (Manchester: Manchester University Press).

Fowler, Norman (1991) *Ministers Decide* (London: Chapman).

Franklin, Mark and Norton, P. (1993) *Parliamentary Questions* (Oxford: Clarendon Press).

Franklin, Mark, Baxter, A. and Jordan, M. (1986) 'Who Were the Rebels? Dissent in the House of Commons 1970–1974', *Legislative Studies Quarterly*, vol. 11, pp. 143–59.

Friedrich, Carl (1963) *Man and his Government: An Empirical Theory of Politics* (New York: McGraw-Hill).

Gamble, Andrew (1994) *The Free Economy and the Strong State,* 2nd edn (London: Macmillan).

Giddings, Philip (1998) 'The Parliamentary Ombudsman: A Successful Alternative?', in D. Oliver and G. Drewry (eds), *The Law and Parliament* (London: Butterworths).

Giddings, Philip and Drewry, G. (eds) (2004) *Britain in the European Union* (London: Palgrave).

Gifford, Zerbanoo (1992) *Dadabhai Naoroji: Britain's First Asian MP* (London: Mantra).

Gifford, D. J. and Salter, J. (1996) *How to Understand an Act of Parliament* (London: Cavendish).

Gilmour, Ian (1971) *The Body Politic,* revd edn (London: Hutchinson).

Golding, John (2003) *Hammer of the Left* (London: Politico's).

Gordon, Strathearn (1948) *Our Parliament,* 3rd edn (London: Hansard Society).

Grant, Wyn (2000) *Pressure Groups and British Politics* (London: Macmillan).

Grantham, Cliff (1989) 'Parliament and Political Consultants', *Parliamentary Affairs,* vol. 42, pp. 503–18.

Grantham, Cliff and Moore Hodgson, C. (1985) 'The House of Lords: Structural Changes', in P. Norton (ed.), *Parliament in the 1980s* (Oxford: Basil Blackwell).

Grantham, Cliff and Seymour-Ure, C. (1990) 'Political Consultants', in M. Rush (ed.), *Parliament and Pressure Politics* (Oxford: Clarendon Press).

Greenway, John (2004) Evidence, *Parliament and the Legislative Process,* Select Committee on the Constitution, House of Lords, 14th Report, Session 2003–4, HL Paper 173–II; pp. 112–25.

Grey, Anthony (1992) *Quest for Justice: Towards Homosexual Emancipation* (London: Sinclair-Stevenson).

Griffith, John A. G. and Ryle, M. (1989) *Parliament: Functions, Practice and Procedure* (London: Sweet & Maxwell).

Hain, Peter (2004) Evidence, *Parliament and the Legislative Process,* Select Committee on the Constitution, House of Lords, 14th Report, Session 2003–4, HL Paper 173–II, pp. 1–16.

Hansard Society (1992) *Making the Law: Report of the Hansard Society Commission on the Legislative Process* (London: The Hansard Society).

Hansard Society (2004) *Issues in Lawmaking: 5. Pre-Legislative Scrutiny,* Hansard Society Briefing Paper (London: Hansard Society).

Hansard Society Commission on Parliamentary Scrutiny (2001) *The Challenge for Parliament: Making Government Accountable* (London: Vacher Dod).

Hazell, Robert (2004) 'Who Is the Guardian of Legal Values in the Legislative Process: Parliament or the Executive?', *Public Law,* Autumn, pp. 495–500.

Hedlund, Ronald D. and Friesema, H. P. (1972), 'Representatives' Perceptions of Constituency Opinion', *Journal of Politics,* vol. 34, pp. 730–52.

Hibbing, John R. (2002) 'Legislative Careers: Why and How We Should Study Them', in G. Loewenberg, P. Squire and D. R. Kiewiet (eds), *Legislatures: Comparative Perspectives on Representative Assemblies* (Ann Arbor, Mich.: University of Michigan Press).

Hofferbert, R. I. and Budge, I. (1992) 'The Party Mandate and the Westminster Model: Election Programmes and government Spending in Britain, 1945–85', *British Journal of Political Science,* vol. 22, pp. 151–82.

Hogg, Douglas (2004) *Parliament and the Legislative Process,* Select Committee on the Constitution, House of Lords, 14th Report, Session 2003–4, HL Paper 173-II, pp. 83–95.

Hollingsworth, Mark (1991) *MPs for Hire* (London: Bloomsbury).

House of Commons Commission (2003) *25th Annual Report,* Session 2002–3, HC 806 (London: The Stationery Office).

House of Commons Information Office (2003), *Sessional Information Digest 2002–2003* (London: House of Commons).

House of Lords (2002) *Annual Report 2001–2002,* HL Paper 153 (London: The Stationery Office).

House of Lords (2003) *Annual Report 2002–2003,* HL Paper 146 (London: The Stationery Office).

House of Lords (2004) *Annual Report 2003–2004,* HL Paper 154 (London: The Stationery Office).

Human Rights Joint Committee (2001) *Criminal Justice and Police Bill,* 1st Special Report, Session 2000–1, HL Paper 42, HC 296 (London: The Stationery Office).

Hurd, Douglas (2003) *Memoirs* (London: Little, Brown).

Independent Commission on the Voting System (1998) *The Report of the Independent Commission on the Voting System,* Cm 4090–I (London: The Stationery Office).

Information Committee, House of Commons (2002) *Digital Technology: Working for Parliament and the Public,* 1st Report, Session 2001–2, HC 1065 (London: The Stationery Office).

Inglehart, Ronald (1977) *The Silent Revolution* (Princeton, NJ: Princeton University Press.)

James, Simon (1992) *British Cabinet Government* (London: Routledge).

Jogerst, Michael (1993) *Reform in the House of Commons* (Lexington, Ky.: University Press of Kentucky).

Johnson, Nevil (1988) 'Departmental Select Committees', in M. Ryle and P. G. Richards (eds), *The Commons Under Scrutiny* (London: Routledge).

Joint Committee on the Draft Communications Bill (2002) *Report of the Joint Committee on the Draft Communications Bill,* Session 2001–2, HC 876, HL Paper 169 (London: The Stationery Office).

Jones, J. Barry (1990) 'Party Committees and All-Party Groups', in M. Rush (ed.), *Parliament and Pressure Politics* (Oxford: Clarendon Press).

Jordan, A. Grant (1991) *The Commercial Lobbyists* (Aberdeen: Aberdeen University Press).

Jordan, A. Grant and Richardson, J. J. (1982) 'The British Policy Style or the Logic of Negotiation', in J. J. Richardson (ed.), *Policy Styles in Western Europe* (London: George Allen & Unwin).

Joseph Rowntree Reform Trust (2004) *The State of British Democracy* (York: Joseph Rowntree Reform Trust).

Jowell, Roger and Witherspoon, S. (1985) *British Social Attitudes: The 1985 Report* (Aldershot: Gower).

Jowell, Roger, Witherspoon, S. and Brook, L. (1987) *British Social Attitudes: The 1987 Report* (Aldershot: Gower).

Judge, David (1990) *Parliament and Industry* (Aldershot: Dartmouth).

Judge, David (1999a) *Representation: Theory and Practice in Britain* (London: Routledge).

Judge, David (1999b) 'Representation in Westminster in the 1990s: The Ghost of Edmund Burke', *The Journal of Legislative Studies*, vol. 5, pp. 12–34.

Judge, David (2004) 'Whatever Happened to Parliamentary Democracy in the United Kingdom?', *Parliamentary Affairs,* vol. 57, pp. 682–701.

Kennon, Andrew (2004) 'Pre-legislative Scrutiny of Draft Bills', *Public Law,* Autumn, pp. 477–94.

King, Anthony (1981) 'The Rise of the Career Politician in Britain – and Its Consequences', *British Journal of Political Science,* vol. 11, pp. 249–85.

Kirchheimer, Otto (1966) 'The Transformation of the Western European Party Systems', in J. LaPolombara, and M. Weiner (eds), *Political Parties and Political Development* (Princeton, NJ: Princeton University Press).

Klug, Francesca and O'Brien, C. (2002) 'The First Two Years of the Human Rights Act', *Public Law,* Winter, pp. 649–62.

Lambert, David, and Navarro, M. (2004) 'Law Making for Wales', in A. Brazier (ed.), *Parliament, Politics and Law Making* (London: The Hansard Society).

Lang, Ian (2002) *Blue Remembered Years* (London: Politico's).

Laugharne, Peter (1994) *Parliament and Specialist Advice* (Liverpool: Manutius Press).

Liaison Committee, House of Commons (2000) *Shifting the Balance: Select Committees and the Executive,* 1st Report, Session 1999–2000, HC 300 (London: The Stationery Office).

Liaison Committee, House of Commons (2004) *Annual Report for 2003–04,* 1st Report, Session 2003–4, HC 446 (London: The Stationery Office).

Locke, John (1960) *Second Treatise on Government* first published 1689; with a introduction by Peter Laslett (Cambridge: Cambridge University Press).

Loewenberg, Gerhard (1971) (ed.) *Modern Parliaments: Change or Decline?* (Chicago: Aldine-Atherton).

Lowell, A. Lawrence (1896) *Government and Parties in Continental Europe* (Cambridge, Mass.: Harvard University Press).

Lowell, A. Lawrence (1924) *The Government of England, Vol. II* (New York: Macmillan).

Lukes, Steven (1974) *Power: A Radical View* (London: Macmillan).

Mackintosh, John P. (1977) *The British Cabinet,* 3rd edn (London: Methuen).

Maer, Lucinda and Sandford, M. (2004) *Select Committees Under Scrutiny* (London: The Constitution Unit).

Major, John (1999) *The Autobiography* (London: HarperCollins).

Marsh, Ian (1986) *Policy-Making in a Three-Party System* (London: Methuen).

Marsh, David and Read, M. (1988) *Private Members' Bills* (Cambridge University Press).

Matthews, Donald R. (1985) 'Legislative Recruitment and Legislative Careers', in G. Loewenberg, S. C. Patterson and M. E. Jewell (eds), *Handbook of Legislative Research* (Cambridge, Mass.: Harvard University Press).

Maxwell, Patricia (1999) 'The House of Lords as a Constitutional Court: The Implications of *Ex p. EOC'*, in P. Carmichael and B. Dickson (eds), *The House of Lords: Its Parliamentary and Judicial Roles* (Oxford: Hart Publishing).

May, Theresa (2004) 'Women in the House: The Continuing Challenge', *Parliamentary Affairs*, no. 57, pp. 844–51.

McKay, William (ed.) (2004) *Erskine May's Treatise on The Law, Privileges, Proceedings and Usage of Parliament*, 23rd edn (London: LexisNexus UK).

McKenzie, Kenneth (1968) *The English Parliament* (London: Penguin).

Melhuish, David and Cowley, P. (1995) 'Whither the New Role in Policy Making? Conservative MPs in Standing Committees 1979 to 1992', *The Journal of Legislative Studies*, no. 1, pp. 54–75.

Mezey, Michael (1979) *Comparative Legislatures* (Durham, NC: Duke University Press).

Miers, David and Brock, J. (1993) 'Government Legislation: Case Studies', in D. Shell and D. Beamish (eds), *The House of Lords at Work* (Oxford: Clarendon Press).

Miller, Charles (1990) *Lobbying: Understanding and Influencing the Corridors of Power*, 2nd edn (Oxford: Basil Blackwell).

Miller, Warren E. and Stokes, D. E. (1963) 'Constituency Influence in Congress', *American Political Science Review*, vol. 57, pp. 45–56.

Mitchell, Neil J. (1997) *The Conspicuous Corporation* (Ann Arbor, Mich.: University of Michigan Press).

Modernisation Committee, House of Commons (1997) *The Legislative Process*, 1st Report, Session 1997–98, HC 190 (London: The Stationery Office).

Modernisation Committee, House of Commons (2002) *Modernisation of the House of Commons: A Reform Programme*, 2nd Report, Session 2001–2, HC 1168–I (London: The Stationery Office).

Modernisation Committee, House of Commons (2004) *Connecting Parliament with the Public*, 1st Report, Session 2003–4, HC 368 (London: The Stationery Office).

Montesquieu, Charles de Secondat, Baron de (1949), *The Spirit of the Laws* [*De L'esprit des lois*], first published 1748 (New York: Hafner).

Moonie, Lewis (2004) Evidence, *Parliament and the Legislative Process,* Select Committee on the Constitution, House of Lords, 14th Report, Session 2003–4, HL Paper 173–II, pp. 111–25.

Moyes, Jonathan (2004) 'What Do All-Party Groups Need to Have in Place to Be an Influential Lobbying Voice?', Undergraduate Dissertation (Hull: Hull University Department of Politics and International Studies).

Negrine, Ralph (1992) 'Reporting Parliamentary Committees: The Investigation of the Rover Group Sale to British Areospace', *Parliamentary Affairs,* vol. 45, pp. 399–408.

Negrine, Ralph (1998) *Parliament and the Media: A Study of Britain, Germany and France* (London: The Royal Institute of International Affairs).

Nixon, Jaqi (1986) 'Evaluating Select Committees and Proposals for an Alternative Perspective', *Policy and Politics,* vol. 14, pp. 415–38.

Norris, Pippa (1997) 'The Puzzle of Constituency Service', *The Journal of Legislative Studies,* vol. 3, pp. 29–49.

Norris, Steven (1996) *Changing Trains* (London: Hutchinson).

Norton, Philip (1975) *Dissension in the House of Commons 1945–74* (London: Macmillan).

Norton, Philip (1978a) *Conservative Dissidents* (London: Temple Smith).

Norton, Philip (1978b) 'Government Defeats in the House of Commons: Myth and Reality', *Public Law,* Winter, pp. 360–78.

Norton, Philip (1979) 'The Organisation of Parliamentary Parties', in S. A.Walkland (ed.), *The House of Commons in the Twentieth Century* (Oxford: Clarendon Press).

Norton, Philip (1980) *Dissension in the House of Commons 1974–1979* (Oxford: Clarendon Press).

Norton, Philip (1981) *The Commons in Perspective* (Oxford: Basil Blackwell).

Norton, Philip (1982a) *The Constitution in Flux* (Oxford: Martin Robertson).

Norton, Philip (1982b) '"Dear Minister…". The Importance of MP-to-Minister Correspondence', *Parliamentary Affairs,* vol. 35, pp. 59–72.

Norton, Philip (1985) 'The House of Commons: Behavioural Changes', in P. Norton (ed.), *Parliament in the 1980s* (Oxford: Basil Blackwell).

Norton, Philip (1986) 'Independence, Scrutiny and Rationalisation: A Decade of Changes in the House of Commons', *Teaching Politics,* vol. 15, pp. 69–98.

Norton, Philip (1987), 'Dissent in the House of Commons: Rejoinder to Franklin, Baxter, Jordan', *Legislative Studies Quarterly,* vol. 12, pp. 143–52.

Norton, Philip (1989a) 'The Constitutional Position of Parliamentary Private Secretaries', *Public Law,* Summer, pp. 232–6.

Norton, Philip (1989b) 'Collective Ministerial Responsibility', *Social Studies Review,* vol. 5, pp. 33–6.

Norton, Philip (1990a) 'Introduction', in P. Norton (ed.), *Legislatures* (Oxford University Press).

Norton, Philip (1990b) 'Public Legislation', in M. Rush (ed.), *Parliament and Pressure Politics* (Oxford: Clarendon Press).

Norton, Philip (1990c) *Parliaments in Western Europe* (London: Frank Cass).

Norton, Philip (1991a), 'Parliament Since 1945: A More Open Institution?', *Contemporary Record,* vol. 5, pp. 217–34.

Norton, Philip (1991b) 'The Changing Face of Parliament: Lobbying and its Consequences', in P. Norton (ed.), *New Directions in British Politics?* (Aldershot: Edward Elgar).

Norton, Philip (1993a) 'Congress: Comparative Perspectives', in D. C., Bacon, R. H. Davidson and M. Keller (eds), *The Encylopedia of the United States Congress* (New York: Simon & Schuster).

Norton, Philip (1993b) 'Questions and the Role of Parliament', in M. Franklin and P. Norton (eds), *Parliamentary Questions* (Oxford: Clarendon Press).

Norton, Philip (1994a) 'The Party in Parliament', in A. Seldon and S. Ball (eds), *Conservative Century* (Oxford University Press).

Norton, Philip (1994b) 'The Growth of the Constituency Role of the MP', *Parliamentary Affairs,* vol. 47, pp. 705–20.

Norton, Philip (1994c) 'Parliament in the United Kingdom: The Incumbency Paradox', in A. Somit, R. Wildenmann, B. Boll and A. Rommele (eds), *The Victorious Incumbent: A Threat to Democracy?* (Aldershot: Dartmouth).

Norton, P. (1994d) 'The Legislative Power of Parliament', in C. Flinterman, A. W. Heringa and L. Waddington (eds), *The Evolving Role of Parliaments in Europe* (Antwerp: Maklu/Nomos).

Norton, P. (1996) 'The United Kingdom: Political Conflict, Parliamentary Scrutiny', in P. Norton (ed.), *National Parliaments and the European Union* (London: Frank Cass).

Norton, Philip (ed.) (1998a) *Parliaments and Governments in Western Europe* (London: Frank Cass).

Norton, Philip (1998b) *Power to the People* (London: Conservative Policy Forum).

Norton, Philip (ed.) (1999a) *Parliaments and Pressure Groups in Western Europe* (London: Frank Cass).

Norton, Philip (1999b) 'The United Kingdom: Parliament under Pressure', in P. Norton (ed.), *Parliaments and Pressure Groups in Western Europe* (London: Frank Cass).

Norton, P. (1999c) *The New Barons? Senior Ministers in British Government,* Goldsmiths College Public Policy Paper (London: Goldsmiths College).

Norton, Philip (2001a) *The British Polity,* 4th edn (New York: Longman).

Norton, Philip (2001b) 'Playing by the Rules: The Constraining Hand of Parliamentary Procedure', *The Journal of Legislative Studies,* vol. 7, pp. 13–33.

Norton, Philip (ed.) (2002a) *Parliaments and Citizens in Western Europe* (London: Frank Cass).

Norton, Philip (2002b) 'The Conservative Party: Is There Anyone Out There?', in A. King (ed.), *Britain at the Polls, 2001* (New York: Chatham House).

Norton, Philip (2002c) 'The United Kingdom: Building the Link between Constituent and MP', in P. Norton (ed.), *Parliaments and Citizens in Western Europe* (London: Frank Cass).

Norton, Philip (2003a) 'Cohesion without Discipline: Party Voting in the House of Lords', *The Journal of Legislative Studies,* vol. 9, pp. 57–72.

Norton, Philip (2003b) 'Governing Alone', *Parliamentary Affairs,* vol. 56, pp. 543–59.

Norton, Philip (2004a) 'The Power of Parliament', *Politics Review,* vol. 14, no. 2, pp. 24–7.

Norton, Philip (2004b) 'The Crown', in B. Jones, D. Kavanagh, M. Moran and P. Norton, *Politics UK,* 5th edn (Harlow: Pearson Education).

Norton, Philip (2004c) 'Parliament', in A. Seldon and K. Hickson (eds), *New Labour, Old Labour,* (London: Routledge).

Norton, Philip (2004d) 'Reforming the House of Lords: A View from the Parapets', *Representation,* vol. 40, pp. 185–99.

Norton, Philip (2004e) 'Parliament and the Courts', in N. D. J. Baldwin (ed.), *Parliament in the 21st Century* (London: Politico's).

Norton, Philip and Wood, D. M. (1990) 'Constituency Service by Members of Parliament: Does it Contribute to a Personal Vote?', *Parliamentary Affairs,* vol. 43, pp. 196–208.

Norton, Philip and Wood, D. M. (1993) *Back from Westminster* (Lexington Ky.: University of Kentucky Press).

Nott, John (2002) *Here Today, Gone Tomorrow* (London: Politico's).

Oliver, Dawn and Drewry, G. (eds) (1998) *The Law and Parliament* (London: Butterworths).

Olson, David M. and Mezey, M. (1991) *Legislatures in the Policy Process* (Cambridge University Press).

Olson, David M. and Norton, P. (eds) (1996) *The New Parliaments of Central and Eastern Europe* (London: Frank Cass).

O'Neill, Aidan (2001) 'Judicial Politics and the Judicial Committee: The Devolution Jurisprudence of the Privy Council', *The Modern Law Review,* vol. 64, no. 4, pp. 603–18.

Ostrogorski, Moisei (1902) *Democracy and the Organisation of Political Parties,* Vol. I (London: Macmillan).

Packenham, Robert (1970) 'Legislatures and Political Development', in A. Kornberg and L. D. Musolf (eds), *Legislatures in Developmental Perspective* (Durham, NC: Duke University Press).

Page, Alan and Batey, A. (2002) 'Scotland's Other Parliament: Westminster Legislation about Devolved Matters in Scotland since Devolution', *Public Law,* Autumn, pp. 501–23.

Parry, Keith (2004) *Webcasting of Parliament*, Standard Note, SN/PC/1761, House of Commons Library, Parliament & Constitution Centre.

Paxman, Jeremy (2002) *The Political Animal* (London: Michael Joseph).

Phillips, A. (1949) 'Post Office Parliamentary Questions', *Public Administration*, vol. 27, pp. 91–9.

Pitkin, Hanna (1967) *The Concept of Representation* (Berkeley, Calif.: University of California Press).

Powell, Christopher (1980) *The Parliamentary and Scientific Committee. The First Forty Years 1939–1979* (London: Croom Helm).

Powell, Enoch (1982) 'Parliament and the Question of Reform', *Teaching Politics*, vol. 11 no. 2, pp. 167–76.

Power, Greg (1996) *Reinventing Westminster* (London: Charter88).

Power, Greg (1998) *Representing the People: MPs and their Constituents* (London: The Fabian Society).

Privy Counsellor Review Committee (2003) *Anti-terrorism, Crime and Security Act 2001 Review: Report*, Session 2003–4, HC 100 (London: The Stationery Office).

Rawlings, Richard (1990) 'The MP's Complaints Service', *The Modern Law Review*, vol. 53, pp. 22–42 and 149–69.

Read, Melvyn D. and Marsh, D. (1998) 'Homosexuality', in P. Cowley (ed.), *Conscience and Parliament* (London: Frank Cass).

Read, Melvyn D., Marsh, D. and Richards, D. (1994) 'Homosexual and Capital Punishment Votes', *Parliamentary Affairs*, vol. 47, pp. 374–86.

Reform Group, All-Party House of Commons (1984) 'Findings of the Survey of MPs' Attitudes to Reform and the Role of the MP', Mimeo, London: House of Commons Reform Group.

Regan, Paul (1987) 'The 1986 Shops Bill', *Parliamentary Affairs*, vol. 41, pp. 218–35.

Renton, Tim (2004) *Chief Whip* (London: Politico's).

Review Body on Senior Salaries (2004), *Review of Parliamentary Pay and Allowances 2004*, Report No. 57, Cm 6354–I (London: The Stationery Office).

Richard Commission (2004) *The Report of the Richard Commission* (Cardiff: National Assembly for Wales).

Richards, Peter G. (1959) *Honourable Members* (London: Faber & Faber).

Richards, Peter G. (1970) *Parliament and Conscience* (London: George Allen & Unwin).

Richardson, Jeremy and Jordan, A. G. (1979) *Governing Under Pressure* (Oxford: Martin Robertson).

Riddell, Peter (1993) *Honest Opportunism* (London: Hamish Hamilton).

Riddell, Peter (1995) 'The Impact of the Rise of the Career Politician', *The Journal of Legislative Studies*, vol. 1, pp. 186–91.

Riddell, Peter (2000) *Parliament Under Blair* (London: Politico's).

Robinson, Geoffrey (2000) *The Unconventional Minister* (London: Michael Joseph).

Rogers, Robert and Walters, R. (2004) *How Parliament Works*, 5th edn (London: Pearson Education).

Rose, Richard (1979) 'Ungovernability: Is There Fire Behind the Smoke?', *Political Studies,* vol. 27, pp. 351–70.

Rose, Richard (1984) *Do Parties Make a Difference?* (London: Macmillan).

Rose, Richard (2001) *The Prime Minister in a Shrinking World* (Cambridge: Polity).

Roskell, John S. (1993) *The House of Commons 1386–1421. 1: Introductory Survey, Appendices, Constituencies* (Stroud: Alan Sutton).

Royal Commission on the Reform of the House of Lords (2000) *A House for the Future,* Cm 4534 (London: The Stationery Office).

Rush, Michael (1979) 'The Member of Parliament', in S. A. Walkland (ed.), *The House of Commons in the Twentieth Century* (Oxford: Clarendon Press).

Rush, Michael (ed.) (1990) *Parliament and Pressure Politics* (Oxford: Clarendon Press).

Rush, Michael (1998) 'The Law Relating to Members' Conduct', in D. Oliver and G. Drewry (eds), *The Law and Parliament* (London: Butterworths).

Rush, Michael (2001) *The Role of the Member of Parliament Since 1868* (Oxford University Press).

Russell, David J. T. (1998) 'The Nocturnal Habits of MPs', Unpublished Undergraduate Dissertation (Hull: Hull University Politics Department).

Russell, Meg (2000) *Reforming the House of Lords* (Oxford University Press).

Schwarz, John E. (1980) 'Exploring a New Role in Policy Making: The British House of Commons in the 1970s', *American Political Science Review,* vol. 74, pp. 23–37.

Searing, Donald (1994) *Westminster's World* (Cambridge, Mass.: Harvard University Press).

Seaton, Janet and Winetrobe, B. (1998) 'The Passage of Constitutional Bills in Parliament', *The Journal of Legislative Studies,* vol. 4, pp. 33–52.

Select Committee on Members' Interests (1990) *Parliamentary Lobbying,* HC 283 (London: HMSO).

Select Committee on Procedure (1992) *Petitions,* 4th Report, Session 1991–92, HC 286 (London: HMSO).

Select Committee on Televising the Proceedings of the House (1990) *Review of the Experiment in Televising the Proceedings of the House,* 1st Report, Session 1989–90, HC 265–I (London: HMSO).

Select Committee on the Sittings of the House, House of Commons (1992) *Report from the Select Committee on the Sittings of the House,* Session 1991–92, HC 20 (London: HMSO).

Self, Peter (1977) 'Are We Worse Governed?', *New Society,* 19 May.

Seyd, Patrick and Whiteley, P. (2001) 'New Labour and the Party: Members and Organisation', in S. Ludlam and M. J. Smith (eds), *New Labour in Government* (London: Macmillan).

Shell, Donald (1988) *The House of Lords* (Deddington: Philip Allan).

Shephard, Gillian (2000) *Shephard's Watch* (London: Politico's).

Shepherd, Robert (1991) *The Power Brokers* (London: Hutchinson).

Silk, Paul (1987) *How Parliament Works* (London: Longman).

Smith, Martin J. (1995) *Pressure Politics* (Manchester: Baseline Book Company).

Sontheimer, Kurt (1984) 'Parliamentarianism in Modern Times – a Political Science Perspective', *Universitas*, no. 26.

Stevens, Robert (2002) *The English Judges* (Oxford: Hart Publishing).

Teeling, William (1970) *Corridors of Frustration* (London: Bodley Head).

Theakston, Kevin (1987) *Junior Ministers in British Government* (Oxford: Basil Blackwell).

Topliss, Eda and Gould, B. (1981) *A Charter for the Disabled* (Oxford: Basil Blackwell).

Tordoff, Lord (2000) 'The Conference of European Affairs Committees: A Collective Voice for National Parliaments in the European Union', *The Journal of Legislative Studies,* vol. 6 no. 4, pp. 1–8.

Trench, Alan (2004a) 'Devolution: The Withering Away of the Joint Ministerial Committee?', *Public Law,* Autumn, pp. 513–17.

Trench, Alan (ed.) (2004b) *Has Devolution Made a Difference?* (London: Imprint Academic).

Trevelyan, George M. (1938) *The English Revolution* (London: Thornton Butterworth).

Tsebelis, George (2002) *Veto Players: How Political Institutions Work* (New York: Russell Sage Foundation/Princeton University Press).

Tyrie, Andrew (2000) *Mr Blair's Poodle* (London: Centre for Policy Studies).

Wakefield of Kendal, Lord (1980), 'Memoir', in C. Powell, *The Parliamentary and Scientific Committee. The First Forty Years 1939–1979* (London: Croom Helm).

Walkland, Stuart A. (1968) *The Legislative Process in Great Britain* (London: George Allen & Unwin).

Walters, Rhodri (2004) 'The House of Lords', in V. Bogdanor (ed.), *The British Constitution in the Twentieth Century* (Oxford University Press).

Westlake, Martin (1994) *Britain's Emerging Euro-Elite?* (Aldershot: Dartmouth).

Wheeler-Booth, Michael (1989) 'The Lords', in J. A. G. Griffith and M. Ryle (eds), *Parliament: Functions, Practices and Procedures* (London: Sweet & Maxwell).

White, Albert B. (1908) *The Making of the English Constitution 449–1485* (London: G. B. Putnam's Sons).

Whiteley, Paul F. and Winyard S. J. (1987) *Pressure for the Poor* (London: Methuen).

Winetrobe, Barry K. (2002), 'Scottish Devolved Legislation and the Courts', *Public Law,* Spring, pp. 31–8.

Winetrobe, Barry K. (2004), 'Making the Law in Devolved Scotland', in A. Brazier (ed.), *Parliament, Politics and Law Making* (London: The Hansard Society).

Wiseman, H. Victor (1966) (ed.) *Parliament and the Executive* (London: Routledge & Kegan Paul).

Woodhouse, Diana (1994) *Ministers and Parliament* (Oxford: Clarendon Press).

Woodhouse, Diana (2002), 'The Law and Politics: In the Shadow of the Human Rights Act', *Parliamentary Affairs,* vol. 55, no. 2, pp. 254–70.

Wootton, Graham (1975) *Pressure Groups in Britain 1720–1970* (London: Allen Lane).

Young, Ross, Cracknell, R., Tetteh, E., Griffin, G. and Brown, D. (2003) *Parliamentary Questions, Debate Contributions and Participation in Commons Divisions*, House of Commons Library, Research Paper 03/32 (London: House of Commons Library).

Index